Policy Horizons and Parliamentary Government

Also by Paul V. Warwick

THE FRENCH POPULAR FRONT: A Legislative Analysis

POLITICAL COHESION IN A FRAGILE MOSAIC: The Yugoslav Experience (*co-author with Lenard Cohen*)

CULTURE, STRUCTURE, OR CHOICE? Essays in the Interpretation of the British Experience

GOVERNMENT SURVIVAL IN PARLIAMENTARY DEMOCRACIES

Policy Horizons and Parliamentary Government

Paul V. Warwick

Professor of Political Science
Simon Fraser University, Canada

palgrave
macmillan

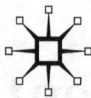

First published 2006 by
PALGRAVE MACMILLAN
Houndmills, Basingstoke, Hampshire RG21 6XS and
175 Fifth Avenue, New York, N.Y. 10010
Companies and representatives throughout the world

PALGRAVE MACMILLAN is the global academic imprint of the Palgrave Macmillan division of St. Martin's Press, LLC and of Palgrave Macmillan Ltd. Macmillan® is a registered trademark in the United States, United Kingdom and other countries. Palgrave is a registered trademark in the European Union and other countries.

ISBN-13: 978–1–4039–9779–1 hardback
ISBN-10: 1–4039–9779–9 hardback

This book is printed on paper suitable for recycling and made from fully managed and sustained forest sources.

A catalogue record for this book is available from the British Library.

Library of Congress Cataloging-in-Publication Data
Warwick, Paul, 1947–
    Policy horizons and parliamentary government / Paul V. Warwick.
        p.   cm.
    Includes bibliographical references and index.
    ISBN 1–4039–9779–9 (cloth)
    1. Coalition governments—Europe, Western. 2. Political planning—Europe, Western. 3. Europe, Western—Politics and government.
    I. Title.
    JN94.A979W37 2006
    324.094—dc22   2005056585

10   9   8   7   6   5   4   3   2   1
15   14   13   12   11   10   09   08   07   06

Printed and bound in Great Britain by
Antony Rowe Ltd, Chippenham and Eastbourne

Contents

v

List of Figures and Tables

Figures

Tables

Preface

This study is motivated by the conviction that coalition behaviour in parliamentary systems must be, at its base, simple. By this, I do not mean that a simple theory is all that will be required in order to account for it, or that the gathering and assessment of evidence for such a theory should be relatively uncomplicated – far from it, as this study will reveal. Rather, the simplicity in question pertains to the decisions made by the political leaders who conduct the business of forming and maintaining governments in coalitional contexts. I do not believe that these leaders perform complex calculations of strategies in order to determine their best moves, as many game theoretic accounts would have us believe, nor that they collect and distil large amounts of precise information on the utility functions or policy preferences of voters, activists, or other parliamentary parties. Instead, I suspect that they operate on the basis of few relatively basic considerations, assessed impressionistically rather than precisely.

The objective of this study is to evaluate one possible consideration: that party leaders are limited in the extent to which they can accept policy compromises for the purpose of participating in coalition governments. In a general sense, this suggestion is hardly surprising. It is a well-established fact that coalition governments tend to be formed of parties whose policy preferences are relatively similar, and it is natural to assume that this flows from the desire of leaders to fulfil policy commitments to the fullest possible extant and the need to have compatible coalition partners. What I have in mind, however, is something much more specific and much less obvious. This is that parties in West European parliamentary systems have distinct *bounds* on how far they can abandon policy commitments for cabinet seats. Each party's bounds, I suggest, define a 'policy horizon' surrounding its declared policy or ideological position and create a very simple criterion for making coalition decisions: the party may entertain or advance a proposal to form a government only if the policy stance that government will implement falls within the party's horizon. Any other coalition possibilities must be cast aside, regardless of what other advantages they would hold for the party or its leaders.

The study thus proposes the existence of an imagined entity, policy horizons, and much of it is devoted to establishing that this imagined entity is not, in fact, imaginary. This task involves several challenging requirements, the first of which is to find out where the policy horizons of individual parties, if they exist, are located. I seek measurement of policy horizons indirectly from the coalition behaviour of parties in fourteen West European parliamentary systems and more directly by means of a new survey of political experts on these systems, the results of which are also reported in this book. With horizons estimated, the next requirement is some means of determining which groups of parties in any given legislature have horizons that mutually intersect, which would allow the parties to find some common policy position around which they could form a government. For this task, a new computer programme, *Horizons 3D*©, has been created; its functionality and operating instructions are also detailed in this study (the programme itself is available at no charge from my website). The final task is to assemble this information and test various implications of the concept of policy horizons, including, most obviously, the proposition that governments tend to be formed by groups of parties with intersecting horizons.

Needless to say, considerable resources were required to undertake this project. The financial wherewithal was provided by a research grant from the Social Sciences and Humanities Research Council of Canada, for which I am extremely grateful. In terms of human resources, the project benefited at various stages from the work of research assistants Andrea Balogh, Anthony Maragna, Scott Matthews, and Michael McNamara, and from student programmers Byron White, Rob Slifka, and especially Monica Jercan. With impressive speed and skill, David Eberly of Magic Software, Inc. created the code that turns limits of compromise into three-dimensional policy horizons and determines whether and to what extent they intersect. James Adams deserves a special note of appreciation for his unfailing support of this research and for urging me to turn it into a book; he willingly embraced the necessary corollary, which is to read and comment on the entire manuscript. The book also benefited from comments on selected chapters from James Druckman and Ben Nyblade. Stephen Easton was a most helpful muse through much of the early gestation of the policy horizon idea. Finally, a note of thanks should be extended to the *European Journal of Political Research*, the *British Journal of Political Science* and the *American Journal of Political Science* for allowing me to publish, in revised form, certain material that originally appeared in their pages (Warwick 2000, 2005a, 2005b).

1
Introduction

Parliamentary politics inevitably involves compromise among divergent points of view. It is easy to lose sight of this reality when parliamentarism is equated with its Westminster variant, which, in its pure form, envisages a single, highly disciplined party in firm control of both the executive and the legislative branches of government. But even leaving aside the possibility that the ruling party may not be as united as it appears and the probability that it is at odds with some influential outside interests, this image would still be false for most of the established parliamentary systems in Western Europe for the simple reason that they seldom produce single-party majorities. Whenever two or more parties must cooperate in order to form a viable government, as is the norm in these systems, trade-offs and compromise must become the order of the day.

The need to accommodate inter-party differences over policy poses a clear challenge in these situations, but how great a challenge is it? Contemporary theoretical work on parliamentary government provides at least two perspectives in which its significance is downplayed. The first is embodied in the 'portfolio allocation' model of government formation and survival advanced by Laver and Shepsle (1996). This model assumes that parties do not have to reconcile differences in their policy positions to form coalition governments; they simply divide up the cabinet portfolios and allow each party to implement its own policies in the portfolios it controls. Certainly, this involves compromise in the sense that no one party gets everything it wants, but it is bound to be a lot easier to allocate policy jurisdictions than to hammer out compromise positions in each of them.

The idea of ministerial autonomy upon which Laver and Shepsle base their model is an intriguing one because it provides a simple answer to the vexing question of how parties manage to cooperate with one

1

another, as they clearly do in many parliamentary systems. Yet it has not fared especially well when placed under the microscope by specialists of West European parliamentary systems (Laver and Shepsle 1994), nor in more quantitative investigations (e.g. Warwick 1999). Laver and Shepsle (1999) have disputed the latter claim, but it is unlikely that they would dispute the impression that most knowledgeable observers do not see ministerial autonomy as the basis for the formation of viable governing coalitions in these systems.

What, then, do most observers believe? A premise that enjoys near-universal support is that parties prefer government policy to be as similar as possible to their own policy preferences, other things being equal.[1] Parties, in the parlance of the scholarly literature, are 'policy-seekers'. This premise is embodied in formal models of legislative bargaining via the stipulation that a party's utility is a negative function of the difference, or sometimes the squared difference, between its policy position and that of the government. Few theorists today assume that policy costs are the only thing that matters to parties – parties, or at least their leaders, are usually assumed to covet cabinet portfolios as well – but it is invariably taken as the key element in party motivations.

Like the ministerial autonomy assumption, the policy distance assumption conveys a very simple image of party behaviour: parties evaluate potential governments according to the degree to which they offer policy stances compatible with their own and, other things being equal, act accordingly. Unlike that assumption, however, the notion that minimizing policy differences guides party behaviour has plenty of empirical evidence in its support. For instance, in previous work (Warwick 1996, 1998), I found that a party's odds of joining a governing coalition in West European parliamentary democracies decrease with increasing distance between its policy position and that of the party designated to form the government, which suggests that the *formateur* party, as it is known, seeks out coalition partners from among the parties that are close to it in policy terms. In a similar vein, Martin and Stevenson (2001) have shown that parties that are more united in policy terms have higher odds of forming coalition governments, a tendency that will also reveal itself in the present investigation.

Despite its inherent plausibility and the wealth of empirical evidence in its favour, however, the policy distance assumption is not sufficient onto itself. This is because, if policy-seeking has free rein, the outcomes of legislative bargaining ought to fall within the embrace of the well-known chaos theorem (McKelvey 1976, 1979). The gist of this theorem is that, so long as there is more than one policy dimension over which parties compete, it is highly likely that at least one party in any governing coalition or potential coalition will be able to find another coalition willing to provide it a better policy deal. This makes any coalition vulnerable to immediate dissolution and ought to lead to a perpetual cycling of proposals as parties, like revellers at vernal bacchanalia, switch partners with wild abandon.

A great deal of the formal theorizing in the last 20 years has focussed on providing some means by which this theoretical expectation of profligate promiscuity – which, happily, is absent from actual parliamentary systems – can be neutralized. Since the office-seeking propensities of politicians are generally not seen as useful in achieving this end, various other constraints have been proposed; Laver and Shepsle's ministerial autonomy assumption is one such device. Despite the amount of attention given to grappling with the non-chaotic nature of parliamentary reality, however, there is one possibility that is universally ignored: that there may be something wrong with the policy-seeking assumption itself. Yet it is not difficult to find instances where it appears to break down. One such example occurred in Sweden in the autumn of 1978. The government at that time consisted of a coalition among the Centre party, the Liberals, and the Moderates, headed by a Centre prime minister. Although sharing much common ground, the three parties were divided over the issue of nuclear power, with the Centre party opposed and the other two parties in favour. A carefully crafted compromise hammered out in 1976 guided the government's handling of the nuclear issue for two years, but it ultimately broke down over the Centre party's proposal that the nuclear power issue be put to a referendum and the prime minister resigned.

If we ask why the Centre party instigated the coalition's demise, it is difficult to find an answer consistent with a policy-seeking and/or an office-seeking perspective. As the median party on the left–right dimension, the Centre party was in the best position to switch sides by forming an alliance with the very large Social Democratic party located immediately to its left. Since the previous Social Democratic government had advanced the nuclear agenda, however, the chances of getting a more favourable deal on nuclear policy from that party were remote at best. Another possibility is that its central location may have induced the Centre party to believe that it could form a viable single-party government by playing off the one side against the other. If this was its strategy, it failed miserably: a single-party government did emerge, but it was formed by the Liberals. The referendum proposal suggests that it might have been looking further ahead, anticipating that its anti-nuclear stand would garner it more seats and hence more influence in the next legislature. This would imply a 'vote-seeking' motivation (Strøm 1990a). If so, it miscalculated badly: the party lost one-quarter of its parliamentary strength in the next election. So long as we assume that the Centre party was simply looking for the best available way to advance its own policy, office or short-term electoral interests, its decision appears to have been singularly self-defeating.

A similar conclusion applies to the French Communist party in the Socialist–Communist governments of the 1980s. The two parties had been (occasionally truculent) allies since the early 1970s, and in the aftermath of the 1981 legislative elections the Socialists invited the Communists to join them in a governing coalition. This was a generous gesture on the part of the Socialists since they in fact had won a majority of seats in those elections. By 1984, however, the Communists had become increasingly critical of the rightward drift in the government's economic and industrial policy and after failing to obtain assurances that government policy would reverse course, they decided to withdraw their participation. This represented no threat at all to the Socialists' survival in power and the effect on government policy could only have been to remove any resistance their presence in cabinet would have had to its further drift to the right. In terms of getting the best available policy deal, the Communists would therefore have been no worse off, and possibly better off, by staying in the government; the advantages of holding office – which include not just the associated perks but also access to patronage for supporters and control over decisions in their departments not requiring cabinet approval – pointed to the same conclusion. Yet the Communists left.

Both examples illustrate behaviour that challenges the standard notion of how parties deal with the need to accommodate their policy differences. Parties as policy-seekers are assumed to support the most favourable policy deal available to them, other things being equal. One of those 'other things' is clearly office benefits, which implies that parties might give up some ground on policy if it is offset by office benefits or vice versa. The problem here is that the Swedish Centre party and the French Communists sacrificed on both fronts: they lost their cabinet posts and opened the door to a movement in government policy away from their policy preferences. Their decisions might have made sense if they had allowed the parties to amass more votes in the next election, perhaps by capitalizing on the government's unpopularity. In both cases, however, their parliamentary representation declined. It is tempting to conclude that the parties simply miscalculated, but this position – which is dangerously close to asserting that the theory is right and the real world wrong – is one that most theorists are reluctant to adopt.[2] But unless we do so, we must conclude that something else figured in their calculations.

What might this extra consideration be? The decision to abandon a governing coalition would not seem to be an especially attractive one for party leaders, since they presumably covet cabinet office and might be tempted to justify substantial policy concessions if it could be argued that no better alternative is available. This temptation would only prevail, however, if office-holding matters more to them than staying true to their policy goals, which may be an excessively cynical view of their motivations (in some cases at least). Moreover, even if that cynicism were warranted, it need not follow that it should be extended to party supporters. Apart from the relatively small numbers of supporters who may expect to benefit from government patronage, there is little in office-holding *per se* that advantages them. What they may want above all is for their leaders to respect their policy commitments, regardless of the portfolio or other costs that might be entailed. In other words, the accurate representation of a party's policy positions in the political arena may be valued in its own right by party voters, and the party's longer-term electoral prospects may depend more on its reputation for sticking to its commitments than on the frequency with which it can find a place for itself at the cabinet table.

The same logic might also guide decisions to join or not to join coalition governments. There are no better illustrations of this than the Communist parties of Western Europe (before 1991). In some cases, their exclusion from government derived from their association with the West's main Cold War adversary, the Soviet Union. But exclusion was more often the consequence of simple policy incompatibility: no government programme could be devised that would have been acceptable both to the Communists and to sufficient other parties to command a parliamentary majority. In some cases, it was the Communist party itself that refused the offer. After the fall of the Socialist–Communist government in France in 1984, for instance, the Communists rejected a Socialist offer of a place in a new government (for the same reasons that caused them to leave the previous one).

There is an interesting footnote to this example. Aware that they stood little chance of retaining their parliamentary majority in the 1986 elections, the subsequent Socialist government decided to change the electoral system to one based on proportional representation. The principal consequence of this change was to eliminate the parliamentary under-representation of the National Front (its seats increased from 0 to

35). The Socialists' purpose was not to help the Front, of course, but it may not have been to improve their own electoral prospects (as was reported at the time), either. Instead, many observers suspected that the real objective was to make the policy incompatibility between the Front and the other parties of the Right (the UDF and the Gaullists) a significant factor in parliamentary politics; in other words, to create on the Right the same kind of dilemma the Socialists had faced, and might face again, on the Left.[3]

These examples suggest that the possibility that parties are constrained in their coalition behaviour by their policy commitments is far from being implausible. Not only would it account for the relative absence from government of many parties of the extreme Left and Right in the post-War period, but it would also explain how it was possible for them to survive electorally for decades in several West European countries despite this lack of access to power.[4] In fact, the possibility has appeared, directly or indirectly, in research on both voting and coalition behaviour. The notion that voters might expect substantial compliance with policy commitments even if it results in a greater policy cost is implicit, for example, in party competition models that see 'abstention from alienation' as a factor that parties must take into account.[5] With respect to government formation, Luebbert (1986, p. 46) advanced the proposition that party leaders are primarily concerned with maintaining their leadership positions and may occasionally forgo opportunities to participate if they calculate that the proposed government's policies would be unpalatable to party members. Similarly, Strøm (1990b, p. 45) reasoned that minority governments may be formed when too many parties anticipate that the policy compromises associated with membership would hurt them in future elections.

Despite these observations, formal models of government formation largely ignore this possibility. This may be because it is assumed that the degree of supporter alienation increases with policy differences and is therefore embedded in the policy-seeking assumption. But the possibility raised here is quite different: it implies the existence of a discrete limit on the amount of policy compromise that party supporters are willing to tolerate. In other words, the suggestion is that, while party supporters presumably accept that coalition-building requires that party leaders be given some flexibility in policy matters, they do so only up to a certain point. Beyond that point, they prefer their party to stay out of government – even if it means that the government that is formed will implement policies that are even more remote from the party's (and their) ideals.

The purpose of this book is to propose and test this possibility. Specifically, it will test the hypothesis that parties in West European parliamentary systems have discrete thresholds or 'policy horizons' that mark the maximum extent of policy compromise that they are prepared to undertake in order to participate in government. In the absence of horizons, parties would potentially be willing to enter governments whose proposed policies are very remote from their own, if that is the best available option. With horizons, there are definite limits to the willingness of parties to compromise on policy regardless of the consequences.

The policy horizon hypothesis immediately raises two very important questions: how can we detect horizons and why should we care whether they exist? The first question poses a very fundamental dilemma, the dilemma of measurement. Without the ability to measure these imagined entities, the policy horizons of parliamentary parties, the hypothesis becomes mere idle speculation. It is evident that we cannot ask party officials for this information – they would have no incentive to be frank about how far their parties are willing to compromise. Other means must therefore be found and a good deal of this book is dedicated to this task. The second question, fortunately, is much more easily addressed, since it can be shown that the existence of horizons has the potential to transform the way in which parliamentary government formation is understood and modelled. The next section sketches the main contours of this argument and, in so doing, provides a rationale for launching a thorough search for policy horizons in extant parliamentary systems.

An overview of the policy horizon hypothesis

Policy horizons and their potential impact are best explored within the context of a spatial voting framework, which is the standard tool for analyzing coalition behaviour in parliamentary contexts. In that framework, the policies of individual parties are represented by points, known as 'ideal points', in a space whose dimensions reflect the major axes of party competition in the system.[6] One such dimension in the ideological space of West European systems is inevitably the left–right dimension, but others – such as a clerical/secular dimension or a materialism/postmaterialism dimension – may be present as well. The practice of representing the policy positions of parties by single points rests on the assumption that each party is united behind a single policy stance that it would like to see implemented by government. This 'unitary actor' assumption is a simplification of the actual state of affairs in many parties but not an unreasonable one for most purposes, since it is almost always the case that parties arrive at single policy platforms that, officially at least, is endorsed by all their parliamentary members.

The policy position of any government or proposed government can also be represented by a point in the ideological space and its attractiveness to a given party depends on how distant it is from the party's ideal point (and, as noted earlier, how important the various issue dimensions are to the party). This policy distance assumption is common to both the standard and the policy horizon approach. Where the latter differs is by postulating that each party's ideal point is surrounded by an outer boundary or 'policy horizon' that demarcates the party's limit of acceptable compromise. According to the hypothesis, a party will normally take up an opportunity to participate in a governing coalition only if that coalition intends to adopt and implement a policy position that lies within the party's horizon. In other words, the hypothesis recognizes that parties will have to compromise to form governments whenever no party is in command of a parliamentary majority, but it adds the stipulation that there is a definite limit to the extent to which any party is willing to do so.

What changes when we introduce the concept of policy horizons? The key point about horizons is that, if they exist and are relatively narrow, then the points in the ideological space upon which viable governments can be constructed will be correspondingly limited. This can have very important implications for government formation, as Figure 1.1(a) illustrates. The figure shows a two-dimensional ideological space occupied by three parties, whose ideal points are labelled A, B, and C. None of these parties possesses a parliamentary majority, but any two of them can form a majority coalition. To keep the illustration as simple as possible, the two policy dimensions are assumed to be of equal importance or salience for each party. This implies circular policy horizons (see Chapter 2), which are drawn around each party's ideal point.

In the absence of policy horizons, the scenario portrayed in Figure 1.1(a) would represent a classic instance of non-stability according to the chaos theorem: no matter what policy point is adopted as the basis for a governing coalition, there is at least one other point in the space that is preferred by some legislative majority. In fact, any point in the space can be reached by some process of outbidding; nothing constrains outcomes to be close to any of the parties. Once policy horizons are introduced, however, the situation changes drastically. Now, the only areas of the space that can serve as the policy basis for a government are the areas enclosed by the three policy horizons;

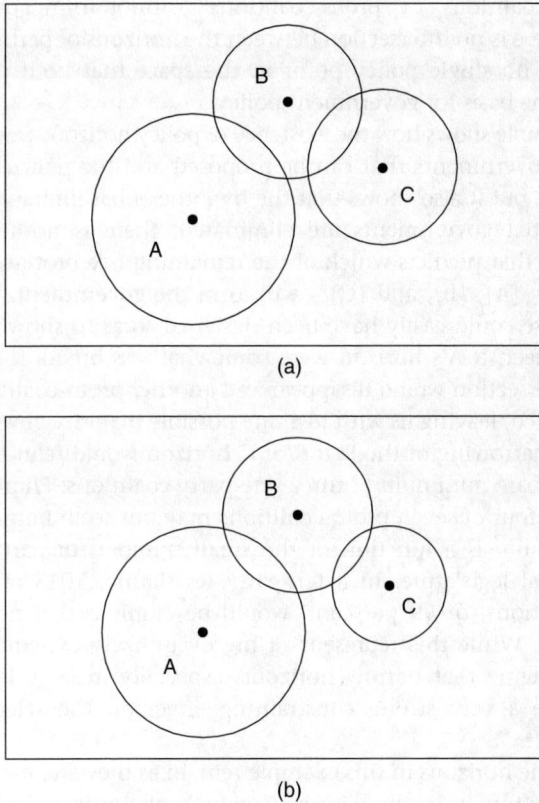

Figure 1.1 Ideal points and policy horizons in a hypothetical three-party legislature.

proposals based on policies lying outside these circles would neither be advanced nor supported by any of the parties. Moreover, for a majority government to form, acceptable policies would have to fall within the considerably smaller petal-like areas created by horizon intersections. Only in these regions can policy points be found that meet the horizon requirements of at least two parties.

In terms of the composition of governments, the range of possibilities is also simplified. Under the policy distance assumption, not only is it possible for any policy in the space to be proposed, but it is also possible for any party or combination of parties to make proposals. Of the seven possible governments in this example, however, the policy horizon hypothesis rules out two: the coalition of parties A and C, denoted {AC}, and the grand coalition of all three parties, {ABC}. These two potential coalitions, or 'proto-coalitions', cannot form governments because there is no intersection between the horizons of parties A and C and hence no single policy point in the space that both parties can accept as the basis for government policy.

This example shows how the existence of policy horizons would narrow both the governments that can be proposed and the policies they can implement, but it also shows that the hypothesis has limitations. While two potential governments are eliminated, there is nothing in the hypothesis that predicts which of the remaining five proto-coalitions – {AB}, {BC}, {A}, {B}, and {C} – will form the government. Of course, the example could easily have been designed so as to show a stronger horizon effect. If A's horizon were somewhat less broad, for instance, the AB intersection would disappear and another proto-coalition would be eliminated, leaving us with just one possible majority government; a moderate narrowing of the B and/or C horizon would reduce possibilities to the bare minimum of three one-party coalitions. Eliminating no more than four of seven proto-coalitions may not seem impressive, but this maximum is a function of the small numbers of parties in this hypothetical legislature. In a ten-party legislature, 1013 of the 1023 proto-coalitions, or 99 per cent, would be eliminated if no horizons intersected. While this represents a highly unlikely extreme, one can readily imagine that narrow horizons, especially in large legislatures, could have a very strong constraining effect on the selection of a government.

Even if the horizons in this example remain as they are, moreover, we are not left totally in the dark as to which of the five eligible proto-coalitions will form the government. Since no single party commands a parliamentary majority by itself, we can anticipate that the two-party proto-coalitions have better odds of emerging as the government than any single party (other things being equal). We might further anticipate that, of the two intersecting majority proto-coalitions, the one composed of B and C has a better chance than the one composed of parties A and B. This would follow from policy distance considerations, since B's ideal point is closer to C's than it is to A's, but it might also follow from the fact that B and C have a larger horizon intersection, making it easier for them to find a policy they can agree on and easier to find acceptable alternatives should circumstances necessitate a change in course.

The latter interpretation suggests a subsidiary horizon hypothesis: within the set of proto-coalitions with intersecting horizons, those with larger intersections are more likely to form the government. In this example, we cannot assess its viability because policy distances mirror intersection sizes, but consider the slightly altered version of this legislature shown in Figure 1.1(b). The only change from Figure 1.1(a) is that party C's horizon is now somewhat narrower. It still intersects B's horizon, but the intersection has become smaller than the {AB} intersection – even though B's ideal point remains closer to C's than to A's. If distance considerations prevail, we would still expect that {BC} would be more likely to form than {AB}, but if what really matters is the range of policies that the coalescing parties would find mutually acceptable, then {AB} becomes the more likely government. Thus, it is possible that horizon intersections influence the choice of government not just by their existence but by their size, and this additional influence can be detected so long as policy distances and horizon intersection sizes do not always move in lockstep.

In sum, the horizon hypothesis can tell us a lot about coalition government formation, but it cannot tell us everything. Since it is always possible under the hypothesis for a party to form a government by itself, and since any legislature that we would be interested in will have at least three parties, there will always be three or more possible governments that might form under the hypothesis. A complete account of government formation must be able to identify which of these alternatives, if any, will emerge as the government. This need not mean that the contribution of policy horizons is an unimportant one, however. Policy horizons can play a powerful role in the government formation process if they are narrow enough to rule out a substantial proportion of possible governments (and perhaps to make others less likely because of small intersection sizes); conversely, very large horizons would eliminate few alternatives and thereby yield little explanatory purchase on the formation process. This means that policy horizons can affect outcomes significantly only if parties are obliged to take policy commitments seriously, which is, of course, a fundamental premise of the entire approach.

The policy horizon hypothesis thus has the potential to transform the way in which parliamentary government formation is understood and modelled. At this stage, however, it is only a potential. Not only must it be established that parties operate within the constraint of horizons, but the horizons must be sufficiently narrow to convey a major constraining influence on the choice of a government in coalition situations. Of more immediate import is that fact that nothing can be established unless we can find some means of measuring these imagined entities. The next section considers this pivotal issue.

Finding a horizon effect

It has already been noted that the most direct approach to measuring horizons – simply asking party officials how far their parties would be willing to compromise in government – is unlikely to elicit truthful responses. Officials might not only indicate less flexibility than actually exists, but declare that there are strict bounds when in fact there are none. More indirect means must therefore be found and an obvious place to begin is with the parties' past behaviour in coalition formation situations. Since a party's horizon represents the limit of its willingness to compromise for the purposes of government participation, it stands to reason that some indication of where that limit lies will be detectable in the amounts of compromise it has accepted in the past.

The most straightforward way to do this would be to look at the instances in which a party participated in a government, calculate the distance between the party's policy position and that of the government it joined in each case, and take the maximum of these distances as defining the party's limit of compromise. This method requires that we have some means of measuring party and government positions and it also requires that the party in question be present in enough formation situations to reveal its propensity for compromise with reasonable accuracy. These are practical matters that can be addressed, as we shall see. A more demanding feature of the method is its assumption that parties never miscalculate in their coalition decisions and never make exceptions, even in extraordinary circumstances. Fortunately, this latter assumption can be relaxed by resorting to a second behaviour-based method. This method uses a logistic regression of government membership on party–government policy distances to locate the distance at which the probability of being a government member reaches 50 per cent for each party, which is then identified as its limit of compromise.

Both methods will be employed in the estimation of party horizons in West European parliamentary systems and a comparison of their results will enable us to offset their particular weaknesses to some extent. But there is one potential weakness that cannot be offset in this way because they both may be susceptible to it. This is the risk that the use of behaviour-based horizons will lead to explanations that are circular or endogenous. This risk is present because the methods utilize information on the coalition behaviour of parties in the estimation of their policy horizons, then employ those horizons to account for which coalitions took office.

This is clearly a possibility that must be evaluated with great care. But even if that evaluation process were to allay concerns about endogeneity (which it does), it would still be desirable to submit the horizon hypothesis to tests in which the measurement of policy horizons is separate from the testing itself. One avenue might be to use horizons estimated from coalition behaviour in one period to test for a horizon effect in the coalition formations of a subsequent period; closer examination will show, however, that this solution is not as viable as it might appear. A better approach would be to measure horizons from a source other than coalition behaviour. To realize this goal, a new survey of experts in the politics of 13 West European parliamentary democracies was undertaken. In this survey, respondents were asked not only to locate party positions on a number of policy dimensions, but also to estimate the bounds or limits of acceptable compromise for each of those parties on those dimensions (without reference to their coalition behaviour). There is no guarantee that this approach will provide more accurate estimates of horizons – respondents may never have considered whether parties have horizons, much less where to locate them – but at least they are (and, in fact, can be shown to be) uninfluenced by coalition behaviour.

The use of multiple measurement strategies is driven by the realization that no single strategy exists that can provide a completely satisfactory measurement of the concept of policy horizons. Given that the existence of horizons has only been hinted at in previous research, this is hardly a surprising state of affairs, but it does mean that establishing the truth value of the policy horizon hypothesis will be no easy matter. The hope is that the use of alternative measures will yield a pattern of findings that is consistent enough to sustain a firm conclusion concerning its validity.

It is not enough, however, simply to measure the limits of compromise for parties with some accuracy. For one thing, compromise limits must be translated into horizons. The translation process is a straightforward matter in the case of the behaviour-based methods, since they produce a single distance for each party that represents its limit of compromise in all directions. This means that the horizon for each party is a circle or sphere centred on the party's ideal point with a radius equal to that distance. For the survey-based horizons, however, no such constraint operates. Respondents were not required to estimate spherical or any other kind of symmetrical horizon and they did not do so. Freedom from this constraint allows for a more realistic estimation of horizons, since there is no reason why a party should not be willing to compromise more on one dimension than another or, indeed, more in one direction on a given dimension than in the other. But it underscores the importance of a hitherto unmentioned requirement for testing the hypothesis: some means of constructing policy horizons from information on each party's limits of compromise and then of determining which horizons intersect in any given legislature.

This is no simple task; in fact, a substantial portion of the research effort was consumed by the process of developing the specialized computer software to address it. The outcome of this process is *Horizons 3D©*, a computer program that has the capacity to construct a (possibly irregularly shaped) horizon for each party in a legislature from information on its position and compromise limits in up to three policy dimensions and to display these horizons visually.[7] It also determines which of all proto-coalitions have common horizon intersections and calculates the size of each of them. To test the horizon hypothesis against its natural foil, the hypothesis that compact proto-coalitions are more likely to form governments because they tend to impose lower policy costs on their member-parties, the program calculates the distance spanned by each possible coalition (taking due account of dimension saliences, where necessary). Finally, since the measurement of parameters such as the location of parties' positions and horizons is bound to be imprecise, the program contains a simulation capability that allows the researcher to vary parameters randomly, either according to some global error specification or according to the specific error associated with each parameter, in order to obtain estimates of the likelihood that a horizon intersection exists, given that error.

It will be apparent by now that the testing of the horizon hypothesis requires a substantial stockpile of new weaponry (the *Horizons 3D©* program) and ammunition (the various sets of horizon estimates). What justifies the scope and complexity of the testing procedure is the potential import of the hypothesis for the study of coalition government: as we have seen, it could alter fundamentally our understanding of how parliamentary systems function in the absence of a majority party. In the remainder of this chapter, I outline how this book will explore and assess this potential.

The plan of attack

The plan of attack unfolds more or less in the order in which the hypothesis and its testing have been laid out in the foregoing comments. I begin in Chapter 2 with a more precise statement of the policy horizon hypothesis and a more detailed exploration of its implications for research on coalition government in parliamentary systems. This chapter will also relate the concept of horizons to its theoretical predecessors. Attention then turns to the methodology to be used for testing the hypothesis, including an exposition of the specific capabilities of the *Horizons 3D*© program and their relevance to the research tasks at hand.

In Chapter 3, the two methods for estimating policy horizons from the coalition behaviour and policy positions of parties are developed. The possibility of endogeneity is also addressed, including an analysis of simulated data to demonstrate that the methods, although utilizing coalition behaviour in the estimation process, are highly unlikely to create a false or artefactual horizon effect. The methods are then applied to post-War government formations in 14 West European parliamentary democracies, using party positions derived from Comparative Manifestos Project (CMP) data. The analyses reveal that the horizons estimated by both methods have a strong structuring effect on the outcomes of these formation processes, even when other significant influences are controlled and especially when simulations are used to take account of the possibility of random measurement error in the position and horizon estimates.

Although the behaviour-based horizons do not generate false horizon effects, we have seen that it would still be valuable to derive a set of horizon estimates that are independent of coalition behaviour. This would assist not only in laying the endogeneity concern to rest but also in overcoming certain inherent limitations in the behaviour-based methods. Most notable among these is the assumption of circular or spherical horizons, which imply that compromise in all policy directions is equally costly to parties. Chapter 4 addresses these concerns by introducing a new data source, a custom-designed survey of experts on 13 West European parliamentary systems. This survey facilitates the derivation of an appropriate multidimensional ideological space for each system, provides estimates of the saliences of the dimensions, and locates both the positions and the compromise limits of each party on each dimension.

The use of the survey estimates also comes with costs. One cost is the substantial risk of measurement error inherent in asking respondents to estimate a set of parameters that is both large and, to some extent, novel. Substantial attention is therefore devoted in this chapter to establishing the reliability and validity of the survey results, especially those concerning the estimation of horizon bounds.

The estimates of party and horizon parameters derived from the survey responses are utilized in new tests of the horizon hypothesis in Chapter 5. The results show that survey-estimated horizons have a net structuring effect on government formation, albeit not as strong an effect as the behaviour-based horizons displayed. Further investigation reveals that the discrepancy results from the positions and horizons estimated for a very small number of parties on certain dimensions (for the most part, Christian Democratic parties and their partners on a clerical–secular dimension) and that the failure is one of measurement rather than of the hypothesis itself. By using a multiple imputation technique to adjust for these anomalies, a much stronger horizon effect is uncovered.

The book to this point has largely concentrated on measuring policy horizons in West European coalition systems and determining whether they provide an additional constraint on coalition formation beyond that entailed by policy distance costs. In Chapter 6, a variety of other issues suggested by the policy horizon approach is explored, including the possibility that policy horizons can cast some light on the formation of minority governments. The hypothesis, suggested in the discussion of Figure 1.1(b), that some or all of the remaining policy distance effect (i.e. the part not already attributed to horizon intersections) should more properly be attributed to intersection size will be a particular focus of this investigation.

Chapter 7 expands the perspective further by exploring the implications of policy horizons for the survival of governments in coalition situations. It brings into the analysis a range of factors demonstrated in previous research to influence survival, but is especially concerned with horizon-related issues such as whether governing coalitions based on large horizon intersections, which presumably have more room to manoeuvre without violating the horizons of any member-party, tend to outlast other governments. The focus in previous chapters on the attributes of all possible coalitions facilitates the introduction of a perspective largely ignored in systematic empirical explorations of government survival: does the survival of a government depend on the properties possessed by other coalitions that might be formed? The investigation thus seeks to open new methodological as well as new substantive ground in the investigation of this central issue in parliamentary governance.

Chapter 8 pulls together the results presented in the previous six in order to evaluate the overall status of the policy horizon hypothesis. It also explores how the policy horizon framework might influence the evolution of theorizing on, and especially formal modelling of, parliamentary government in coalition situations. As we shall see, much depends on matters about which we know very little. For instance, it is possible that the odds of minority governments being formed are conditioned by 'support horizons', that is discrete limits on how far parties can go in providing parliamentary support for minority governments. Regardless of how questions like this are ultimately answered, it will be evident that the existence of policy horizons does much more than add a modest qualification to the way in which policy distance is conceptualized in formal models; it opens the door to a very different view of the government formation process in parliamentary systems.

2
The Nature and Testing of the Policy Horizon Hypothesis

Parliamentary parties are usually treated in theoretical work as both policy-seekers and office-seekers, and the policy horizon approach accepts much that is implied by this perspective. Under the horizon approach, for instance, parties still prefer government policy to be as close as possible to their own policy stances (taking due account of dimension saliences) and they may covet cabinet portfolios as well. Indeed, under certain circumstances they may even trade policy for offices. But the horizon approach also anticipates that a party might refuse an opportunity to join a proposed government even though this refusal would result in policy outcomes diverging further from the party's preferences (and, of course, costing it office benefits as well). Such a decision would fit poorly within the standard framework.

Parties might make such a choice, however, if they care not just about which policy is implemented but also about who implements it. In particular, the choice might follow from an unwillingness on the part of party leaders to participate in governments whose intent is to implement policies that are too far away from the party's stated commitments. The notion of being 'too far away' implies the existence of a threshold for each party delimiting the policies it considers acceptable as a basis for government participation, and this, in essence, is what the horizon hypothesis proposes. This threshold should hold regardless of any office benefits that might be on offer (which means that policy can only be traded for offices up to but not beyond the threshold) and regardless of how it affects the subsequent evolution of the coalition formation process.

At this point, all that we can say about policy horizons is that their existence is plausible and that it could entail a substantial change in the way coalition behaviour is understood. The purpose of this chapter is to advance matters by developing the concept of horizons and its implications more rigorously and then by exploring what would be required to establish their relevance in actual parliamentary systems. The first of these tasks is undertaken in the next section, which highlights the uniqueness of the approach by differentiating it from others in the literature that might appear to bear a certain resemblance to it. The remainder of the chapter introduces the methodology that will be enlisted to test the horizon hypothesis, including the specialized software that has been developed for this purpose.

Policy horizons and their consequences

The nature of policy horizons

In order to explore further the concept of policy horizons and its potential impact on government formation, let us return to the spatial voting framework introduced in Chapter 1. Recall that policies in that framework are represented by points in an ideological space of one or more dimensions and that the proximity of points in the space reflects the similarity of the positions they represent (other things being equal). The policy horizon concept can be represented by surrounding each party's ideal point (most preferred position) with a boundary that circumscribes the set of policies acceptable to the party as a basis for government participation. Only policies within this boundary or horizon would meet the criterion of acceptability, although a party might prefer those that entail lower distance costs.[1]

This method of representing policy horizons brings to mind the indifference contours that are often used to join policy points of equal utility in spatial representations, especially those drawn through some status quo (SQ) or reversionary point. Figure 2.1(a) shows indifference contours of this type for two parties, A and B. They are drawn through the SQ point which represents the policy stance currently being implemented by the government. All points on each contour have the same policy utility for the party they enclose as the SQ policy, which is why the party is indifferent among them. The party in question would prefer any policy located inside its contour, however, since they are all closer to its ideal point, while points outside it are more distant and hence have less utility for it. Thus, each contour divides the space into the set of policies that the party prefers to SQ – and hence would be willing to take action to bring into effect – and the set that it does not. If that action includes joining a government that plans to implement one of

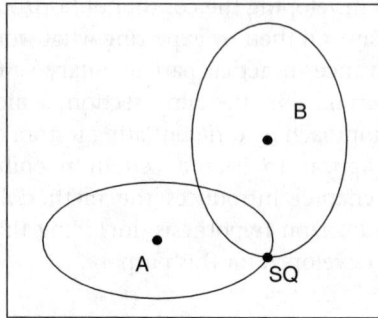

(a)

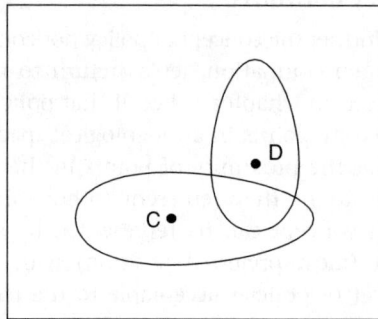

(b)

Figure 2.1   Examples of standard indifference contours and policy horizons.
(a) Standard indifference contours through an SQ point (b) Non-symmetrical
policy horizons.

the policies inside the indifference contour, the contour begins to look
very much like a policy horizon.

Although policy horizons are indifference contours, they nevertheless
differ from what is portrayed in the figure. The most obvious difference
is that horizons are not drawn with respect to the SQ or any other reversionary or baseline policy. To take a simple illustration, suppose that
the conservatives control government policy in an ideological space
defined by a single left–right dimension. For a left-wing party such as
the Communist party, any policy to the left of the conservatives' position (the current SQ) would be preferable and its indifference contour
would therefore pass through that point. But given its ideological
commitments, it is highly unlikely that the Communists would be

willing to participate in the implementation of all policies in this range; the party's policy horizon may not even extend as far as the Socialists' position. Another difference is that an indifference contour of this type will change with every change in government policy. If the conservative government is succeeded by a liberal government, the Communists' indifference contour would be altered accordingly, but there is no reason to expect its ideological commitments, and hence its horizon, to change. Horizons represent much more long-term commitments and therefore do not change with every change in current government policy.[2]

The fact that policy horizons are indifference contours is nonetheless instructive. Like other types of indifference contour, policy horizons may not treat policy distance in all directions equally. This is represented graphically by contours that do not extend the same distance in all directions. The indifference contour for party A in Figure 2.1(a), for example, extends considerably further along the horizontal dimension than along the vertical one. The SQ point located close to the right extreme of the contour is therefore much further away from A's ideal point than a policy located at the contour's highest point, even though the party would be indifferent between them. This indicates that distance in the vertical dimension is more costly to A: each unit of distance lowers its utility more on this dimension than on the horizontal dimension. Thus, the elliptical contour surrounding A's ideal point conveys the information that party A attributes a much higher importance or *salience* to policy differences on the vertical dimension. By the same token, the fact that B's indifference contour extends further in the vertical dimension indicates that B attributes more salience to the horizontal dimension.

Policy horizons are especially likely to take this property one step further. Since it is perfectly possible for a party to be willing to associate itself with larger policy concessions in one direction than another, a horizon may lack the symmetry about the party's ideal point that is typical of indifference contours. This means that the cost a party attributes to a given policy distance may vary not just across dimensions but also within them, depending on the direction in which they are taken. The horizon drawn around party C in Figure 2.1(b) illustrates this possibility. It shows not only that C attributes more salience to policy in the vertical dimension than in the horizontal dimension, but also that C finds compromise less costly to its right on the latter dimension than to its left. Similarly, the asymmetrical horizon drawn around D's ideal point indicates that D is more tolerant of policy compromise above its position on the vertical dimension than below it.

The easy translation of the concept of policy horizons into the standard spatial modelling framework suggests that it may have been anticipated in previous modelling efforts. Perhaps the most obvious candidate is the concept of a 'region of acceptability' in the directional theory of voting proposed by Rabinowitz and Macdonald (1989). On any given issue, this theory posits that voters prefer parties to the extent that they adopt their side of the issue and articulate that position with great intensity. Yet intensity is likely to alienate rather than attract voters if it becomes excessive and for this reason it must be kept within bounds that are considered 'acceptable' in the political system in question. These bounds enclose the region of acceptability.

Policy horizons and directional theory's regions of acceptability share the property that they both delimit what is acceptable in party behaviour in a given political system. But their apparent affinity is deceptive; in fact, they differ from each other in two fundamental respects. First, the spaces in which they exist are different. Rabinowitz and Macdonald's regions demarcate the limits on acceptable levels of emotional intensity, not acceptable policy positions (a point frequently overlooked in the literature). Second, the region of acceptability in any party system applies to all of its parties, or at least all 'acceptable' (i.e. non-extremist) parties; it does not define party-specific limits. Thus, even if it were referencing positions rather than intensities, the concept would only rule out governments in which extremist parties participated. In the context of government formation, the explanatory value of this achievement would be very limited. The policy horizon approach aims to achieve a good deal more.

Linking policy horizons with directional theory's regions of acceptability is thus a false path. But there is another path that does bring us much closer to the concept of policy horizons. Consider the formulation of party utility employed in a formal model of coalition government proposed by Sened (1995, 1996). It follows the standard practice of seeing a party's utility as a function of the portfolio payoff it receives and the policy distance cost it must bear, the latter represented by the squared distance between government and party policy positions.[3] The key innovation is that Sened attributes no policy cost to parties that are not in government because he assumes that they are not held responsible for government policy. The consequence is that a party will only join a government if its payoff in portfolios exceeds the cost of being associated with policies other than its own. Since the total utility to be had from cabinet portfolios is assumed to be fairly limited (Sened 1995, p. 294), this specification implies the existence of an outer bound on the policy distance costs that a party can accept by entering government. The greater the relative importance of policy to party utility, the narrower this bound will be.

A limit on the extent to which parties can compromise in government is therefore implied by Sened's definition of party utility and for a reason very similar to the one proposed here for horizons: supporters hold parties responsible for policies implemented by governments they join. But the resemblance is far from total. The policy horizons created by Sened's definition are a function not of the policy stances to which the party is committed, but of the value of the various cabinet portfolios. Add more portfolios to the cabinet and Sened's party horizons will expand. In addition, given the very strong evidence that portfolios are allocated according to the legislative sizes of coalition parties (e.g. Warwick and Druckman 2001), Sened's horizons will tend to be larger for larger parties. The bigger the party, the more it can give up on policy because the more it can expect to get in terms of portfolios.

While this conception has the merit of introducing a constraint on coalition behaviour emanating from outside the parliamentary arena, the picture it paints is unconvincing. How likely is it that large parties are less rigid on policy matters because they can command more cabinet portfolios? In fact, what we tend to observe is the opposite: large parties getting their way more often at the cabinet table because their presence is greater.[4] The core problem with Sened's conception of party utility is that it fails to take account of the asymmetry in the two sources of party utility: the cost of policy compromise is borne by all party supporters but the benefits of cabinet office go largely to the party leaders who hold them.[5] This asymmetry means that, if a party trades policy for offices, party supporters lose on the former but gain little on the latter. Although supporters may tolerate this behaviour to some extent – they may get some psychic or other benefits from having their leaders in office or they may not be fully aware of what is happening – it is unlikely that the unfettered exploitation of this type of trade-off would go down well with them. The policy horizon approach recognizes this by allowing policy trade-offs only within a limit that is not fungible: the policy horizon itself.

The sources of policy horizons

If policy horizons are not the by-product of the limited availability of office benefits, where do they come from? One possibility is that the capacity for policy compromise may be limited because party supporters expect reasonably faithful representation of their views and leaders fear that they will become disaffected if that expectation is not met. In his *Economic Theory of Democracy*, Downs (1957, pp. 103–9) saw such an expectation as following from the desire of voters to reduce uncertainty over future outcomes. The non-simultaneous nature of this exchange of votes for policies clearly puts voters at a disadvantage, and it would not be surprising if some of them were to sanction parties that failed to deliver on their side of the bargain. In fact, recent evidence indicates that voter abstention in US presidential elections emanates in substantial measure from alienation from candidates' policies, rather than just indifference about the outcome (Adams *et al.* 2001). In West European parliamentary systems where more choice is generally available, one can readily imagine that vote-switching would be the more likely outcome.

Another possibility is that the main external constraint comes not from voters but from party activists. After all, it is the activists that contribute the time and money that make it possible for the party to fight elections. While party leaders may be tempted to alter party positions to attract new electoral support, the expectations of their policy-motivated activists may limit their freedom to do so. According to Aldrich (1995, p. 183), 'The political role of this part of the party is to attempt to constrain the actual leaders of the party, the ambitious office seekers, as they try to become the party-in-government by appealing to the electorate.'

These explanations suggest a principal-agent framework in which voters and/or activists provide needed resources (votes, money, effort) to parties in order to have their views articulated and advanced in the political arena and are prepared to punish those that betray that responsibility. But they also raise a problem: which views are to be represented faithfully? After all, not all voters or activists of a party share the same political stance. If their ideal points are spread out in the vicinity of the party's ideal point and if each expects reasonable representation of his or her position, this would imply the existence of a plethora of overlapping but largely non-coincident supporter horizons – which ones should the party respect?

It may be that decisions to join or not join coalitions are based on calculations of the extent to which they satisfy the individual horizons of their voters or activists, taking due account of the costs and benefits of altering policy positions so as to attract new support. These calculations are likely to be highly complex, however, and to the extent that they are, their credibility as a decision-making mechanism diminishes. Quite apart from the infeasibility of knowing the locations of individual voter or supporter horizons with sufficient precision, the image of party leaders or advisors engaging in complex mathematical calculations to determine whether accepting a given coalition offer will preserve or enhance their electoral base lacks verisimilitude. Political decisions, one suspects, are arrived at much more simply.

Formal voting models often assume that parties avoid complexities such as this by focussing their attention on the median voter or party supporter, but it is not yet clear whether this is an accurate description of behaviour or merely a device to make their models tractable. Something quite different may be at work: party leaders may believe that their party's longer-term interests (and their own as well) are best served by cultivating and preserving a distinct ideological identity for the party, regardless of whether it maximizes support at any one time. This interpretation corresponds to an advertising or 'brand label' framework. Indeed, rather than accepting voter positions as given, parties may set out to mould the electoral landscape by pitching a particular ideological brand; once brand loyalty has been established, it then becomes paramount for the party to adhere reasonably faithfully to it. After all, if supporters of a party have come to accept the message that its ideological stance provides the correct strategy for confronting the country's problems and challenges, a party's decision to participate in a government that intends to implement an essentially different agenda is bound to undermine its *raison d'être*. This does not mean that the party's position and horizon cannot evolve, but the evolution – since it involves changing the beliefs of existing supporters rather than seeking out a new clientele – is likely to be gradual.

Good examples of the problems involved in attempting to loosen the constraints of prior policy commitments can be found in German politics. In 2002, the *Washington Post* (reprinted in the *Guardian Weekly*, 28 February 2002) reported that the Greens, the junior partner in the Social Democrat-led coalition government, were facing an identity crisis after the party leadership chose to remain in the government and accept the participation of German troops in the US-led invasion of Afghanistan. In view of the Greens' long-standing pacifism, 'voters are wondering what the Greens stand for now', the article noted. It also cited a following assessment by a prominent party defector (Wolf-Dieter Hasenclever): 'The leaders of the party want to govern, but I think they need to go into opposition to refresh themselves. The soul of the party is gone.' A similar situation confronted the Social Democrats over Chancellor Schröder's economic reform programme, which, the *Guardian Weekly* (12 February 2004) reports, 'has caused an exodus of party members, who feel the SPD is betraying its socialist principles'.

The idea of brand loyalty naturally suggests a concept long familiar and, especially in non-American contexts, long debated: the concept of party identification. If the concept is intended to capture an emotional or non-rational commitment to a party, however, it actually takes us away from the idea of horizons. A voter may become emotionally attached to a particular party under the horizon approach, but this attachment is to the ideological stance or image conveyed by the party. In other words, loyalty is conditional rather than blind; it must constrain coalition behaviour rather than giving party leaders *carte blanche* to do what they like.

The discussion of cultivating allegiance to an ideological brand conjures up an image of manipulative, unprincipled leaders, but there is no reason why this need be the case. While leaders must be mindful of maintaining the allegiance of supporters, it is not beyond the realm of imagination that party leaders themselves may be sincerely committed to a particular ideology or political programme and reluctant to compromise those beliefs beyond a certain point. Although leaders bear the office costs of excluding the party from government, these costs may be offset by the value they place on their own political convictions – convictions strong enough to have led them to seek careers in politics in the first place. Extreme cynicism concerning politicians' motivations also lacks verisimilitude.

These observations concerning the sources of horizons are, of course, impressionistic rather than rigorous. I shall have more to say about the possible sources of horizons in the concluding chapter, but it should be understood that there are limits on what can be established in this study. This is because the data that have been collected for this investigation allow us to detect the presence of horizons, but provide no convincing evidence concerning their sources.[6] Nevertheless, the preceding comments make it clear that the existence of horizons would rule out certain possibilities. For instance, even if leaders care only for preserving and growing their electoral base, the notion that parties have policy horizons is not the same as saying that they are vote-seekers, as the term is normally understood. Parties must concern themselves with their survival, to be sure, and survival ultimately depends on attracting votes in parliamentary elections. But a vote-seeking party would not let principles and past commitments stand in its way; if there are more votes to be had by re-positioning itself, it would do so. While the positions and horizons of parties may evolve over time, we have seen that the need to take policy commitments seriously imposes limits on the ability of parties to manoeuvre in the ideological space, at least in the short term. One would not be able to draw a horizon around a true vote-seeking party.

The policy horizon hypothesis

If we are limited in what we can say about the sources of policy horizons, this is not the case with respect to their impact. The important point about horizons is that their existence may affect the government formation process by limiting the choice to proto-coalitions composed of parties with intersecting horizons. The reason is evident: if a set of parties lacks a common horizon intersection, they cannot come together to form a government because there is no point in the space that they would all accept as the policy basis for that government. The policy horizon hypothesis thus takes the form of a two-pronged necessary condition: (1) for a *party* to participate in a government, the government's proposed policy position must fall within the horizon surrounding the party's ideal point that circumscribes the set of policies acceptable to it as a basis for government participation, and therefore (2) for a *government* to form, the horizons of all parties participating in the government must intersect one another in the ideological space.

Two aspects of the potential impact of this hypothesis deserve emphasis. The first is that the hypothesis cannot provide a complete explanation of government formation in parliamentary systems because the necessary condition it stipulates can never be uniquely satisfied. The hypothesis, in other words, proposes a necessary condition for government formation but not a sufficient one. As noted in Chapter 1, this is because the hypothesis is only of interest for legislatures that have more than two parties and, since any party can form a government by itself that satisfies the condition (by implementing a policy that falls within its own horizon), these legislatures will always have at least three possible governments. The hypothesis therefore has the more limited purpose of advancing a change in the way in which a key building block of any complete theory, the cost of policy compromise, is conceptualized.

The second point to note is that limited changes may nonetheless have major consequences. Under the hypothesis, parties do not evaluate potential governments simply on the basis of the policy distance costs they would entail (along with office or other inducements they would provide); instead, coalition options may be ruled out absolutely on the basis of policy, regardless of other considerations. How much this condition affects outcomes depends largely on the degree of tolerance parties have for policy compromise. Broad horizons (i.e. high tolerance for compromise) imply little impact, but if horizons are narrow enough to eliminate a substantial proportion of potential governing coalitions, the dynamics and outcome of the government formation process could be profoundly altered.

Testing the hypothesis

Although the policy horizon hypothesis is relatively simple to state, it is by no means simple to test. Determining whether policy horizons impose a significant constraining influence on the coalition game in parliamentary government requires three capabilities: (1) the ability to estimate the limits of compromise for individual parties, (2) the ability to construct horizons for parties from this information and to determine their intersections, and (3) the ability to assess the role that these intersections play in the government formation process. The methods that will be used to locate the compromise limits themselves are best developed in the context of the data analysis and their full elaboration is deferred until then. The remainder of this chapter will focus on the other components of the testing process: the construction of horizons and the testing of their impact.

The primary purpose of this discussion is to lay out the stages of the testing procedure as well as to introduce the custom-built software that is required in order to implement it. But there is a second, no less important purpose: to provide further clarification concerning the nature of the horizon hypothesis and, in particular, to bring into focus certain assumptions that are entailed in moving its evaluation to an empirical level. We begin in the next section with the final stage, the actual testing of the hypothesis.

Requirements and basic tools

The most appropriate statistical tool for testing the horizon hypothesis, and in fact any hypothesis concerning coalition government formation, is the McFadden's (1973) conditional logit model. This model estimates the effects of various traits on the odds of achieving some outcome, conditional on being a member of the choice set or set of alternatives at play. For any given government formation situation, the choice set consists of every possible combination of parties or 'proto-coalition' and the outcome in question is the emergence of one of these proto-coalitions as the government. Thus, the method has the advantage of taking all possibilities in any formation situation into account, while avoiding complications arising from variations in the number of possibilities across formation situations by making the situation itself the unit of analysis (Martin and Stevenson 2001, pp. 38–9).[7]

Using the conditional logit procedure to test the horizon hypothesis is contingent upon the capacity to determine which of a potentially large number of proto-coalitions in a legislature have horizons that mutually intersect. Because this requirement is unique to the horizon hypothesis, it is not surprising that no existing computer software can address it. It was therefore necessary to develop new software for this purpose. The result is *Horizons 3D*[©], a stand-alone Java program that displays party horizons and calculates not only their intersections but also a variety of other useful quantities. *Horizons 3D*[©] is freely available to interested readers and complete instructions for installing and operating it are provided in Appendix 1. In the remainder of this discussion, I outline the tasks that it can perform and their relevance to the present investigation.

The first point to note about *Horizons 3D*[©] is that its capacity extends to ideological spaces of two or three dimensions.[8] Limiting spaces to three dimensions reflects in part the need to keep calculations within tractable bounds (as we shall see, they can still involve large amounts of computer time). More significantly, it meets or exceeds what is typically attributed to West European party systems. To cite a few prominent examples, the Manifesto Research Group's (Budge *et al.* 1987) analyses of party manifestos generally turned up two dimensions per system; Laver and Shepsle's (1996) testing of their portfolio allocation model of parliamentary government utilized two or three dimensions per system; and Müller and Strøm's (2000) compendium does not allocate more than three dimensions for any system.

The most basic task that *Horizons 3D*[©] must address is the construction of horizons in ideological spaces of these dimensionalities. The program provides three means for doing so, depending on the kinds of assumptions that are made about the horizons. The simplest form of horizon is a circular (two dimensions) or spherical (three dimensions) horizon, which represents the situation in which dimensions are equally salient for the party in question in the sense that a unit of policy distance in any direction costs it the same loss of utility. All that is needed for *Horizons 3D*[©] to create this type of horizon is the location of the party's ideal point and a radius, that is the distance from the ideal point to the horizon. A single radius or compromise distance is, in fact, the type of horizon information that the two behaviour-based methods generate for each party and, as a result, all horizons estimated via those methods take on this shape (and the assumptions that underlie it).

If a party does not see all dimensions as equally salient, but still treats distance in either direction on any one dimension as equivalent, the result is an elliptical or ellipsoidal horizon. The creation of horizons of this shape in *Horizons 3D*© requires separate radii for each dimension. Since policy compromise is still symmetrical within dimensions, the horizon is centred on the party's ideal point. The radii define how far the horizon is from that point in each direction. Thus, a two-dimensional horizon with radii of two units on the horizontal dimension and three units on the vertical dimension would locate the horizon bounds at two units above and below the ideal point and three units to its left and right. The four points would then be joined in a smooth elliptical curve to create the horizon.

If we relax the assumption that distance costs are symmetrical about the ideal point, a much more complex horizon is implied. It corresponds to the case in which a party not only treats compromise on different dimensions differently, but also treats compromise in one direction of a dimension differently from compromise in the other direction. For instance, a party might be more willing to compromise on the clerical/secular dimension than on the left/right one and it might also be more willing to tolerate compromise on the former dimension if it entails greater secularism than if it entails greater clericalism. These are referred to in *Horizons 3D*© as 'user-defined horizons' and their construction requires the locations of the upper and lower bounds or limits of compromise on each dimension (these can be entered either as distances from the ideal point or as positions on the various dimensions). *Horizons 3D*© creates the horizon by joining up these bounds in a smooth, concave perimeter surrounding the party's ideal point.

With a horizon of this type, the constraint that the ideal point should be located at its geometric centre is relaxed and, with it, the constraint that the horizon should take on a regular shape such as a sphere or an ellipsoid. The sole assumption that is made about the shape is that parties trade off concessions in one dimension against those in another. This implies that when a party has reached its limits of compromise on one dimension, it will not also be making concessions in other dimensions. This assumption, which also applies to the other horizon types, is based on the idea that a horizon is an indifference contour that joins points of equal policy cost to the party.

In reality, horizons might not have this property. Its absence might mean that horizons are square (two dimensions) or box like (three dimensions) in shape, which would indicate that parties would be willing to go to their compromise limits in one dimension, regardless of how much they have compromised in the other dimension(s). Another possibility is that horizons are 'non-separable', that is they are slanted diagonally so that the compromise limit on one dimension is reached at a point where some degree of compromise is also entailed on at least one other dimension. This would mean, for example, that the high points in C's and D's horizons in Figure 2.1(b) would not be located directly above their ideal points, but somewhere to their left or right. What makes these alternatives implausible is that they imply that parties will tolerate greater policy costs in directions that are not parallel to dimensional axes than in directions that are. Virtually no spatial modellers endorse such an interpretation. Horizons are therefore constructed with concave contours and extremes in direct or non-diagonal alignment with ideal points.

Horizons 3D© displays these horizons in two or three dimensions so that the user can visually examine the pattern of horizon intersections in a given legislature. One such display, a three-dimensional rendering of the 1972 Italian parliamentary party system, is shown in Figure 2.2. It is based on party locations and horizon bounds derived from the expert survey (to be discussed in Chapter 4). Since respondents were not directed or constrained to provide regularly shaped horizons, the results, as might be expected, are quite irregular. Although the party ideal points are not shown, the fact that the shapes are not ellipsoidal indicates that the ideal points are not centred inside them.

The reproduction in Figure 2.2 lacks two important features of the original – the colour coding for the parties and the ability to rotate the configuration in all three dimensions. Both features greatly facilitate the ability to visualize the space and, in particular, the horizon intersections. Nevertheless, by specifying the wire-frame method of portraying horizons (a solid-surface method is also available), it is possible to get some sense of the dimensionality of the shapes as well as to gain a better idea of how they are actually constructed. As the wire-frame figures illustrate, horizons are represented in *Horizons 3D©* as convex polyhedra (objects with numerous flat facets), which proved to be the most efficacious method of representation for the purpose of calculating intersections.[9]

Visual displays of the horizons and horizon intersections of any legislature can often be of considerable heuristic value, but the prime function of the program is to generate information on the various proto-coalitions of a legislature that can be used in the conditional logit analyses. Foremost among the kinds of information we seek for each

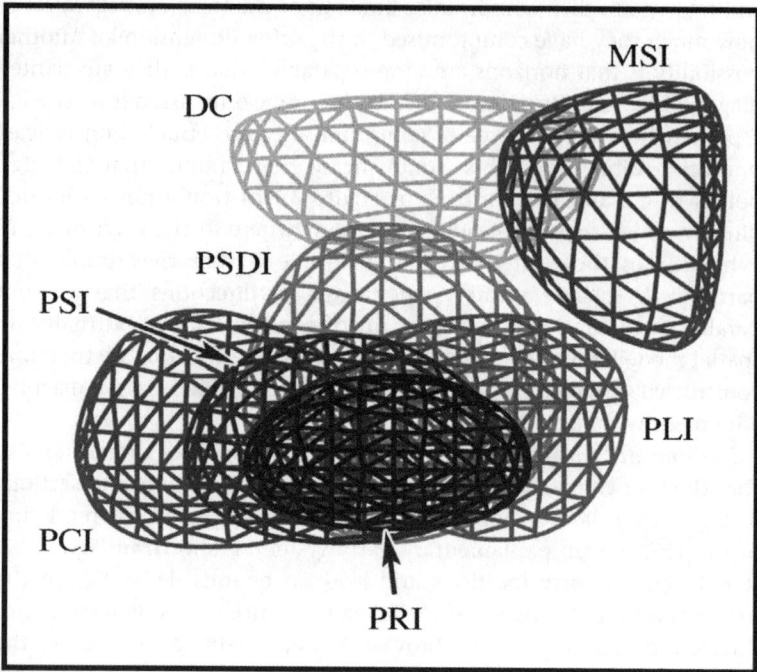

Figure 2.2 Spatial display of party horizons: Italy (1972). *Note*: The left–right dimension is represented on the horizontal axis and the clerical–secular dimension on the vertical axis. In this graphic representation, party horizons appear to be super-imposed when in fact they intersect. Key: PCI = Communists; PSI = Socialists; PSDI = Social Democrats; DC = Christian Democrats; PLI = Liberals; PRI = Republicans; MSI = Italian Social Movement (Neo-Fascists).

proto-coalition is whether or not there exists some policy that satisfies the horizons of all its member-parties. For multiparty proto-coalitions, this condition is satisfied if the horizons of all of its parties intersect with one another; any policy point within the region defined by that intersection would be consistent with the horizon hypothesis. For single-party proto-coalitions, any point within its own horizon would meet the condition. *Horizons 3D*© therefore calculates a *Horizon Intersection* variable that receives a score of '1' if all horizons intersect (or if the coalition consists of only one party) and '0' otherwise.

A proper evaluation of the horizon hypothesis must also take into account the policy distance spanned by each proto-coalition. If parties are policy-seekers, they seek to minimize policy costs and the chances of doing so are likely to be greater in proto-coalitions composed of parties that are located close to one another in the ideological space. Hence, other things being equal, one would expect proto-coalitions that span larger policy distances to be less likely to become governments. I shall refer to this as the policy distance hypothesis.

We have seen that the propensity for policy distance to be inversely related to the likelihood of forming a government is already well established. But policy distance is also highly likely to be correlated with horizon intersections since the farther apart parties are, the less likely it is that their horizons intersect (other things being equal). This means that any effect attributed to horizon intersections could easily be due to policy distance – and vice versa. In fact, the horizon hypothesis may serve as a refinement of the distance hypothesis: both allow that the odds of any set of parties forming a government tend to decrease with the distance among them (taking due account of salience differences), but the horizon hypothesis postulates a threshold or cut-off point whereas the distance hypothesis sees only a smoothly declining probability. Thus, what we seek is evidence that the policy distance relationship is qualified by a threshold effect and both variables must be measured to make such a determination.

Horizons 3D© addresses this requirement by calculating how much distance is spanned by the two most distant parties in each proto-coalition. This operationalization of the concept of policy distance is predicated on the idea that, since any member-party can destroy a coalition by leaving it, the policy viability of a potential governing coalition is reflected in the maximum policy divergence among its members.[10] There is, however, a complication. Strictly speaking, it is not policy distance *per se* that we are interested in but policy costs and these depend on the importance or salience that the party in question attributes to the various policy dimensions. This distinction is evident in the indifference contours of Figure 2.1(a). Each of these contours joins policy points of equal utility to the party whose ideal point they circumscribe, but the points on the contours are not equally distant from the party's ideal point. For party A, a unit of distance along the vertical dimension entails a greater cost than a unit along the horizontal dimension; party B, in contrast, would sustain greater costs on the horizontal dimension.

It is reasonable to assume that the ability of policy distance or compactness is to serve as a proxy for policy or ideological compatibility will depend to some degree on whether these differences have been taken into account. If party-specific dimension saliences are available, this can be achieved by the relatively simple expedient of calculating salience-weighted distances. For example, the (Euclidean) distance between parties A and B in this two-dimensional space from party A's point of view would be given by:

$$Dist_{AB} = \sqrt{w_{x.A}{}^{2}(x_A - x_B)^2 + w_{y.A}{}^{2}(y_A - y_B)^2},$$

where the w's are the saliences or weights party A assigns to the two dimensions, x and y. (Note that the use of unit weights reduces the formula to the standard Euclidean distance equation.)

It is evident that this distance may not be the same from party B's point of view, since B may apply different salience values to these dimensions. If the distance is greater in A's view, it would mean that A sees an {AB} coalition as less viable in policy terms than B does. *Horizons 3D©* therefore calculates two salience-weighted distances between every pair of parties in each proto-coalition and selects the overall maximum distance to represent the salience-weighted version of each proto-coalition's policy diversity.[11]

Taking account of dimension saliences has another benefit: it largely neutralizes the impact of assuming a particular dimensionality for any given ideological space. Consider the survey data gathered for this research project, which provide party positions and horizon bounds in three dimensions for each system. If we ignore differences in dimension saliences, we would implicitly be assuming that each of these systems has three major ideological dimensions of equal importance, which could be a very questionable assumption for many if not all of these systems. Weighting distance calculations by estimates of dimension saliences removes the restriction by allowing the unequal importance of the three dimensions to figure in calculations of policy costs. Even a system with a single dominant dimension can be represented accurately by the simple expedient of attributing very small weights to the other dimensions.

A final reason for using salience-weighted distances is to level the playing field with respect to policy horizons, since horizons also incorporate information on saliences. This is evident in the horizons shown in Figure 2.1: their elongated shapes conveys the information that the parties view policy compromise in some directions as less costly than compromise in other directions. If policy costs functioned identically in all directions, the appropriate horizon shape would have been circular or spherical and policy distance from any given party's point of view could be calculated without weights; all other shapes imply within-party differences in dimension saliences that should be taken into account in computing policy distances as well. As we shall see, the former situation necessarily characterizes the behaviour-based horizons, while the latter characterizes the survey data.

Auxiliary measurements

While the respective roles played by policy distance and policy horizons in government formation are the key issue in this investigation, *Horizons 3D*© also calculates a number of other quantities that may be relevant to the formation and survival of parliamentary governments. The full elaboration of the issues that motivate these calculations is best left to later chapters, but a brief synopsis of the calculations and their purposes can be provided here.

The first group of variables needs little explication, since it consists of very basic types of information on each proto-coalition. These include the number of parties it contains, the percentage of parliamentary seats it controls, whether or not it is majoritarian, and whether or not it is minimal winning. As with other dichotomous variables, the latter two variables are coded '1' for the presence of the trait and '0' otherwise.

Of more immediate relevance to the policy horizon approach is the role that may be played by the size of the region of the ideological space that contains policies acceptable to the proto-coalition. For simplicity's sake, this variable will be called the *intersection size*, although for single-party proto-coalitions, it is really the size of the region enclosed by a single horizon. As suggested earlier, large intersections may be favoured in the government formation process, perhaps because they make it easier for parties both to reach agreement on a government policy position or, in the case of minority governments, to accommodate the policy demands of external support parties. *Horizons 3D*© therefore calculates this quantity for every proto-coalition that has a common horizon intersection. Proto-coalitions with non-intersecting horizons receive scores of zero on this variable.

Another issue that implicates the horizon approach concerns the selection of a government policy. The available evidence, limited though it is, points to a tendency for government policy to accord with the weighted mean position of the parties in the government (Warwick 2001b) – a proportionality result that corresponds to the much better documented tendency for cabinet portfolios to be allocated in proportion to party sizes. If there are strong normative or other pressures favouring this type of policy outcome, it may be the case that proto-coalitions that can accommodate it have an advantage in the formation process. In keeping with the horizon hypothesis, the proto-coalitions in question would be those whose horizon intersections include or encompass the weighted mean of the positions of their members. *Encompassed weighted mean* is a dichotomous variable that indicates whether the proto-coalition has this property.

The final group of variables calculated by *Horizons 3D*© concerns the formation of majority or minority governments. One hypothesis is that minority governments, because they depend on external support in the legislature, are formed of subsets of what I shall term *majority intersections* (majority proto-coalitions that have intersecting horizons). These subsets may be favoured over other minority proto-coalitions because the legislative support they need to survive and implement their policies is provided by parties that could have joined the coalition under the horizon hypothesis and given it majority status but, for one reason or another, did not do so. The *subset of a majority intersection* variable is a dichotomous variable that registers the presence or absence of this property.

Another factor that might affect the formation of minority governments is the amount of additional policy distance a minority proto-coalition would have to take on to command majority support. It is easy to imagine that it might have poor prospects of forming the government if this distance is relatively high. *Horizons 3D* calculates this *assumed majority distance* in salience-weighted and unweighted versions. If a proto-coalition is majoritarian, its assumed majority distance equals its actual policy distance.

Simulations

The last methodological element that needs to be discussed is the use of simulations. Unlike hypotheses that only propose an association between continuous variables, the horizon hypothesis stipulates an all-or-nothing measurement of the key independent variable: either a common horizon intersection exists or it does not. If there is a good deal of inaccuracy in the location of horizon bounds – which there undoubtedly will be, given the measurement methods at our disposal – it is likely that a substantial number of non-intersecting horizons will be miscategorized as intersecting and vice versa. The issue is not just one of measurement error, however. Leaders who must make decisions to join or not to join governments may not know the precise locations of horizons; in fact, precise limits may not exist. A party's leaders may be very confident that compromise within a certain limit is acceptable and that compromise beyond some more distant limit will have negative net consequences, but between those two limits there may exist a grey area where all they have is some notion of the degree of risk they run in accepting compromises.

The best means available for coping with the substantial risk of uncertainty inherent in horizons or their measurement is to incorporate it into the analysis. This can be done by performing a large number of simulations for each legislature in which all of the position and bound values are altered by adding error terms drawn from specified sampling distributions. To illustrate how this might work with the survey data, suppose the mean estimate of the lower bound on a party's willingness to compromise on the left/right dimension is 3.5 (on an 11-point scale). Suppose further that its standard error (*SE*) is 0.5 and that there are five degrees of freedom (*df*), that is six respondents providing the estimate. A new estimate for the location of the bound can be derived by drawing a term from a *t*-distribution centred on zero with the same *SE* and *df* and adding it to 3.5. The next simulation would repeat the process anew to generate another estimate for the bound and so forth. In each simulation, all position and horizon parameters would be altered in this fashion, each according to its own level of uncertainty, and intersections re-calculated. The end result of this process would be a tally of the proportion of simulations in which an intersection occurred for each proto-coalition. This proportion or *horizon intersection rate* can be interpreted as a measure of the probability that the horizons of the proto-coalition's member-parties intersect, given the degree of uncertainty that exists about each of the parameters that influence the outcome.[12]

Horizons 3D© provides two means of performing simulations. The first method involves the use of what are termed 'predefined' errors. These are errors that are specific to a given parameter, as in the above example, and are entered individually by the user when the data file is created. They may be distributed according to a uniform, normal, or *t*-distribution. All the user then has to do is to specify that predefined errors are to be used and the program automatically draws an error for each parameter from its associated distribution in each simulation, as described above.[13]

The second method involves what are termed 'global' errors. In this case, the user specifies a single error distribution that is to be used for all of the parameters. Different specifications can be used for the position and bound parameters and, indeed, predefined errors can be chosen for one and global errors for the other. Although this method is easier to execute in that it does not require the prior entry of an error specification for each individual parameter, the better choice is clearly to enter and utilize such information if it is available. This is the case for the survey data, but for the behaviour-based horizons, there are no parameter-specific error estimates and a global specification must be used for the simulations.

The use of simulations naturally raises the possibility that the crisp threshold effect of the horizon hypothesis may have been dissolved into something resembling a distance effect. In blunt terms, to the extent that the horizon intersection rate for a proto-coalition declines smoothly with the distance separating its two most distant parties, it will tend to mimic policy distance. With a global error specification, this risk can be reduced by introducing a relatively small error, thereby ensuring that the crispness of the postulated horizon threshold is largely preserved. With predefined errors, we are at the mercy of the amount of error inherent in the source data, but in either case the degree to which the horizon intersection rate mirrors distance needs to be evaluated empirically.

Specifying simulations changes some but not all of the output data. Variables that are unrelated to party positions or horizons are unaffected and will return the same results in every simulation. Thus, if 500 simu-lations are specified, a majority proto-coalition will remain majoritarian in all of them and will receive a majority status score of 500; a minority proto-coalition will receive a score of 0. The horizon intersection variable, however, is affected by the random changes and may receive a score that falls between the two extremes. By dividing by the total number of simulations, it can be converted into the horizon intersection rate. For non-dichotomous variables, which include the intersection size variable and all of the various distance variables, the mean scores across the simulations are reported.

The final data file

Once the calculations and/or simulations have been performed for a legislature, the results can be exported as a raw data file using *Horizons 3D©*'s export facility. Because the number of proto-coalitions increases exponentially with the number of parties in the legislature, the size of these files can vary enormously. In fact, with each proto-coalition providing one row of data, they can range from seven rows for three-party legislatures to 4095 rows for twelve-party legislatures (the maximum that *Horizons 3D©* allows).[14]

Exporting results is essential because the quantitative investigation of the horizon hypothesis requires the construction of a data file that combines results for all of the legislatures under scrutiny. In fact, the results for each legislature must be included for each formation situation that occurred in that legislature. Thus, if five governments were formed in a given legislature, the *Horizons* output for that legislature would have to be included five times. Clearly, systems with many parties and multiple formations per legislature, such as Italy, will contribute mightily to the size of this final data file, which can become very large as a result.

At this point, various other variables of interest may be added. In the present investigation, a number of potential causal factors suggested by previous research will be considered. There is one variable, however, that cannot be omitted: a dichotomous variable that identifies which proto-coalition actually became the government in each formation situation. It serves as a dependent variable in the conditional logit analyses.

Discussion

It will be clear enough by now that, even without the task of estimating horizons for parties, the process of testing the horizon hypothesis is no cakewalk. Not only has it been necessary to develop new software to address the unique measurement requirements of the hypothesis, but separate data files must be created for each of the legislatures included in the investigation and separate sets of calculations and simulations performed on each of these files. While the calculations are more or less instantaneous, individual simulation runs performed as part of this investigation have taken as much as 20 hours of computing time using contemporary desktop machines. The results of all these runs then have to be output as raw data files and concatenated to form a final data file, to which other variables – the dependent variable at a minimum – must be added. Only then can the testing of the horizon hypothesis begin.

In this elaborate, multistage process, assumptions must inevitably be introduced. The most important of these concern the shape of policy horizons. While a wide variety of shapes can be accommodated by *Horizons 3D©*, the fact that they are built from information on bounds or limits means that we must assume something about how those points are joined together; the assumption made here is that compromise on different dimensions can be traded off, which creates horizons that are indifference contours with a characteristic concave-inwards form. Another assumption is that the policy viability of proto-coalitions can be represented by the maximum (salience weighted) distance between pairs of coalition members. This is based on the rationale that coalitions, like chains, are only as strong or viable as their weakest link. Both assumptions have plausibility but, of course, no proof in their favour. The representation of horizons by means of convex polyhedra is relatively risk-free by comparison; although it is technically possible that a very small horizon intersection might be missed as a result, simulations would provide the appropriate corrective.

Simple tractability has imposed an assumption of a different type: the assumption that the ideological spaces of West European parliamentary systems can be accurately captured by no more than three policy dimensions. This assumption is made palatable by the knowledge that this limit generally meets or exceeds what other researchers have identified as well as by the fact that dimension saliences can be used to adjust for differences across systems in effective dimensionality. The location of the bounds of horizons in these spaces is, however, altogether a different matter. As the next two chapters will show, there is no method for estimating horizons that is guaranteed to be substantially free of error. The behaviour-based methods are less subjective but depend on assumptions that clearly can be questioned, while the survey-based estimates capture the phenomenon more directly but ask for a type of information that even experts cannot be expected to estimate with great accuracy.

There are tests that can be done to assess the degree of bias in these estimates and the results of these tests are by and large re-assuring, as we shall see. In addition, the existence of more than one estimation procedure will allow us to compare results and, to some extent, offset the weaknesses of each approach. In fact, the strategy pursued here for capturing the concept of policy horizons and measuring its potential impact on coalition behaviour could be described as one of triangulation, and the hope is that different data sources, different measurement procedures, and different assumptions will all point reasonably clearly to a single credible conclusion. In the next chapter, this strategy is launched by seeking out evidence for horizon effects in the actual behaviour of West European parliamentary parties.

3
Behaviour-based Horizons and Government Formation

The previous chapter laid out a fairly elaborate multistage process for evaluating the policy horizon hypothesis. That process depends upon a essential step that has yet to be considered: the measurement of the policy horizons or, more precisely, the limits of policy compromise of individual parties. This task will be addressed in this chapter by using the electoral platforms or manifestos of parties to estimate their policy positions and then using those estimates, in conjunction with information on the parties' participation in government, to derive estimates of their horizon limits or bounds.

The estimation of compromise limits from information that includes the government membership records of parties is likely to be controversial if the intention is to use those estimates to explain the formation of the same set of governments. A tempting remedy for this dilemma would be to split the sample such that the estimation of compromise limits and the testing of the horizon hypothesis are performed on different subsets of cases. This strategy, however, turns out to be less viable that it might appear at first glance. It is therefore essential to establish that the methods, when based on the full set of cases, produce horizon estimates that are capable of providing causally meaningful assessments of the impact of horizons on government formation. Much of the chapter is devoted to this task.

With the validity of the measurement methods established, the first tests of the horizon hypothesis can be undertaken. These tests will be conducted initially against the horizon hypothesis's natural foil, the policy distance hypothesis, but the scope of the tests will subsequently be expanded to incorporate a variety of other causal factors. The results will show a powerful net effect of horizon intersections on the choice of governments and a very substantial weakening of the policy distance

41

effect, consistent with the notion that much of the role allocated in previous research to policy distance belongs instead to the influence of horizons.

Measuring policy horizons from coalition behaviour

Two behaviour-based methods

If policy horizons exist, how could we find them? We have seen that asking party officials to locate their party's limits of compromise is unlikely to bear much fruit: their natural temptation would be to under-estimate, if not deny altogether, the party's willingness to yield on its promises and commitments. Indications of the operation of horizons ought to be detectable in the coalition behaviour of parties, however, since the basic idea is that no party will participate in a government whose proposed policies lie outside the party's horizon. This suggests an obvious measurement strategy: determine in some fashion the policy positions of the governments a given party joined, calculate the policy distance between government and party in each case, and take the maximum distance as the party's limit of compromise. The set of points located at this distance from the party's ideal point would then constitute its estimated horizon.

The great strength of this *Maximum Joining Distance* or MJD method is undoubtedly its simplicity (assuming that government and party policy positions can be measured). But this simplicity rests upon some potentially questionable assumptions. The most obvious is the implicit assumption that the full extent of a party's willingness to accept policy compromises has been demonstrated in the coalition behaviour that has been examined. If a party held legislative seats during only one or two government formations, or if only a few formation situations are utilized in the measurement process, this is unlikely to be the case. For example, the fact that a right-wing party did not join any government in a given legislature may result more from the existence of a viable left-wing majority coalition than the party's unwillingness to compromise; even for the left-wing parties, the amount of policy compromise they accepted in that coalition may not indicate the maximum they would be willing to accept. Clearly, it will take a fair number of observations (formation situations) before a party's horizon can be estimated with an acceptable degree of reliability.

The method also relies on the assumption that each horizon remains constant across the various formation situations for which the party is present. In other words, each party receives a single, fixed horizon for the period covered by the data set. This feature is disadvantageous in the sense that it imposes a constraint – that party horizons do not change over time – that is not implied by the hypothesis. Any attempt to relax it by allowing a party's horizon to change, however, is likely to exacerbate the first problem (the necessity of having a sufficient number of observations to estimate a horizon accurately) and to add a new problem as well: determining when a new horizon should be estimated. More important, the assumption of constant horizons could be regarded as a desirable feature of the method since it tends to allay concerns that horizon estimates could be altered from legislature to legislature to fit the record of government formations. By imposing a more stringent standard than the hypothesis itself implies, it raises the bar considerably and should therefore make any findings in support of the hypothesis more convincing.

Another assumption of the method is that horizons are circular or spherical. It follows from the fact that only a single distance is identified for each party as its limit of compromise, which necessitates using this distance as a radius to describe the horizon. The alternative would be to determine the MJD on each dimension separately, but this approach is unlikely to produce accurate results. The reason is that the amount of compromise a party can accept on a given dimension is likely to depend on how much it must yield on other dimensions, which implies that one can only estimate it accurately if the party has been required to yield as much as it can on that dimension and nothing on the other(s) – an extremely unlikely situation. Fortunately, the use of a factor analytic method to derive party positions can provide an indication of the viability of the assumption of equal saliences by indicating the relative roles of the various dimensions in accounting for variance in policies. In addition, any distortion brought on by the assumption will also affect distance measurements, so that if the goal is to determine whether the policy distance effect is modified by the operation of horizons, both effects will be under-estimated and a reasonably accurate conclusion may still be forthcoming.[1]

A final notable feature of the method is its faithfulness to the necessary condition that the hypothesis embodies. This condition is that, for a party to join a coalition, the intended policies of that coalition must lie within the party's horizon; using the MJD as the horizon ensures that this condition will be met. Nevertheless, this feature, too, cuts both ways. It assumes that party leaders would never violate their parties' horizons through miscalculation, the occurrence of special circumstances (e.g. a national emergency), and so forth. But would the occasional violation of a party's supposed horizon really mean that the horizon is illusory? Or would it simply mean that leaders occasionally make mistakes or display a willingness to make exceptions in exceptional situations?

The second estimation method relaxes this standard somewhat. It establishes the limits of party compromise by determining the policy distance at which it becomes more likely than not that a party will join the government that ultimately forms. This is done by means of a logistic regression analysis covering a substantial number of government formations. The cases in this analysis are the individual parties in these formation situations. The binary dependent variable identifies whether or not they joined the government and the independent variables consist of their policy distance from the government and a set of dummy variables identifying the various parties. The results of this regression are then used to calculate the distance at which the odds of joining reach 50 per cent for each party.[2] The set of points located at this distance from a party's ideal point is then defined as its horizon.

This *logit* method shares with the MJD method the risks that the number of observations for a given party may be too few to locate its policy horizon accurately and that the horizon may not be circular/spherical in shape or constant across the observation period. In addition, the criterion for establishing horizons is arbitrary: why set the horizon at the distance at which the party's probability of joining is 50 per cent? Why not 70 per cent or 90 per cent? There can be no clear-cut answer to these questions since, once one decides to allow for errors, the amount of error that should be tolerated inevitably becomes a matter of judgement. The 50 per cent standard was chosen because (a) a standard close to 100 per cent would essentially reproduce the MJD horizons and (b) it turns out that even with a standard as low as 50 per cent, there are relatively few violations of the horizon principle. Nonetheless, it cannot be denied that the logit method trades one disadvantage (no allowance for occasional errors or exceptional circumstances) for another (an arbitrary cut-point). The hope is that, by applying both methods, we may be able to offset their weaknesses and gain a better grasp on reality.

The validity of the methods

Poor measurement generally has the effect of causing relationships to be under-estimated, and if the two methods outlined above entail so much imprecision that they lead us to make a Type II error (i.e. to reject a true hypothesis), that would be regrettable indeed. But it would be a good deal more regrettable if the methods over-estimated the role of horizons or even manufactured a horizon effect that does not exist at all. These methods would appear to be vulnerable to this risk, since they employ the party memberships of governments to derive horizon calculations that ultimately will be used to explain the formation of the same set of governments. The risk is therefore one that must be examined with some care.

A tempting strategy for circumventing this problem would be to estimate horizons on the basis of a subset of cases and then test the hypothesis on the remainder. Since we will use a standard of five appearances in formation situations as the minimum for estimating a horizon (see p. 57), the most straightforward way of implementing this 'split-sample' design would be to estimate horizons on the basis of parties' first five appearances in formation situations and then use these estimates to account for formation behaviour in the remaining formations in the data set.[3] Further research indicates that a significant horizon effect does emerge under this strategy,[4] but there are two drawbacks. The first is that basing all horizon estimates on just five appearances in formation situations is bound to introduce considerably more measurement error. The second is that the strategy probably cannot achieve its intended purpose.

To see why this is the case, suppose for a moment that the use of horizon estimates from one subsample to explain the government formations of that same subsample is illegitimate because it embeds a measure of circularity or endogeneity. If behaviour is essentially unchanged between the two subsamples, as is likely, then it would follow that the use of those horizons to explain formations in the second subsample should also be considered illegitimate. In other words, if the influence of X on Y is mis-estimated because Y in fact influences X to some extent, and if Y' is a very close correlate of Y because the same underlying processes produce both of them, then regressing Y' on X will produce a similar mis-estimation. Conversely, to the extent that behaviour has changed between subsamples, the test will fail. Thus, all that a successful test of the hypothesis based on this strategy may tell us is that coalition behaviour has not changed from one subsample to the other.

The endogeneity issue therefore cannot be laid to rest by the simple expedient of using a split-sample approach; if endogeneity is embedded in the full-sample approach, it is likely to figure in positive test results based on the split-sample approach as well. But is it present in the full-sample approach? In the next subsection, this issue is examined in detail in order to determine whether behaviour-based methods of estimating horizons are capable of yielding credible findings of a horizon effect, or merely statistical artefacts.

General considerations

An endogeneity or simultaneity problem occurs in statistical estimation procedures when the error term in the model is correlated with an independent variable, causing the role of the latter to be mis-estimated. In essence, its estimated role 'bundles in' the influence of other causal factors represented in the error term. To see how this might occur in the estimation of horizons, suppose that participation in government is influenced by policy distance and one other factor – whether or not the party is basically an office-seeker. Since office-seeking parties place a greater priority on participating in government, they are likely to have higher participation rates, which will tend to cause logit estimates of their compromise limits to be larger (other things being equal). The office-seeking propensity also makes it more likely that their MJD will be greater. This means that the relationship of horizons to government formation will have surreptitiously incorporated the office-seeking propensity of the parties under either estimation method.

This argument is technically valid, but its interpretation as a progenitor of measurement bias is misplaced in the present context. Normally in data analyses, one wants to exclude any possibility of attributing causal influence to one variable that actually belongs to another. In this case, however, that goal does not apply. Both horizon estimation procedures use party–government policy distances to establish horizons, but it is not assumed that distance is a cause of horizons; rather, a party's horizon is affected by factors such as its office-seeking proclivities, its internal distribution of opinion, the expectations of its supporters, and so forth. In estimating horizon radii, the purpose is to gauge where influences such as these cause a party's limit of compromise to be located. Thus, the objective is not to get horizon estimates that are independent of these other factors; the objective is to get estimates that reflect these factors since they are what determines how far a party is willing to compromise.[5]

This point can be made clearer if it is cast in a larger framework. The proposed procedure for testing the horizon hypothesis asks whether government formation in coalition situations displays a pattern that is consistent with the presence of policy horizons. Rather than bringing some exogenous factor to bear on the choice of government, it examines the pattern of formations for signs of an explicit and well-defined threshold effect. This involves using the participation records of parties to estimate where those thresholds, if they exist, are likely to be located and then determining whether those estimates have a net effect when other factors are controlled. The logic is similar to that of likelihood estimation, where the estimation process consists of searching for the parameter values that are most likely to have produced the data being analysed. In this case, we are searching for optimal locations for party horizons and assessing how well horizons, so located, account for the pattern of government formations. The hypothesis would be non-falsifiable if it were assumed that parties may alter horizons at every formation situation; instead, the test incorporates the much tougher assumption that each party's horizon is constant across the entire observation period. If the test proves successful even when other relevant factors are controlled, it would suggest that the pattern of government formations is consistent with the hypothesis that parties have (relatively fixed) policy horizons.

The test is not foolproof, however. What might invalidate it is the possibility that horizons appear to play a role in the choice of government simply because of their association with a known causal factor, policy distance. To some extent, this risk is obviated by the fact that the policy distance utilized in the estimation of horizons is not the same as the policy distance that will be used in the tests of the hypothesis. In the estimation of policy horizons, the key piece of information is the distance between a party's position and the assumed position of the government that is ultimately formed. The test of the hypothesis is based both on a different unit of analysis – proto-coalitions rather than individual parties – and on a different version of policy distance: the distance between the two most distant parties in each possible coalition.

It is nonetheless possible to imagine situations in which the tendency of governments to be formed of parties that are close to one another causes an 'accidental horizon' to appear. To see how horizons could appear accidentally, consider the extreme case in which policy distance is the sole influence on government formation. If governments are invariably formed by parties with similar policy positions, it may appear that parties never stray beyond certain limits or horizons in their coalition behaviour – even though no horizons are operative. What makes this possibility even more threatening is that the horizon effect may be 'privileged' in comparison with policy distance, since it not only reflects distance but it also indirectly incorporates information connected with the dependent variable (specifically, which parties got into government in the various formations).

This is clearly a possibility that needs to be evaluated carefully. The best way to do so is by examining a simulated data set that has been designed to capture this extreme situation in order to see if an artificial horizon effect is produced and, more importantly, if it can be detected. The following subsection presents the results of such an experiment.

Distance and horizon effects in a simulated data set

To keep matters as simple as possible, the data for this experiment consist of three parties of approximately equal size (they hold 35 per cent, 35 per cent, and 30 per cent of legislative seats) that were initially located equidistant from one another in a two-dimensional ideological space. The parties' positions were randomly altered 25 times to generate 25 distinct 'legislatures'.[6] Each legislature is assumed to produce one government. The governments were selected as follows: for six legislatures chosen at random, a randomly selected single party was identified as the government; for the other 19 legislatures, the two closest parties were assumed to form the government.[7] Government formation in these 25 cases is thus a function of policy distance alone (along with a bias in favour of majority governments).

The first step in the analysis of these data is the calculation of party horizons. For this, we need estimates of government positions. Following a common practice in the literature, government positions were measured by the size-weighted mean positions of the parties that compose them.[8] MJD horizons were then determined by calculating the distances between parties and governments and selecting the MJD for each party. For logit horizons, a party-level logistic regression of government membership on party–government distance and two party dummies was run and the results were used to calculate the distance at which each party becomes more likely than not to be a government member.

A graphic representation of these horizons and their intersections for one of the hypothetical legislatures is shown in Figure 3.1. It is evident that the random alteration of party positions has produced a legislature in which B and C are the closest pair of parties and, in line with the policy distance principle, they were identified as forming the government. Note that the intersections for both logit and MJD horizons (shown separately) largely follow policy distances: the {BC} proto-coalition has the largest intersection, followed by {AB}. In contrast, the horizons for the two most distant parties, A and C, do not intersect at all.

As anticipated, the determinative role played by policy distance in government formation generates very sharp, albeit artificial, horizons. In fact, regardless of whether the horizons are estimated by the logit or

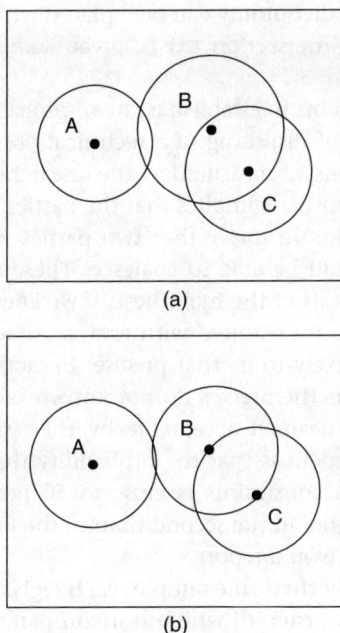

Figure 3.1 Horizon intersections in a hypothetical three-party legislature. (a) Logit horizons (b) MJD horizons.

the MJD method, there are no instances where a party joins a government whose position lies outside its horizon; the necessary condition of the hypothesis, in other words, is perfectly met with either set of horizon estimates. The key question, of course, is whether these artificial horizons generate an artificial horizon effect. For this determination, we must turn to a conditional logit analysis.

The total absence of exceptions to the horizon hypothesis not only suggests that such an effect may have been induced, but also presents an estimation problem. A key characteristic of logit models is that they cannot handle situations in which every positive outcome in the data set possesses (or lacks) a certain trait, as is the case here. The most appropriate remedy in the present context is to allow for the possibility of uncertainty or error in the calculation of horizon intersections; that is, to transform a dichotomy into a continuous variable. As noted in Chapter 2, this can be done by running a series of simulations in which party horizons are randomly altered and a tally is kept of the proportions of those trials in which an intersection occurs. By these means, the horizon intersection dichotomy can be replaced with an estimate of the probability that an intersection exists, given some degree of error in locating horizons.

The use of simulations to establish a rate or probability of intersection is not just a matter of disposing of a technical obstacle. Consider two parties whose horizons, as measured by the researcher, just narrowly fail to intersect. The hypothesis implies that the parties cannot coalesce. By the same token, it would imply that two parties whose horizons just barely intersect should be able to coalesce. These expectations would provide reasonable tests of the hypothesis if we knew that the horizons of the parties had been measured with total accuracy, but no measurement procedure is likely to be that precise. In fact, it may be the case that the party leaders themselves do not know exactly whether such a coalition would be deemed acceptable by their supporters. A much more realistic assessment is that the probability that coalescing would satisfy their horizon constraints is close to 50 per cent in each case (although a little higher in the second than in the first) and this is what the intersection rate would report.

In the present hypothetical example, each legislature was subjected to 500 simulations in each of which horizon parameters were altered by adding error terms drawn randomly from a normal distribution with a mean of zero and standard deviation of 0.25. This introduces a small degree of perturbation and produces intersection rates that are remarkably similar to the original intersection dichotomies: the two variables correlate at $r = .93$ (logit horizons) and $r = .96$ (MJD horizons). Thus, very little is changed in replacing the intersection dichotomy with the intersection rate, but it does facilitate the statistical analysis as well as making for greater realism in measurement assumptions.

Let us turn now to the analysis of government formation in this hypothetical set of legislatures. Three independent variables could influence which coalition forms the government: the coalition's majority status, the policy distance spanned by its member-parties, and the probability that those parties have intersecting horizons. By design, only the first two are actually causative. The third variable might appear to play a role, however, both because it indirectly incorporates information about the dependent variable and because it is highly coterminous with policy distance: as noted earlier, parties never join governments outside their compromise limits. The objective is to determine whether either of these properties tends to induce the spurious conclusion that horizons are actually operative.

The results of the analysis are presented in Table 3.1. As Model 1 of the table indicates, a conditional logit analysis with majority status and policy distance as the independent variables shows that both significantly affect which coalition forms the government.[9] Because of its close association with policy distance in this data set, the horizon intersection rate can also be expected to display a significant (albeit spurious) effect. Model 2, which replaces policy distance with the intersection rate for MJD horizons, confirms this expectation: a false or artificial horizon effect does emerge. When both policy distance and the MJD intersection rate are included (Model 3), however, it is clear that policy distance assumes the dominant role, with the intersection variable reduced to statistical insignificance. The same pattern is produced when logit-based horizons are used: Model 4 shows that the intersection rate is significantly related to government formation, while Model 5 shows that the inclusion of policy distance renders it insignificant. Neither the 'privileging' of the horizon intersection rate nor its overlap with policy distance appear to have helped it very much.

These findings would seem to provide clear evidence that, when governing coalitions are selected on the basis of policy compactness (along with majority status), horizon intersections derived from these data will not show a spurious net effect on government formation so long as policy distance is also included in the model. The results accord with common sense as well. The apparent horizon effect in Models 2 and 4 is generated solely by the fact that all three parties, being essentially

Table 3.1 Testing policy distance and horizons effects in a hypothetical data set

	Model 1	Model 2	Model 3	Model 4	Model 5
Majority status	5.80**	2.25**	4.83**	2.17**	5.10**
	(1.23)	(0.58)	(1.34)	(0.58)	(1.35)
Policy distance	−1.54**	−	−1.07*	−	−1.20**
	(0.38)		(0.49)		(0.49)
Horizon intersection rate:					
– MJD horizons	−	5.31**	2.27	−	−
		(1.84)	(1.97)		
– Logit horizons	−	−	−	6.79**	2.17
				(2.70)	(2.48)
Log-likelihood	−31.70	−33.74	−30.93	−35.01	−31.24

Note: Coefficients derive from conditional logit analyses covering 175 coalitions in 25 hypothetical formation situations. Standard errors are given in parentheses.
* $p < .05$ in a one-tailed test.
** $p < .01$ in a one-tailed test.

interchangeable, have similar horizon distances or radii, which means that intersection rates closely mirror proximity in the space. But one would not expect those rates, which merely reflect the true cause (policy distance), to play a major role when the latter is also included in the analysis.

The problem with this conclusion is that the intersection rate coefficients in Models 3 and 5 have the correct sign. This means that, however unlikely it is that the intersection rate would ever challenge the primacy of policy distance, with sufficient numbers of cases it could become significant in its own right. As noted, this risk exists because the strict application of the policy distance principle actually generates a threshold effect; indeed, not only are there no cases in which a party participates in a government whose policy point lies outside the party's estimated horizon, but there are virtually no cases where a party fails to join a government whose policies lie within that horizon (using either estimation method). As a result, beyond each party's horizon distance, the probability of joining a government falls abruptly from nearly one to zero.

A more realistic scenario, one in which that probability does not collapse so precipitously, can be created by weakening the distance effect somewhat. It is unlikely, after all, that only maximally compact governments take office in any system. Let us assume, accordingly, that two governments were formed in each of the 25 legislatures. One of the governments in each legislature is the same as before, but the second is chosen purely at random. This is intended to capture the idea that there may be other factors, perhaps idiosyncratic factors or at least factors unrelated to policy distance, that also play a role in government formation.

Introducing these extra formations requires that we re-calculate the horizons, since the possibility that non-compact coalitions will occasionally form governments will tend to broaden horizon estimates, especially under the MJD method. Policy distance should still play a significant role (since it is determinative in at least half the cases) and it does, as Model 1 of Table 3.2 attests. But when the intersection rate is added in Model 2 (MJD) and Model 3 (logit), a very different result emerges: not only is the intersection effect highly insignificant in both cases, but it has the wrong sign. Clearly, in this scenario the danger of producing a significant positive effect for horizons intersections simply by expanding the sample size is greatly attenuated.

Table 3.2 Testing distance and horizon effects in a hypothetical data set with random error

	Model 1	Model 2	Model 3
Majority status	2.77** (0.64)	2.89** (0.71)	3.02** (0.74)
Policy distance	−0.52** (0.17)	−0.57** (0.22)	−0.64** (0.25)
Horizon intersection rate			
– MJD horizons	–	−0.59 (1.49)	–
– Logit horizons	–	–	−0.66 (0.99)
Log-likelihood	−86.79	−86.71	−86.58

Note: Coefficients derive from conditional logit analyses covering 350 coalitions in 50 hypothetical formation situations. Standard errors are given in parentheses.
* $p < .05$ in a one-tailed test.
** $p < .01$ in a one-tailed test.

The key lesson that emerges from the analysis of this simulated data set is that, while it is possible to produce a spurious horizon effect, it is likely to require very unusual circumstances. The effect of creating data in which only maximally compact (minority or majority) governments form is to create a false threshold for each party: beyond a certain distance, no party was ever called upon to enter a government because there was always some more compact alternative. Even in this rather unrealistic scenario, however, the horizon effect paled in comparison with the distance effect – the horizons convey a lot less information about joining probabilities than do the policy distances themselves.

It required no more than a modest amount of error to destroy any vestige of a horizon effect. In these circumstances, it is difficult to maintain that the intersection rate is in some way privileged by virtue of its construction. Indeed, what makes the ability to identify distance as the true cause especially noteworthy is that the error that was introduced did not bring the distance and horizons hypotheses into direct conflict. A direct conflict would exist whenever at least one intersecting coalition in a choice set is less compact than at least one non-intersecting coalition, but there are no such occurrences with either the MJD or logit horizons. In general, we may expect that where the conflicting predictions are generated, the two hypotheses will be even more clearly differentiated. Thus, to the extent that intersection rates do not mirror policy distances, the task of determining whether a true horizon effect exists will be greatly facilitated.

Testing distance and horizons in West European systems

The search for a real-world horizon effect will be conducted on government formations in 14 West European parliamentary systems in the period from the start of normal democratic rule after 1945 to about the mid-1990s. The countries are Austria (1949–1990), Belgium (1954–1995), Denmark (1945–1996), Finland (1946–1995), France (1945–1995), Germany (1961–1991), Iceland (1947–1991), Ireland (1961–1997), Italy (1958–1991), Luxembourg (1945–1984), Netherlands (1956–1994), Norway (1961–1997), Portugal (1976–1995), and Sweden (1948–1996).[10] All formation situations for which we have adequate information (as specified below) are included, except for those in which a majority party was present or that did not involve a real choice of government, such as when a prime minister died or retired and the government continued on in office.

As we have seen, the behaviour-based methods for estimating horizons require three types of information: the policy positions of parties, the policy positions of governments, and the parties' government participation records (i.e. which governments each party joined) in the legislatures upon which the estimates will be based. The last-mentioned item is a matter of public record, but party and government positions must be measured in some way. We therefore begin with this measurement task.

Estimating positions and horizons

The best available source of standardized information on the policy positions of parties in West European systems is the content analysis of party manifestos undertaken by the Comparative Manifestos Project (CMP).[11] The CMP is a multi-national research effort that analyses manifestos by recording the amount of attention they give to each of fifty-six policy areas or positions. Although there is some debate over both the use of experts to code manifestos and the particular set of coding categories adopted by the CMP (Laver and Garry 2000, pp. 620–1), studies have shown that the CMP data can yield position estimates that match up well with human judgements of party positions (Gabel and Huber 2000) and even with estimates produced by the recent computer-based methods of analyzing content (Laver and Garry 2000; Laver *et al.* 2003). Moreover, the CMP data are unmatched in the comprehensiveness of their coverage of both countries and elections. The coverage by election means that, unlike expert judgements, the CMP data can readily be used to produce separate position estimates for each legislature, thereby allowing the analysis to take account of changes in party positions over time. These features make the CMP data invaluable for present purposes; in fact, the selection of countries and periods noted in p. 54 was largely dictated by the coverage of the CMP data set.

Party and government positions

The standard procedure for establishing an appropriate multidimensional ideological space and deriving party positions in that space is to subject data such as the CMP policy variables to some form of dimensional analysis. The technique chosen for this purpose here is principal components analysis (PCA). In the present application, the analysis was conducted across the countries and periods listed in p. 54, with weights applied so that the number of cases contributed by each country was equalized. The decision to conduct a cross-national analysis was not inevitable: separate analyses could have been done for individual countries, which would have obviated the concern that estimates of party positions in any one country are influenced by positions in the other countries (Budge *et al.* 2001, p. 60). Gabel and Huber (2000, p. 98) have found, however, that left/right positions derived from a cross-national factor analysis accord better with expert judgements than do estimates based on separate country analyses. Consistent with this finding, the current data reveal that the position estimates produced by the cross-national PCA yield a noticeably stronger distance effect on government formation than estimates from country-specific analyses. Since the horizon effect is only slightly altered at most,[12] the overall result of deriving party positions from a cross-national analysis is to favour distance over horizons. This is a useful feature because it reduces the possibility that any support that emerges for the horizon hypothesis will have derived from a relative under-estimation of the role played by policy distance.

The first two orthogonally rotated components from the PCA were taken as defining the relevant ideological space. The decision to retain two dimensions is arbitrary, although not unprecedented (e.g. Budge *et al.* 1987; Crombez 1996). It can be justified on other grounds as well. The first two principal components account for approximately equal amounts of variance (5.8 and 4.9 per cent) and thus provide reasonable compliance with the assumption of equal dimension saliences (on average). Moreover, both components are readily interpretable. As shown in Table 3.3, the items loading highest ($|0.4|$ and above) on the first principal component consist of negative mentions of free enterprise, incentives, and economic orthodoxy and positive mentions of

Table 3.3 Rotated loadings on the first two principal components of the comparative manifestos project data

	Rotated loadings	
	First component	Second component
104. Military: negative	.49	−.07
106. Peace	.42	−.03
401. Free enterprise	−.56	−.15
402. Incentives	−.41	–
413. Nationalization	.40	−.08
414. Economic orthodoxy	−.48	−.27
701. Labour groups: positive	.48	−.16
107. Internationalism	.09	.44
305. Political authority	.03	−.43
501. Environmental protection	.12	.44
502. Culture	−.04	.58
506. Educational expansion	−.10	.48
705. Underprivileged minority groups	.14	.42

Note: The entries are loadings from an orthogonal rotation of the first two components of a PCA of 56 CMP variables, with equal weighting applied to the 14 West European countries included in the analysis. Only variables with a loading of 0.4 or above are shown.

nationalizations, peace, anti-militarism, and labour groups. This pattern strongly suggests a basic left/right dimension. With respect to the second component, the high loadings for positive mentions of internationalism, environmental protection, culture, educational expansion and the protection of underprivileged minorities and negative mentions of political authority indicate a 'new politics' or postmaterialism dimension.[13]

The parties' positions on these dimensions for each election in which they participated can be readily measured by their principal component (factor) scores.[14] But we also require measurement of the positions of the various governments, a need that the CMP has only addressed in limited measure. Fortunately, the available evidence (Warwick 2001b) suggests that they can be approximated reasonably well by the size-weighted mean position of the government parties. Since this measurement requires policy data for every party in government, any government formation that lacked complete CMP data for all government parties must be excluded from the analysis. This rule mainly involves cases where a very small party happened to find a place for itself in government.

This is not the only basis for excluding cases. In order to focus the analysis on bargaining situations for which information is essentially complete, it is also necessary to exclude legislatures without data for sizeable non-government parties. The criterion used here is that any legislature that lacks data for a party holding more than 5 per cent of legislative seats is excluded. Although the CMP data occasionally omit a sizeable party (principally due to party splits occurring between elections), this criterion came into play mainly with regard to the estimation of parties' compromise limits, to which we now turn.

Compromise limits

It is evident that a party's tolerance for compromise can only be estimated adequately by behaviour-based methods if the party has appeared in a reasonable number of formation situations. Yet, setting the minimum number of appearances at a high level would leave a substantial number of significant parties without estimates and thus would cause many legislatures to be discarded. It is therefore necessary to adopt a criterion that balances these two concerns. The criterion adopted here is that there must be a minimum of five appearances in formation situations for a horizon to be estimated; if any party with at least 5 per cent of legislative seats did not meet this criterion, the entire legislature was excluded. Whether this criterion leads to poor measurement of horizons will become evident in due course, but at least it leaves us with a reasonable number of cases: the remaining data consist of 273 government formation situations in 157 legislatures across the 14 countries. The distribution of cases by country is shown in Table 3.4.

The MJD method estimates a party's horizon simply by identifying the largest party–government distance it tolerated in government. The logit method is more complex, since it is based on a statistical estimation procedure. There are 2199 cases of parties appearing in formation situations in the data set and the procedure consists of regressing government membership (i.e. whether or not the party joined the government) across these cases on party–government distance and a series of dummy variables identifying the various parties (but one). As one would expect, the results show a very strong and highly significant relationship between party–government distance and government membership ($\beta = -2.516$, $S.E. = 0.154$, $p < .001$). Based on this regression, the distance at which the odds of belonging to the government reach 50 per cent was identified for each party.

The application of the logit method to these data requires two adjustments (neither of which came into play in the analysis of the

Table 3.4   The manifesto-based data set coverage

	Period covered	Number of proto-coalitions	Number of formations
Austria	1945–1990	100	12
Belgium	1954–1995	9,640	24
Denmark	1945–1996	8,775	25
Finland	1946–1995	6,430	34
France	1946–1995	10,894	34
Germany	1961–1991	91	13
Iceland	1947–1991	226	14
Ireland	1961–1997	189	11
Italy	1958–1991	12,894	34
Luxembourg	1945–1984	180	12
Netherlands	1956–1994	561	15
Norway	1961–1997	1,391	17
Portugal	1976–1995	215	9
Sweden	1948–1994	685	19
Total		52,271	273

hypothetical example). First, it is possible that the estimated distance at which a party becomes more likely than not to join a government is negative, a circumstance that usually crops up with parties that have never participated in government. Given that negative horizon distances have no meaning, they were set to 0.001 (*Horizons 3D*© requires a horizon radius greater than zero). The second adjustment was necessitated by the opposite situation, that in which a party is always in government. In the absence of evidence that the party would ever refuse to join a government, the logit method tends to produce extremely large horizon distances. In this situation, which affects just six parties (of 157), the horizon distances were adjusted downwards to fit the general pattern.[15]

Testing the hypothesis

We can now proceed to the testing of the horizon hypothesis using the two sets of horizon estimates. The first step in the testing procedure is to enter the party data – seat sizes, positions, and horizons – into the *Horizons 3D*© program for analysis. Data for each legislature had to be entered twice – once using the MJD horizon estimates and a second time using the logit-based horizons. For both versions of each legislature, 500 simulations were performed in which the party and horizon data were randomly altered according to the same specifications used in the hypothetical example (errors ~ N (0, 0.25)). The 314 files of output from these analyses were then concatenated to produce a final data file covering 52,271 proto-coalitions in the 273 formation situations.

The key variables produced by the *Horizons* analyses are the proto-coalition's policy distance, whether or not it has a common horizon intersection, and the probability of such an intersection, as estimated in the simulations. The proto-coalition's policy distance is again opera-tionalized in terms of the (Euclidean) distance between the two parties in the proto-coalition that are the furthest apart. As noted in Chapter 2, this decision is based on the idea that, since any disagreement can rupture a coalition, coalitions are only as viable as their weakest link – the two parties are most likely to disagree over policy.

We begin by examining the necessary condition that governments are formed of parties with intersecting horizons. The MJD method of calculating horizons ensures that this condition is always met, but what about the logit method which allows for violations? Ragin (2000, p. 111) has suggested that the 'fuzziness' of social science data warrants adoption of the lower standard of 'almost always necessary', which he defines as 80 per cent compliance with the necessary condition. The actual rate at which the necessary condition is met with the logit hori-zons estimated here is 85.3 per cent, which is significantly greater than Ragin's standard ($t = 2.22$, $p < .05$ in a one-tailed test). Thus, for these data, the logit method can be regarded as a viable means of generating horizons that meet the necessary condition in essence.

As we saw with the analysis of the simulated data, meeting the neces-sary condition does not guarantee explanatory power; for this determi-nation, we must move to a conditional logit analysis. This analysis will focus on the role played by the intersection rate rather than the horizon dichotomy for a couple of reasons. The first is that the causal role of the MJD-based horizon dichotomy variable cannot be estimated, since MJD horizons always satisfy the necessary condition of the hypothesis. The second and more significant reason is that intersection rates, by taking account of the inevitable presence of error or uncertainty surrounding the locations of horizons, are likely to bring a greater realism into the testing procedure. Before proceeding, however, it would be appropriate to examine how things change when simulations are introduced.

With simulations, a proto-coalition's policy distance becomes its mean distance across the simulations. The unbiased nature of the random errors generated in the simulations means that little is changed in this process; in fact, the correlation between this version and the original distance variable is .995. (The small discrepancy is due to the fact that adding random errors to party positions cannot be allowed to make the distance between them negative). For the horizon intersections, however, the correspondence will not always be so exact. If the original horizons of two parties narrowly fail to intersect, for instance, intersections are likely to occur in a fair proportion of the simulations. Similarly, if the original horizons just barely intersect, non-intersections should turn up quite often in the simulations.

The extent to which this is the case depends on the amount of error introduced in the simulations. With the hypothetical data, very little changed because of the relatively small error specification, and the fact that we are using the same error specification here suggests that a similarly high level of correspondence will appear. This turns out to be accurate: for logit horizons, the correlation between the intersection dichotomy and the intersection rate is 0.934; for MJD horizons, the corresponding correlation is 0.945. The bar chart in Figure 3.2 provides

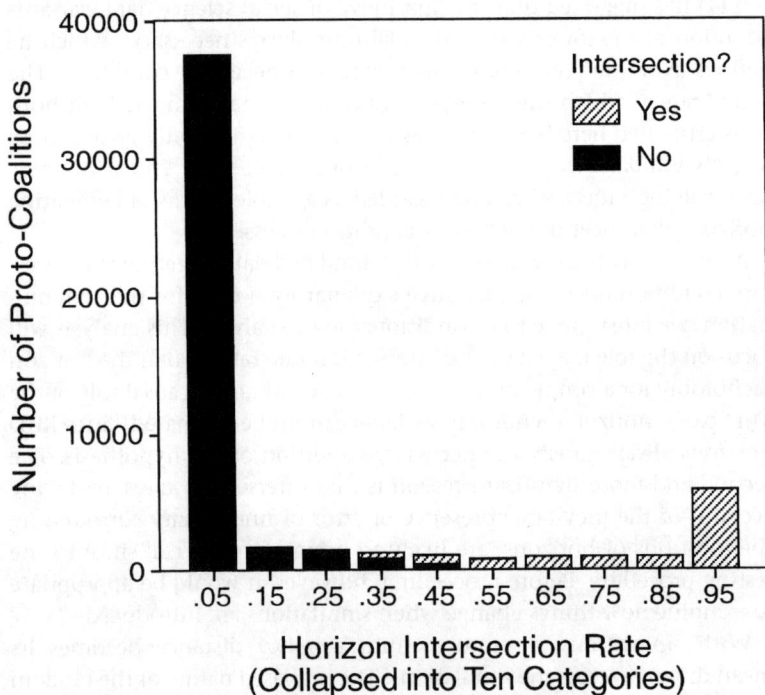

Figure 3.2   Logit horizon intersections and intersection rates.

further insight into the nature of this correspondence. In the figure, the logit-based intersection rate is grouped into ten categories of equal width and the bars are shaded to separate the proto-coalitions that had a common intersection according to the (logit) intersection dichotomy from those that did not. It is evident that the vast majority of proto-coalitions have intersection rates that are close to one extreme or the other (0 or 1); these cases mirror the categorization of the intersection dichotomy very precisely. The ambiguous cases – those with middling intersection rates – are not only few in number but also tend to follow the intersection dichotomy closely: most proto-coalitions with intersection rates between 0.1 and 0.5 originally had non-intersecting horizons, while virtually all those with rates in the 0.5–0.9 range had intersecting horizons.

Thus, the intersection rate is very similar, in fact identical, to the intersection dichotomy for the vast majority of cases. Where it differs is mainly over the small number of 'near-misses' and 'near-hits', for which it captures the considerable uncertainty that exists concerning the presence of an intersection. This pattern supports the argument that the intersection rate is a more reasonable rendering of the state of our knowledge about these situations, and presumably also the state of knowledge of the political actors making coalition decisions in these situations, but how well can its role be differentiated from that played by policy distance?

We saw earlier that the possibility of confusing a horizon effect for a distance effect increases when the variables measuring the two are highly correlated. This was the case in the hypothetical example before the random outcomes were added: the correlations between policy distance and the intersection rate were $r=-.80$ for MJD horizons and $r=-.77$ for logit horizons. The reason for these strong correlations is that the high level of symmetry in the bargaining system produced similar likelihoods of government participation for all three parties, which meant that the closer parties were, the greater the chance that their horizons intersected. Introducing some random error lowered these correlations to $-.58$ and $-.70$, respectively and made it much easier to identify the spurious horizon effect. With the actual parliamentary data, the correlations between intersection rates and distances are even less strong: $r=-.56$ (MJD horizons) and $r=-.60$ (logit horizons). Because real-world parliamentary systems lack the symmetry of the hypothetical example, the degree of collinearity between distance and intersection rates is much less and the chance that one will be mistaken for the other is correspondingly diminished.

The hypothetical example showed a strong policy distance effect because it was designed to do so, but is policy distance a major factor in real-world government-building? This question cannot be answered simply by looking at how policy distance affects the log-odds of emerging as the government; the size of the proto-coalition must also be taken into account. As in the hypothetical example, this involves separating majority from minority proto-coalitions: although the former are likely to be more ideologically diverse, the majority principle on which government survival and legislative effectiveness are based creates a bias in their favour.[16] Since real-world minority proto-coalitions (unlike the hypothetical ones) vary widely in size, however, there may also be a bias favouring those that are closer to majority status, despite the likelihood that closeness will bring with it extra parties and hence extra policy distance. Thus, what we should be considering is the effect of policy distance controlling not just for whether a proto-coalition is majoritarian but also how close it is to majority status. The latter effect can be captured by the *Size Gap*, a variable that records the percentage of parliamentary seats a proto-coalition falls short of majority status (it is set to zero for majority proto-coalitions).[17]

Let us turn now to the conditional logit analyses which are reported in Table 3.5. Model 1 assesses the effect of policy distance on the log-odds of emerging as the government, with majority status and closeness to it (the size gap) controlled. The results reveal a highly significant

Table 3.5 Testing policy distance and horizons effects in 14 West European systems

	Model 1	Model 2	Model 3	Model 4
Majority status	0.75** (0.19)	0.92** (0.19)	0.76** (0.18)	0.61** (0.18)
Size gap	−0.11** (0.01)	−0.11** (0.01)	−0.10** (0.01)	−0.10** (0.01)
Policy distance	−1.86** (0.12)	−0.75** (0.13)	−0.45** (0.14)	−1.00** (0.13)
Horizon intersection rate				
– MJD horizons	–	4.70** (0.36)	–	–
– Logit horizons	–	–	4.40** (0.30)	–
Horizon intersection (logit)	–	–	–	2.50** (0.22)
Log-likelihood	−946.0	−825.7	−819.4	−871.5

Note: Coefficients derive from conditional logit analyses covering 52,271 coalitions in 273 formation situations. Standard errors are given in parentheses.
* $p < .05$ in a one-tailed test.
** $p < .01$ in a one-tailed test.

impact: net of proto-coalition size, the more compact the proto-coalition is, the greater its chances of forming the next government.[18] As anticipated, the odds of forming the government are also significantly higher for majority proto-coalitions and increase as minority proto-coalitions approach majority status. In addition, further testing (not shown) indicates that there is no significant interaction effect between distance and majority status. This indicates that although majority governments are more likely to form than minority ones at any given level of compactness, changes in compactness affect the log-odds of forming a government in essentially the same way for both types of proto-coalition.

The fact that policy distance plays a significant net role in Model 1 is hardly a surprise, since it is consistent not only with the policy-seeking assumption of most formal models but also with previous empirical research on coalition formation and membership in West European democracies (e.g. Warwick 1996, 1998; Martin and Stevenson 2001). But what about the horizon hypothesis? If policy horizons are operative, then the probability that the parties in a proto-coalition have intersecting horizons should influence its chances of becoming the next government, independent of how far apart those parties are from one another. This possibility is examined in Models 2 and 3, which add the intersection rate based on MJD and logit horizons, respectively. In both models, the horizon intersection rate clearly shows a highly significant net impact on the log-odds of becoming the government. Again, further testing reveals no significant interaction effect with majority status, indicating that the intersection rate enhances the odds of formation similarly for both majority and minority proto-coalitions.

It does not seem to matter which method of horizon estimation is used, since the two methods result in highly similar effect coefficients. But does it matter that we have used intersection rates rather than a dichotomous measure that simply records whether or not each proto-coalition has intersecting horizons? This question cannot be answered with the MJD horizons for the reasons noted earlier, but it is possible to address the issue with the logit horizons. Model 4 shows the results when the logit-based intersection rate is replaced by the corresponding intersection dichotomy: the horizon effect is somewhat weaker, as one would expect, but still highly significant. While the intersection rate is the better measure since it allows for some degree of error or uncertainty, it is reassuring that both versions point to the same fundamental conclusion.

It is important to remember that the existence of a horizon effect does not totally undermine the basic policy distance assumption that guides most formal modelling. There is nothing in the policy horizon hypothesis that would rule out the possibility that, within the set of coalitions that have intersecting horizons in a given formation situation, the more compact will be more likely to form the government. One should therefore not expect the distance effect to disappear when the horizon effect is taken into account and indeed it does not. Models 2 and 3 make it clear, however, that the introduction of horizon intersection rates does cause a very large reduction in the policy distance effect. This suggests that much, perhaps most, of the impact formerly attributed to policy distance actually belongs to the operation of policy horizons.

How strong is the explanatory impact of these models? One means of assessing the impact of independent variables in logit models is to calculate the rate at which the model makes correct predictions. Following Martin and Stevenson (2001), a correct prediction can be said to occur when the predicted probability of becoming the government is higher for the proto-coalition that actually formed the government than it is for any of the other proto-coalitions in the choice set. This standard is very demanding: if the successful proto-coalition has a predicted probability that is only slightly lower than that of some other proto-coalition, the case would count as a prediction failure. Nevertheless, Models 2 and 3 do quite well under this standard. Since there is a mean of 191.5 coalitions per formation situation, the odds that any one of them would emerge as the government through chance alone tend to be very small; they average just 3.45 per cent across the 273 formation situations. Model 2, however, picks the government correctly over 20.5 per cent of the time, while Model 3 does so in 22.3 per cent of cases.

These rates of predictive success reveal something else as well. A comparison of the horizon effects in Models 2 and 3 might have suggested that the MJD method of measuring horizons produces a stronger horizon effect. But note that the distance effect is also stronger when MJD horizons are used and it offsets the horizon effect. The result is that Model 2, despite its stronger distance and horizon effects, has a lower log-likelihood and fewer predictive successes. Since the measurement of the other three variables is identical in the two models, these findings suggest that the MJD method of measuring horizons may not be quite as good as the logit method.

Model assumptions

Earlier in this chapter, considerable attention was devoted to assessing whether the estimation of horizon radii from the government participation records of the various parties is likely to produce a false horizon effect. This is not the only assumption that warrants examination, however. There are two others of particular importance: the 'independence from irrelevant alternatives' assumption that underpins the conditional logit model used to produce the effects shown in Table 3.5 and the assumption that those results hold when other influences on government formation are controlled. In this section, both assumptions are examined, beginning with the former.

The IIA assumption

In logit models, the estimation of covariate effects depends on an assumption known as 'independence from irrelevant alternatives' or IIA. This assumption stipulates that the relative probabilities of any two choices emerging as the outcome do not depend on the other choices present in the choice set. Thus, the fact that one might lack data on a particular party (and hence have omitted all proto-coalitions containing it) should not affect the relative formation probabilities of the remaining proto-coalitions in the choice set.

Following a suggestion by McFadden (1974), Martin and Stevenson (2001) tested this assumption in their models of government formation by dropping a random 10 per cent of proto-coalitions from each formation situation (excluding the proto-coalition that formed the government) and applying the Hausman test to determine if the estimated coefficients changed significantly.[19] If the IIA assumption is met, the removal of these choices should not affect the results. They performed this test 20 times on each model and reported the average *p*-value across the tests. These *p*-values were well above the .05 level, suggesting that the coefficients were not significantly affected by these reductions in the choice sets.

The models in Table 3.5 also survive this test, but it is less than clear that the test is adequate to the task. The reason is that it is based on fairly restrictive assumptions.[20] *Stata: Release 8* (StataCorp 2003) contains a generalization of the Hausman test that overcomes these limitations. When this test was applied to intersection rate effect in Models 2 and 3, significant differences did emerge in most of the trials. These differences, however, are very small. As Panel A of Table 3.6 shows, the mean effect across 20 trials of removing a random 10 per cent of

Table 3.6 Testing the IIA assumption

	All proto-coalitions (from Table 3.5)	Random 10% of proto-coalitions per choice set removed	Random 20% of proto-coalitions per choice set removed	Proto-coalitions containing a party with 2% or fewer seats excluded
Panel A: MJD horizons				
MJD intersection rate	4.70 (0.36)	4.71	4.73	4.38 (0.38)
Mean difference from full-sample coefficient	–	–0.010	–0.034	–
Standard error of difference	–	0.010	0.012	–
Panel B: Logit horizons				
Logit intersection rate	4.40 (0.30)	4.40	4.39	4.21 (0.33)
Mean difference from full-sample coefficient	–	0.007	0.020	–
Standard error of difference	–	0.008	0.008	–
N (proto-coalitions)	52,271	47,043	41,817	33,838

Note: Coefficients are from conditional logit analyses with majority status, the size gap, and policy distance also included in the specification. Standard errors are given in parentheses. The means for analyses with randomly removed proto-coalitions are based on 20 trials. All estimated coefficients are significant at $p < .001$ level in one-tailed tests.

each choice set is to cause the MJD intersection rate coefficient to deviate from its full-sample value of 4.70 by just 0.010, with a standard error of 0.010. When 80 per cent samples are specified, that is, a random 20 per cent of choices are discarded from each choice set, the mean deviation is 0.034 units *(SE* = 0.012). The corresponding deviations in the logit intersection rate coefficient of 4.41 (Panel B) are 0.007 *(SE* = 0.008) and 0.020 *(SE* = 0.008).

These results suggest that any dependency that may exist among choices has a very limited impact on the estimation of the role played by the intersection rate. In other words, the effects reported in Table 3.5 do not appear to be artefacts of using a statistical model that does not capture linkages among choices. However, this conclusion is based on removing choices randomly, which may not be the most appropriate way to proceed in the present context. Consider, in particular, the situation with respect to very small parties. The presence of these parties in a legislature is usually quite inconsequential for coalition bargaining and, for that reason, legislatures that lack information on one or more of these parties (defined as those holding less than 5 per cent of legislative seats) were not excluded from the data set. But the omission of any party, not matter how small, is far from inconsequential for the size of the choice set: it cuts that size approximately in half. It would be very disturbing if the substantial reduction in the size of the choice set that results from the exclusion of even one small party were to have a significant effect on the results of the conditional logit analyses. In fact, given the usual irrelevance of these parties to the government formation process, any dependence of results on whether or not they are included would constitute not just a technical violation of the IIA assumption but a major substantive problem for researchers. One can easily imagine that the issue of which proto-coalitions should be considered relevant to the government formation process could overwhelm the issue of what causal factors drive the process.

That the presence of small parties has a profound effect on the size of choice sets is evident in the fact that more than one-third of proto-coalitions in the data set contain a party that held no more than 2 per cent of legislative seats. This reflects the decision taken here to include even the smallest parties, provided information is available on their policy positions. Whether there are consequences to this decision can be assessed by the simple expedient of re-estimating Models 2 and 3 without these choices. The re-estimated intersection rate effects are reported in the final column of Table 3.6. If the IIA assumption holds, these effects should not be altered in any major way by the exclusion of these choices. Although the coefficients are changed somewhat, application of the generalized Hausman test reveals that these changes are not significant at the 0.05 level.

Ceteris Paribus?

As with all statistical models, the evidence for a horizon effect reported in Table 3.5 only holds on the assumption that other things are equal. The other things that we need to take into account here are numerous; Martin and Stevenson (2001, p. 45), for example, identify some nine variables that appear to exercise a significant net influence on the log-odds of forming the government. Since that study represents the most recent attempt to explain government formation in West European coalitional systems (and the only one to base the analysis on proto-coalitions rather than individual parties), it shall provide our inventory of 'other things' to be considered.

Unsurprisingly, size and policy differences loom large in the Martin and Stevenson model. The three size variables for which they find significant effects are dichotomous indicators of whether the proto-coalition (1) is minimal winning, (2) includes the largest party, and (3) is minoritarian in a system that requires a vote of investiture. The last-mentioned variable captures the hypothesis that minority coalitions should be disfavoured only if a proposed government must pass a formal parliamentary vote of investiture in order to take office. Policy differences figure directly in two independent variables: the proto-coalition's left–right ideological division and the anti-system presence in it. The latter is measured by the highest anti-system score (derived from the CMP data) held by a proto-coalition member and is intended to capture the idea that certain parties in West European party systems hold views so extreme or unacceptable to other parties that they are 'non-coalitionable', that is, they are effectively excluded (and/or exclude themselves) from coalition bargaining.[21] In addition, policy may undergird another dichotomy: whether or not the parties in the proto-coalition entered into a pre-electoral pact.

Parliamentary size and policy also influence the chances that a party is a 'very strong party' or VSP in the sense used in Laver and Shepsle's (1996) portfolio allocation model of parliamentary governance. VSPs are large, centrally located parties that, according to the model, should dominate the government formation process. Martin and Stevenson find both those proto-coalitions that include a VSP and those that consist solely of a VSP are more likely to take office. Finally, they detect a degree of institutional inertia in the tendency for the coalition that formed the last government to form the next one.

In the analyses that follow, these variables will be measured as in Martin and Stevenson, with two exceptions.[22] First, ideological divisions within a proto-coalition will be measured by the policy distance variable developed here, rather than with their one-dimensional version. Second, the operationalization of the notion that certain governments are rendered improbable or impossible by the presence of non-coalitionable parties will be effected by means of a dichotomous variable, *Extremist party presence*. This variable is based on Powell's (1982, pp. 233–4) definition of an extremist party as one that (1) espouses a non-democratic ideology, (2) proposes a fundamental alteration in national boundaries, or (3) represents a diffuse protest, alienation, or distrust of the political system. Powell's list of these parties was updated and any proto-coalition containing one of them receives a value of '1' on the variable; all other proto-coalitions are coded '0'.[23] Testing reveals that this variable has a much stronger effect on government formation than the manifesto-based version used by Martin and Stevenson.

Because of differences in the time period and countries covered, certain of the Martin–Stevenson variables are not available for all cases in the present data set.[24] Since the exclusion of these cases would eliminate about one-third of the data set, multiple imputation was utilized to fill in these data gaps. The inspiration behind this technique is that the correlations among variables in a data set ought to enable us to make reasonable guesses about the values of missing data entries. While guessing is not the same as knowing for sure, it should be superior to assuming that we have no idea what the missing scores should be, which is what we do when we leave the entries blank. Following King *et al.*'s (2001, p. 57) recommendation that all variables to be utilized in the subsequent data analysis be included in the imputation process, the imputation procedure included not just the Martin and Stevenson variables, but also those in our four-variable model as well as variables such as the mean intersection size and the probability of an encompassed weighted mean (EWM) that will figure in subsequent analyses. The procedure was implemented by means of Honaker *et al.*'s (2003) *Amelia* program, which generated five new data sets, each sporting imputed values for the missing data and the original data elsewhere.[25]

Model 1 of Table 3.7 shows the effects of these nine variables on the log-odds of government formation. The estimated effect coefficients are simply the means from separate analyses of the five partially imputed data sets (the standard errors, however, are somewhat more complex

Table 3.7   Testing horizons effects in the Martin–Stevenson model

	Model 1	Model 2	Model 3	Model 4
Minimum winning status	0.95** (0.18)	0.35* (0.20)	−0.04 (0.20)	−0.16 (0.21)
Coalition has largest party	1.03** (0.18)	−0.07 (0.20)	0.06 (0.21)	−0.19 (0.21)
Minority coalition in Investiture system	−0.55* (0.27)	−0.03 (0.31)	0.01 (0.32)	−0.10 (0.31)
Anti-system presence	−2.26** (0.27)	−2.34** (0.27)	−1.61** (0.27)	−1.39** (0.28)
Pre-electoral pact	3.64** (0.86)	3.28** (0.76)	2.67** (0.74)	3.59** (0.80)
Coalition has VSP	0.88** (0.31)	0.60* (0.33)	0.68* (0.34)	0.61* (0.33)
Coalition consists of VSP	0.87** (0.34)	0.51 (0.37)	0.68* (0.38)	0.66* (0.37)
Incumbent government	2.32** (0.18)	2.09** (0.18)	1.85** (0.18)	1.78** (0.18)
Policy distance	−0.69** (0.09)	−1.40** (0.13)	−0.62** (0.15)	−0.52** (0.16)
Majority status	–	0.61* (0.28)	0.99** (0.29)	0.96** (0.28)
Size gap	–	−0.10** (0.01)	−0.09** (0.01)	−0.09** (0.01)
Horizon intersection rate				
– MJD horizons	–	–	3.72** (0.40)	–
– Logit horizons	–	–	–	3.34** (0.35)

Note: Coefficients derive from conditional logit analyses of five data sets, each covering 52,271 coalitions in 273 formation situations with imputed data for missing Martin–Stevenson scores. Standard errors are given in parentheses.
* $p < .05$ in a one-tailed test.
** $p < .01$ in a one-tailed test.

since they take into account variance within as well across data sets). The results indicate that all of Martin and Stevenson's variables are significantly related to government formation, which suggests that their model is well replicated with these data, despite the differences in coverage between this study and theirs.[26]

Our concern, of course, is not with replicating that model but with determining whether policy horizons continue to show a significant net impact on government formation once these other effects are controlled. In order to do this, however, we must ensure that the policy distance effect is adequately captured. This requires controlling for proto-coalition size by means of the majority status and size gap variables. As Model 2 shows, the result is a very large increase in the magnitude of the policy distance effect, as well as substantial weakening in the effects of some of the Martin–Stevenson variables. In Model 3 (logit horizons) and Model 4 (MJD horizons), the horizon intersection rate is added to the specification. As before, the results are consistent between the two models and therefore point to a single conclusion. In this case, the conclusion is striking: the intersection rate not only continues to display a highly significant net impact on the log-odds of forming the government, but its presence reduces the influence of policy distance strikingly.

These results are strongly supportive of the hypothesis that policy horizons condition government formations. There is no guarantee that Martin and Stevenson tested all other potential causal factors; indeed, we shall be considering the impact of some novel horizon-related variables in Chapter 6. Nevertheless, the ability of the horizon effect to survive so well the introduction of nine previously identified causal factors adds considerable credibility to the case for a horizon effect in coalition government formations.

Discussion

One of the more surprising aspects of the analysis undertaken in this chapter is that it has proven possible to estimate policy horizons from information on government membership and policy distance in a set of formation situations and then to use those estimates to detect the operation of horizons in the same situations – and in the process to challenge an explanation based on policy distance itself. The reason we can estimate horizons in this way is that there is nothing inevitable about the explanation they provide: if the government membership record of parties does not reflect the presence of horizons, then estimating a horizon for each party via these methods will not manufacture a horizon effect. Indeed, even when policy distance so closely determines government formations that accidental horizons are produced, as in the hypothetical data, it still proved to be relatively easy to identify the true cause. Any privileging of the intersection rate variable by virtue of the horizon estimation procedures in no way inhibited the achievement of that outcome.

Differentiating policy distance from horizon effects becomes even more straightforward when the two are not so highly correlated. This is the situation in the West European parliamentary data analysed here. Despite the fact that party–government distances are a major component in the estimation of horizons, the final product of that procedure – the horizon intersection rates – bears no more than a passing resemblance to the policy distances spanned by proto-coalitions. To illustrate the discrepancy, consider situations where a majority government was formed. These coalitions always have intersecting MJD horizons and almost always have intersecting logit horizons. They are seldom, however, the most compact choices available: there are, on average, about 15 majority alternatives per formation situation that are more compact. Of these alternatives, however, only about one-third (35.1 per cent) have intersecting logit-based horizons.[27] In other words, a substantial number of these alternatives do not have intersecting horizons, even though the parties that compose them are closer together in the space. Clearly, in the actual (as opposed to the hypothetical) data, horizon intersections do not move in lockstep with policy distance.

Another curiosity of the analysis is that there appears to be very strong horizon effects in the parliamentary data using both the logit and MJD horizons, even though the two can often be quite dissimilar.[28] One reason that this does not lead to different results is that, despite locating the horizons somewhat differently, the methods tend to agree on whether an intersection is likely to exist. If we take an intersection rate of 50 per cent or greater as indicating the probable existence of a horizon intersection, for instance, the two reach the same verdict for 84.5 per cent of the proto-coalitions. The second reason is that, while the MJD method guarantees that all governing coalitions will have horizon intersections (and therefore high intersection rates in all probability), the method also generates larger prediction sets.[29] In other words, the gain in predictive successes is offset by a substantial increase in incorrect predictions.

The consequence is that the data analysis provides no clear indication as to which method of estimating horizons is to be preferred. The logit method is perhaps more realistic in allowing for measurement errors, calculation errors by politicians, or the occurrence of exceptional circumstances, but its criterion for defining horizon distances is arbitrary. The MJD method meets the necessary condition of the hypothesis in full, but it rules out fewer coalitions. Both methods, moreover, assume (1) that horizons are circular and fixed for the duration of the observation period and (2) that joining behaviour in as few as five coalition formation situations is adequate to establish a party's limits of compromise.

In view of these limitations to the horizon measurement procedures, it is striking how strongly a proto-coalition's odds of becoming the next government are related to the probability that its member-parties have intersecting horizons, as measured here. It appears that much of the influence normally attributed to policy distance, the key ingredient in most conceptualizations of party utility, more properly belongs to this factor. The horizon effect, moreover, is largely independent of other influences on government formation that have been identified in the literature; as a comparison of Tables 3.5 and 3.7 reveals, their presence in the models scarcely alters its magnitude. We cannot say how strong the effect truly is, given the measurement concerns discussed above, but this evidence suggests that it is considerable indeed.

4
Expert Estimates of Ideological Spaces and Party Bounds

The empirical analysis thus far has been based on party positions as derived from content analyses of manifestos conducted by the Comparative Manifesto Project (Budge *et al.* 2001). The advantages of using manifestos rather than the judgements of experts to establish party positions are twofold. First, the tendency of parties to issue new manifestos with every election allows changes in party positions to be tracked over time very readily; second, reliance on the CMP data reduces the element of subjectivity in the estimation process. While human judgement plays a significant role both in the content analysis of the manifestos and in the dimensional analysis of the results, this is still a far cry from having experts directly make guesses about policy positions.

Despite these advantages, the use of expert surveys should not be discounted. This is because expert surveys allow researchers to tackle important inferred concepts in a much more direct fashion. The key such concept for present purposes is the concept of policy horizons. In the preceding chapter, horizons were derived indirectly from the parties' positions and their records of government participation. While various steps were taken to demonstrate that the methods of doing so are valid, nothing in the procedure links the horizon estimates to their supposed source, the expectations of party supporters. Asking experts to estimate horizon bounds provides a means of establishing a much closer linkage.

A second inferred concept for which an expert survey can provide valuable leverage is the relevant ideological space for each political system. Dimensional analyses, despite the name, are not especially good at this. Although they provide an indication of the explanatory power of each dimension, the researcher must still decide how many dimensions to retain as significant or important. In Chapter 3, not only was the decision to retain two dimensions inevitably arbitrary, but the goal of generating the most accurate estimates of party positions necessitated a cross-system analysis, which meant assuming the same two dimensions for every system. Another shortfall of the approach adopted in Chapter 3 is the absence of some viable means of introducing dimensional saliences into the picture. This necessitated the assumption that horizons are circular in shape and the calculation of distances in simple Euclidean terms, both of which imply that the two dimensions have the same importance for every party.

Expert surveys are the essential tool for relaxing these restrictions; as Laver and Hunt (1992, p. 39) note, it would be almost impossible to collect reliable information on the relevant ideological space for a system by any other means. But this is only achievable if the survey specifically targets an appropriate conception of the ideological space under investigation, which will often mean going beyond the simple one-dimensional characterization frequently used in the past. The survey must also expand the interpretation of the relevant features of the space to include party-specific dimension saliences.

This chapter reports the results of a new expert survey covering 13 West European systems that is specifically focussed on these tasks. Much of the chapter is devoted to describing the methodology of the survey and subjecting the results to various reliability and validity tests. Among other things, these tests will sustain the contention that the survey responses provide estimates of party horizons that are independent of coalition behaviour – and therefore a valuable new resource for testing the policy horizon hypothesis.

The design and implementation of the new survey

The expert survey undertaken with these measurement goals in mind covers the same West European parliamentary systems that were the subject of the investigations in the previous chapter: Austria, Belgium, Denmark, Finland, France, Germany, Iceland, Ireland, Italy, Luxembourg, the Netherlands, Norway, Portugal, and Sweden. This selection is dictated in large measure by the need to focus on systems where majority parties are relatively uncommon. The first objective of the survey was to establish an appropriate ideological space for each of these systems. As the experience of Huber and Inglehart (1995) indicates, this is not as simple a matter as it might appear. Their expert survey asked respondents to locate the parties both on a left/right scale and any other policy dimension that they deemed to be relevant to the system in question. What they found was surprisingly little agreement among experts in the various systems on what that second dimension should be. In fact, among European countries, only for Norway, Sweden, and Switzerland did more than one-third of expert respondents agree on the identity of a second dimension.

This suggests that a more focussed approach is required. Fortunately, other research provides some guidance as to how to proceed. In their expert survey conducted in 1989, Laver and Hunt (1992) identified eight basic issues that they regarded as fundamental to West European political systems and asked their expert respondents to rate parties on each of them. The issues cover public expenditures ('taxes vs. spending'), social permissiveness, public ownership, clericalism/secularism, urban/rural interests, decentralization of decision-making, environmental protection vs. growth, and friendliness towards the Soviet Union. In previous research (Warwick 2001a), I performed a PCA of party positions on these scales across 16 West European countries and found that they can be reduced to just three dimensions: left/right (comprising public expenditures, public ownership, and Soviet relations), 'social control' (social permissiveness, clericalism, and urban/rural interests), and materialism/postmaterialism (environmentalism and decentralization).[1] These dimensions account for an impressive 89 per cent of the variance in the original eight scales.

The left/right, social control, and materialism/postmaterialism dimensions would therefore appear to constitute a good starting-point in characterizing ideological spaces in West European systems. It would be desirable, however, to make some finer distinctions within the second dimension: while clericalism/secularism might still constitute the core of this dimension in some systems, in others it has much more to do with what is sometimes called 'libertarianism/authoritarianism'.[2] In addition, some allowance should be made for the possibility that other policy dimensions may assume a major importance in the various systems. For these reasons, the present survey asked respondents to estimate party positions on a left/right dimension, a materialism/postmaterialism dimension, and either a clerical/secular dimension or a libertarian/authoritarian dimension – respondents were free to indicate which designation was more appropriate for the system in question. Respondents were also asked to indicate any other dimension that they regarded as important for the country in question and locate the parties on it as well.

Respondents could therefore designate up to four policy dimensions and situate parties on them. But it is also essential to know how important these dimensions are. For many purposes, a space of just two or three dimensions may be perfectly adequate, but which dimensions should they be? In particular, are any of the user-specified dimensions more important than the three specified dimensions? As we have seen, dimension saliences are also essential if more realistic estimates of policy compatibility based on salience-weighted policy distances are to be calculated. Respondents were therefore asked to assume that the left/ right dimension has a basic salience value of '1' and assign saliences to the other dimensions in proportion to the degree to which they exceed or undershoot that value. For instance, a salience of 0.8 attributed to a dimension would indicate that it is 80 per cent as salient as the left/ right dimension, a score of 1.5 would indicate that it is 50 per cent more salient, and so forth. To capture the possibility that individual parties differ in their assessments of the salience of any given dimension, respondents were given the option of designating party-specific salience scores.

Respondents were thus presented with a semi-structured choice of dimensions, but with complete freedom to rule individual dimensions in or out of contention as important axes of party competition through the allocation of salience scores. Within this dimensional format, party positions were to be estimated. The survey utilized the standard device of asking respondents to place parties on a continuous scale (in this case, a scale calibrated with integers from '0' to '10') but, unlike other expert surveys, it sought information both on present parties and parties no longer represented in the legislature. The reason is, of course, to provide as much coverage as possible of the post-War democratic era in each country. Priority was given to the present state of affairs, however, and parties no longer in existence were only included when (1) the current party system was adequately covered within a limit of twelve parties and (2) there was an expectation that their parameters could be estimated with reasonable accuracy.

These constraints were adopted simply to keep the task manageable, but they do entail the loss of a sizeable number of formation situations covered in the analyses of Chapter 3, including those in the Netherlands before the amalgamation of religious parties into the Christian Democratic Union in the 1970s and all formations in the French Fourth Republic. In the case of Italy, the total transformation of the party system in the early 1990s would have made the losses even greater. To prevent so great a loss of cases, the survey sought separate sets of estimates for the two eras, which considerably expanded the burden imposed on respondents.

The final element in the survey design is the request for estimates of the bounds or limits of compromise for the various parties. It is important to note that this request did not force respondents to accept that these bounds exist: they were specifically instructed that placing a party's bounds at the end of a policy scale would be equivalent to saying that there are no limits on the amount of policy compromise that the party could accept on that dimension. Respondents were thus free to eviscerate the horizon hypothesis' substantive content while conforming totally to the demands of the survey. Respondents were also instructed to base their estimates on their 'understanding of the degree to which the party's policy on the dimension is taken seriously, and faithfulness to policy commitments valued highly, by party members and supporters – *not on the extent of policy compromises the party has accepted in past governments'* (emphasis in original).[3] The reason for this request was to gain estimates of the limits of compromise that are not based on the phenomenon they will be used to explain.

As a guide in providing the requested information, respondents were presented with an example, shown in Figure 4.1, of a party judged to be located at 5.5 on the left/right dimension and considered to be free to enter only those governments whose proposed policies fall in the 4.5–6.5 range without incurring significant internal dissent or alienation. In the survey itself, the same 11-point scale was presented for each party on each dimension, with upper and lower extremes labelled (e.g. the lower ends of the three designated dimensions were identified as 'Extreme Left', 'Secular/Libertarian', and 'Postmaterialist', respectively). Respondents who identified a country-specific dimension were asked to supply their own labels to identify its extremes. A box located to the right of each scale allowed the respondent to indicate a party-specific salience, if different from the overall salience they attribute to the dimension.

It will be evident by now that the survey asked a lot of its respondents. Not only were they expected to provide estimates of positions on three or four policy dimensions for up to twelve parties (even more for Italy), but they also had to provide salience estimates for these dimensions and, where appropriate, for individual parties as well. In addition, they

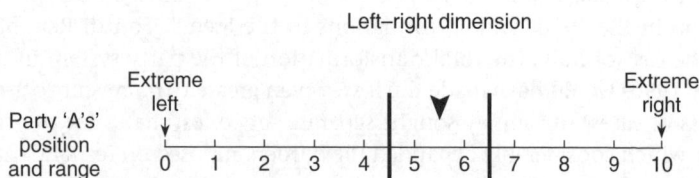

Figure 4.1   Locating party positions and bounds in the survey questionnaire.

were asked to provide a novel type of information: estimates of the limits of compromise surrounding each of the party positions.

To accomplish these tasks, respondents would clearly need a substantial degree of political knowledge. The search for respondents therefore focussed on social scientists with expertise in one of the countries under investigation. Potential respondents were identified initially from the list of respondents to Huber and Inglehart's (1995) survey, which covered almost all of these systems. This was supplemented by names taken from the members' directory of the *European Consortium for Political Research* and from bibliographic searches.[4] Respondents were also encouraged to suggest names of other qualified individuals and many did.

The initial mailing of surveys took place in the autumn of 2000 and the winter of 2001. As new names were identified, more questionnaires were mailed. By the summer of 2002, replies from 169 respondents had been received, representing 23.1 per cent of the 731 individuals sent questionnaires. This response rate is similar to the rate of 28.9 per cent reported for the Laver and Hunt (1992, p. 36) survey, which was also quite demanding of respondents. Considerable effort was made to ensure an adequate number of respondents for each country and this was achieved in large measure: all countries but one are represented by at least ten respondents, which is double the minimum of five that Laver and Hunt set for their survey (Laver and Hunt 1992, p. 37). The exception is Luxembourg, for which it proved impossible to identify a sufficient number of respondents and which is excluded from further consideration for that reason.[5] For the remaining countries, the numbers of respondents compare well with those of other expert surveys.[6]

The survey results: Coverage, reliability, and validity

The presentation of the survey results begins with the key policy dimensions of the various systems, as identified by our expert respondents. This information is summarized in Table 4.1, which also lists the number of respondents providing information on each system. The dimensions are presented in the order discussed in the previous section, beginning with the left/right dimension. As noted earlier, the second dimension may take the form of either a libertarian/authoritarian or a clerical/secular dimension; the version listed for each system is the one chosen by a majority of its respondents. The third and fourth dimensions are, respectively, the materialism/postmaterialism dimension and a user-specified or country-specific dimension. In most countries, either

Table 4.1 The nature and salience of key dimensions

	First dimension			Second dimension		Third dimension		Fourth dimension		
	N	Policy area	Salience	Policy area	Salience	Policy area	Salience	Policy area	N	Salience
Austria	14	Left/right	0.97	Lib./auth.	0.95	Mat./postmat.	0.98	None		
Belgium	12	Left/right	1.07	Clerical/secular	0.99	Mat./postmat.	0.92	Centralization/decentralization	7	1.30
Denmark	13	Left/right	1.00	Lib./auth.	0.78	Mat./postmat.	0.78	None		
Finland	11	Left/right	1.02	Clerical/secular	0.83	Mat./postmat.	0.93	Urban–Centre–Pro-EU/Rural–Peripheral–Anti-EU	8	1.29
France (V)	10	Left/right	1.00	Lib./auth.	0.74	Mat./postmat.	0.73	None		
Germany	13	Left/right	1.03	Clerical/secular	0.88	Mat./postmat.	0.73	None		
Iceland	10	Left/right	1.00	Lib./auth.	0.53	Mat./postmat.	0.51	Nationalist–isolationist/internationalist–pro-West	6	0.93
Ireland	15	Left/right	1.03	Clerical/secular	0.96	Mat./postmat.	0.73	Northern Ireland	7	1.23
Italy (before transformation)	13	Left/right	0.99	Clerical/secular	1.07	Mat./postmat.	0.54	None		
Italy (after transformation)		Left/right	0.96	Clerical/secular	0.99	Mat./postmat.	0.57	None		
Netherlands	13	Left/right	0.99	Clerical/secular	1.08	Mat./postmat.	0.73	None		
Norway	18	Left/right	1.04	Clerical/secular	0.70	Mat./postmat.	0.61	Centre–urban/periphery–rural	8	0.78
Portugal	15	Left/right	1.03	Clerical/secular	0.99	Mat./postmat.	0.73	None		
Sweden	12	Left/right	0.98	Lib./auth.	0.68	Mat./postmat.	0.51	None		

Note: Salience entries are party saliences averaged across respondents and parties. The *N* for the fourth dimension refers to the number of respondents identifying the dimension in question as salient.

few respondents identified a country-specific dimension or there was no substantial agreement on its nature; the five showing a fourth dimension in the table are the systems in which there was substantial agreement on one particular choice.[7] The number of respondents sharing this opinion is also reported.

Associated with each dimension identified in Table 4.1 is a salience value. About one-quarter of the time, respondents simply provided a single salience value for an entire dimension, but usually they indicated that one or more parties differed from that score. The salience levels listed in Table 4.1 were derived by calculating the mean salience scores for each party on the dimension in question, then averaging across the parties of the system. What is perhaps most notable about the scores is the relevance of multidimensional conceptions of the ideological spaces: there is never a dimension less than half as salient as the left/right dimension and six of the systems have a dimension that is more salient. This result goes against the assumption sometimes made in empirical analyses that policies in West European systems can be adequately captured by a single left–right dimension.[8]

Although Table 4.1 furnishes information on the key dimensions of the various systems, it says nothing about how parties are located on those dimensions. This much more extensive type of information can be found in Appendix 2, which lists the mean party positions for the three most important dimensions in each system. These dimensions were identified by counting the number of respondents that placed each dimension in the top three in terms of overall salience.[9] Appendix 2 also reports mean party-specific salience values for these dimensions as well as the mean locations of the lower and upper horizon bounds on each dimension. Each mean is accompanied by its standard error and the number of respondents supplying estimates so that confidence intervals can be calculated.

Missing data

One characteristic of the data reported in Appendix 2 is that the numbers of respondents supplying salience and bounds estimates is consistently less than the numbers providing position estimates. This is partly the result of the survey design. The original intention was to spare respondents the difficult task of estimating bounds for parties on all dimensions by asking only for bounds on the left/right dimension and then using the dimension saliences to re-scale those bounds to fit other dimensions. This approach was based on the idea that the more important a policy dimension is to a party, the less it ought to be willing to compromise on it. Take, for example, a respondent who estimated bounds for a party spanning four units on the left/right dimension and who left the salience for that dimension at the default value of '1'. If the respondent estimated the party's salience score for the second dimension at '0.8', it would indicate that, in the respondent's view, issues in this dimension were only four-fifths as important to the party. This implies a greater willingness to compromise on these matters, which could be captured by expanding the party's left/right bounds by 25 per cent (5/4) to produce a compromise region spanning five units. Unfortunately, analysis of the surveys of respondents who provided bounds for all dimensions indicated that the expected inverse association between salience values and bound widths was weak at best, which effectively nullified the measurement strategy.[10] Many respondents were therefore re-contacted with requests to estimate bounds for the other dimensions but, as one might expect given the difficulty of the task, not everyone did.

An attractive option when data are missing is to employ a multiple imputation technique to fill in the blanks, as we did in Chapter 3. In the present case, there tend to be very strong correlations between party positions and party bounds: the higher a party's position is on the scale in question, the higher are its lower and upper bounds. Therefore, rather than assuming total ignorance when respondents did not supply bounds, we should be able to use the party positions they provided as well as the correlations between positions and bounds (calculated across cases where both types of information were provided) to make sensible guesses about where the missing bounds estimates would lie.

Considerable experimentation was performed to see if the bounds estimates might be enhanced along these lines but, unfortunately, the results were disappointing. Honaker *et al.*'s (2003) *Amelia* program produced parameter estimates and standard errors very similar to those produced using the original data, but with much higher degrees of freedom. This implies greater estimation precision, but unfortunately the degrees of freedom tended to be implausibly high, typically much higher than the total number of respondents. This perplexing outcome has been noted before and the imputation procedure implemented in SAS statistical package (SAS Institute 2001) incorporates the Barnard–Rubin correction factor to cope with it, but the estimated degrees of freedom it produces were so low (and the parameter estimates and standard errors remained so similar) that no clear improvement over the original data could be detected.[11]

This result, although certainly disappointing, is far from catastrophic. For one thing, it is evident from the results reported in Appendix 2 that the shortfall in the numbers of respondents providing bounds estimates affects only the second and third dimensions; the number providing bounds estimates for the left/right dimension exceeds the minimum criterion (five) adopted by Laver and Hunt in every country. Even for the other dimensions, moreover, the number of respondents is almost always at least four, just one short of the Laver–Hunt criterion. Finally, we have seen that there is a highly effective means of dealing with uncertainty over the locations of horizon bounds: incorporate it into the measurement of horizon intersections by means of simulations.

Reliability

An accurate estimate of expert opinion on any matter depends not just on how many experts are consulted but also on how well they agree with one another. An indication of the level of agreement among respondents can be garnered from the standard errors of the means reported in Appendix 2. Consider the first or left/right dimension. There seems to be substantial agreement on the location of parties on this dimension; the average standard error for a party location is just 0.25 units. The average standard errors for the location of horizon bounds, however, are noticeably larger at 0.32 units for the lower bound and 0.30 units for the upper bound. For the second dimension in the various countries, all three scores are approximately doubled (to 0.48, 0.62, and 0.65 for the position, lower bound, and upper bound estimates, respectively), and for the third dimension, the standard errors for the bounds are higher still (the corresponding figures are 0.48, 0.73, and 0.69). Thus, the standard errors indicate that there is less certainty in estimating horizon bounds than in estimating positions and less certainty in estimating all parameters for dimensions other than the first.[12]

Although the sizes of the standard errors give some sense of the extent of agreement across respondents, a better gauge of inter-rater reliability can be derived from intraclass correlations (ICCs). For a given group of raters and set of objects, ICCs assess reliability by comparing the variance in ratings across objects to the total variance across objects and raters. An ICC for party positions on a given dimension for a given country, for example, would consist of the ratio of the variance in positions across parties to the total variance in positions.[13] The higher this ratio, the more reliable the measurement.

The most common ICC is Cronbach's alpha. For present purposes, however, this measure has a weakness: it takes no account of absolute differences in score values. For instance, if one respondent placed five parties at integers beginning with '1' on the left/right scale and another placed them in the same order but at integers starting with '6', the alpha score would be 1.0, indicating perfect reliability – despite the fact that all five parties are left-wing for the first respondent and right-wing for the second. When absolute differences are taken into account, the ICC in this example drops to 0.286.

Absolute differences in scores for positions and bounds clearly matter here, so the latter version of the ICC will be used to assess reliability.[14] Table 4.2 presents a summary of the findings in the form of the ICCs for the position and bounds estimates for the three main dimensions, averaged across countries. As one would expect, there is greater inter-respondent agreement on positions than on bounds and greater agreement on all parameters for the left/right dimension than for the other two dimensions. Nevertheless, the differences are relatively minor; even the bounds estimates, a novel form of data request, are only marginally less reliable than the positions estimates. More significantly, all mean values are well above the level of 0.7 conventionally used as the minimum acceptable level. These means, moreover, do not hide huge variations in reliability across systems; in fact, only 9 of 126 country-level coefficients fall below that standard.

Knowing that the respondents tend to agree reasonably well with one another on where to locate the ideal points and horizon bounds of parties is reassuring, but it would also be useful to know if they tend to agree with other experts. Previous expert-based measurement efforts have involved both expert surveys (Castles and Mair 1984; Laver and Hunt 1992; and Huber and Inglehart 1995) and author-based assessments (Dodd 1976; Browne *et al.* 1984b).[15] Although the numbers of assessors in those studies are also fairly small (see note 6) and although party positions may have shifted in the interim, a high degree of agreement between the estimates they yielded and those of the present survey

Table 4.2 Intraclass correlations for positions and bounds estimates, averaged across systems

	First dimension	Second dimension	Third dimension
Lower bound	.886	.840	.835
Position	.968	.889	.939
Upper bound	.928	.862	.848

Note: Entries are means of the country-level average-measure ICCs (using a two-way random effect model with an absolute agreement definition).

would go a long way towards dispelling concerns that the latter are based on country samples that are unrepresentative of the larger universes of country experts. This comparison with the results of other expert surveys will be confined to position estimates, since these are what previous sources concentrated on.

The comparison is effected in Table 4.3 mainly by means of (product-moment) correlations of the party positions derived here with the party positions presented in the other sources cited above.[16] Of the latter, only Laver and Hunt's (1992) expert survey and Dodd's (1976) own position estimates encompass the clerical/secular dimension and only Laver and Hunt provide scales that touch on libertarianism/authoritarianism (the social permissiveness scale) or materialism/postmaterialism (the environmentalism vs. growth scale). While the comparisons that can be made are limited, they clearly have the virtue of consistently indicating a high degree of comparability. Particularly noteworthy in this respect is the very strong correlation between the present survey's left/right positions and those produced by its most recent predecessor, the Huber and Inglehart (1995) survey. Other comparisons, even those extending back a quarter-century, are still very impressive.[17]

The fact that mean party positions estimated in the present survey correspond closely with mean positions estimated in other surveys does not establish reliability in a larger sense, however, since it may be the case that all expert-based results are biased. Budge (2000, p. 109), in particular, has argued that expert judgements of positions are likely to be influenced by coalition behaviour, making them unsuitable to explain it. In other words, there may be a tendency for experts to place parties closer together if they have frequently coalesced, with the consequence that the connection between policy distance and coalition formation may be exaggerated.

Although this danger should not be dismissed, there are significant mitigating considerations. The first is that the danger depends on a high degree of recurrence in coalition patterns; placing parties too close together if they happen to form, say, the current government would undermine the relationship if these parties did not also form governments often in the past. Second, if any bias of this sort has infected estimates, it is likely to advantage the policy distance hypothesis over the horizon hypothesis. This is because it is relatively easy to place parties close together if they coalesce often, but not so easy to decipher which sets of positions will produce intersecting horizons in a multidimensional space. (The possibility that knowledge of coalition behaviour also affects the location of horizon bounds is examined in the following section.)

Table 4.3 Correlations of survey-based party positions with other position measures

Dimension	Comparison measures			
	Castles and Mair (1984)	Browne *et al.* (1984b)*	Laver and Hunt (1992): Cut taxes vs. raise spending	Laver and Hunt (1992): Pro- vs. anti-public ownership	Huber and Inglehart (1995)
Left/right	.936 ($n=72$)	.867 ($n=96$)	.909 ($n=91$)	.893 ($n=91$)	.969 ($n=87$)
Clerical/secular	Dodd (1976) .869 ($n=22$)	Laver and Hunt (1992) .957 ($n=48$)			
Libertarian/ authoritarian	Laver and Hunt (1992): Social permissiveness .705 ($n=28$)				
Materialist/ postmaterialist	Laver and Hunt (1992): Environment vs. growth .902 ($n=83$)				

Note: These correlations are based only on systems that have the dimension in question as one of their three main dimensions.
* The Browne *et al.* (1984b) scales are a revision of Dodd's (1976) economic conflict scales. They have been further updated for this comparison.

Validity

The strong correlations shown in Table 4.3 also support the validity of the measurement of party positions undertaken here. Referents such as 'left' and 'right' may mean different things to different respondents, as Budge (2000, p. 107) observes, but the fact that several different sets of experts at different times have given highly similar ratings to parties suggests that those ratings are all tapping into the same general dimension.[18] Huber and Inglehart (1995, p. 77–80) make a similar point with respect to their own survey results and back it up by exploring the meaning that respondents attach to the left/right dimension. That exploration reveals considerable consensus in developed countries that the dimension refers predominantly to economic or class conflict (Huber and Inglehart 1995, pp. 83–90). The comparisons for other dimensions in Table 4.3, although fewer in number, also support a conclusion of measurement validity.

Examining the validity of the position estimates is facilitated by the existence of previous measurement efforts, but what can we say about a new concept such as the bounds or limits of compromise? Since its meaning was explained to respondents in very explicit terms, it is natural to suppose that they must have attempted to provide what was asked for. There is, however, one major area in which the instructions may have proved impossible to follow. This is the instruction not to base estimates on the parties' coalition behaviour.

This instruction was motivated by the same sort of endogeneity concerns that Budge (2000) expressed about expert judgements of party positions and that were a major focus of attention in the last chapter. It is therefore appropriate to recall the outcome of that discussion, which is that the presence of endogeneity of this sort would not invalidate hypothesis tests. Thus, if a researcher suspected the existence of discrete limits on the willingness of parties to compromise in a particular country and found after careful scrutiny of coalition formations that each party did indeed adhere to certain identifiable limits, he or she would be entitled to conclude that they structure that behaviour (assuming other things are equal); it would be equivalent to having detected a pattern in the dependent variable. Nevertheless, our objective in undertaking the expert survey is to obtain limits that are not based on coalition behaviour because in that case we would have not only the effect but also the cause (or something related to the cause) as well. Respondents were therefore asked to base their estimates of bounds on their general impression of the extent to which parties are expected by their supporters to respect policy commitments. The question is, did the respondents achieve this objective or did knowledge of the parties' past coalition behaviour creep into their estimates?

This may seem an impossible question to answer, but there is one area where any tendency to use knowledge of coalition behaviour to estimate bounds would be apparent. This is in the standard errors of the bounds estimates themselves. These errors reflect the uncertainty that respondents have over where bounds should be located and, if respondents were taking their cues from coalition behaviour itself, one would expect the degree of uncertainty to be less for parties that have participated in numerous coalition governments. There are confounding factors, however. One such factor is the size of the party. Larger parties tend to survive better and hence to be available more often for government participation, but their size may also mean that respondents are more knowledgeable about them. In addition, there may be significant variation across systems in the extent to which the experts polled were familiar with party compromise limits. A test of whether the size of the standard error for a bound estimate is related (negatively) to the number of times a party was in government should therefore be performed with party size and country controlled.

This test is less than perfect in the sense that respondents may have been better able to locate the bounds for parties that are frequently in government for reasons unconnected with their coalition behaviour; they may simply know more about the internal dynamics of these parties because they are major players in the political system. The test, in other words, may be biased against the hypothesis that the independence condition has been met. Nevertheless, despite this possible bias, the test consistently fails to reveal any such linkage. Consider, for example, the results for the left/right dimension. When the standard error for the lower bound was regressed on the number of post-War governments a party participated in, its mean size over that period and a set of country dummies, the number of governments variable showed the correct negative effect but that effect was highly insignificant ($p=.490$ in a one-tailed test). The same is true for the corresponding analysis of the lower bound ($p=.280$). In fact, as Panel A of Table 4.4 shows, non-significance was also the outcome when the upper and lower bounds of the second and third dimensions were analysed.

It may be that the number of governments a party entered is not the relevant independent variable; perhaps it is simply the number of formation situations for which a party was present. After all, not joining a government may also reveal something about a party's willingness to compromise. When the tests were repeated using the number of

Table 4.4 Testing the independence of horizon estimates from party behaviour

	First dimension		Second dimension		Third dimension	
	Lower bound	Upper bound	Lower bound	Upper bound	Lower bound	Upper bound
Panel A						
Number of governments joined by party	0.000 (0.003)	−0.001 (0.003)	−0.001 (0.007)	−0.005 (0.006)	0.001 (0.008)	0.002 (0.007)
Panel B						
Number of formation situations at which party was present	−0.004 (0.003)	−0.004 (0.002)	0.007 (0.006)	0.001 (0.006)	0.002 (0.007)	−0.005 (0.006)

Note: Entries are unstandardized slopes (with standard errors in parentheses) from regressions of the standard errors associated with estimates of party bounds. Each regression equation also included the mean size of the party plus a set of country dummy variables. None of the effects is significant at the .05 level in one-tailed tests.

government formations for which a party was present in the legislature, however, essentially the same outcome was obtained. As Panel B of Table 4.4 shows, half of the regression coefficients for this variable are wrongly signed and none is statistically significant.

It is appropriate to conclude this section with a note of caution: conformity to the injunction not to base estimates of horizon bounds on coalition behaviour does not mean that the measurement of the concept is valid in other respects. Substantial measurement invalidity, if present, should become apparent when the horizon hypothesis is tested in the next chapter, but there is occasional evidence in the responses themselves that misunderstandings may have affected the judgements of our respondents. By far the likeliest instance of this occurred in the case of Finland, where the existence at the time of the survey of the 'rainbow coalition' government embracing parties from the former Communists to the conservatives (the National Coalition) caused several respondents to place the bounds for all parties at or near the extremes of the left–right scale. While it may be the case that all of these parties have become this open to compromise, it seems more likely that the range of policy positions acceptable to all parties as a basis for government participation is considerably smaller. In other words, it is not clear that these respondents distinguished between the situation where all major parties are willing to agree on some policy or set of policies and the situation where all parties would agree to virtually any policy at all.

Discussion

The central task of this chapter has been to report and evaluate the results of an expert survey that incorporates design features that are in some respects novel, but in all respects important to the goal of generating data suitable for testing the policy horizon hypothesis. These design features aim (1) to identify appropriate multidimensional spaces for West European coalition systems, (2) to locate parties on the key policy dimensions of their system and determine how much importance or salience they attribute to each of them, and (3) to provide estimates of horizon bounds that derive from the expectations of party supporters rather than from coalition behaviour. All features are important for a more thorough, less constrained testing of the horizon hypothesis.

There is no reason to believe that experts can measure these parameters with perfect accuracy, to be sure. In general, error may be systematic or random. With respect to systematic error, Budge (2000) has drawn attention to the possibility that estimates of party positions may be influenced by the respondents' knowledge of common coalition patterns in their countries; by extension, this could also be true of horizon estimates. If this type of bias is present, however, it is likely to have the opposite effect for other formations in the country's post-War experience that failed to conform to the same patterns. More important, any bias of this sort is much more likely to favour the distance hypothesis than the horizon hypothesis. There are two main reasons for this. First, the operation of policy distance is probably more transparent to respondents than the operation of horizons and therefore more easily captured in parameter estimates. Second, respondents were specifically admonished not to base bounds estimates on coalition behaviour and the available evidence indicates that the estimates they provided satisfy this injunction. Thus, if systematic bias of this sort is present, its likely consequence is to disadvantage the horizon hypothesis vis-à-vis its main rival.

If the measurement error is random in nature, it may be expected to weaken support for any causal hypothesis that is tested. But more can be done than simply noting this possibility. We have seen that the simulation facility in *Horizons 3D*© can utilize the uncertainty over positions and compromise limits to achieve better measurement of the causal concept about which the greatest doubts are likely to exist, the concept of horizon intersections. There is no need, in other words, to take the bounds estimates reported in Appendix 2 as exact values in measuring this challenging concept.

The use of simulations cannot overcome every measurement error, to be sure. If respondents have mis-estimated the willingness of a party to compromise on policy goals, that mis-estimation will still influence the outcome of the simulations. Nor can simulations make estimates taken in 2000–2002 accurate for earlier times if party positions, compromise limits, or dimensional saliences have changed in the interim. Thus, the resort to survey data is no panacea: it sacrifices some virtues, such as the ability to capture changes over time, in order to achieve others. One should therefore not expect that it will yield stronger support for the horizon hypothesis, merely that it yields support that is substantial and credible. The next chapter assesses whether these expectations are met.

5
Survey-based Horizons and Government Formation

The main challenge to testing the policy horizon hypothesis is that it necessarily involves the measurement of a very elusive entity, the policy horizons of parties. In Chapter 3, two measurement methods were introduced to meet this challenge. Both methods have significant limitations, of which the most important relates to the use of coalition behaviour in the estimation procedure. Contrary to what might be supposed, the risk of circular explanation is not the prime concern. Although false or accidental horizon effects can be generated with these methods, we have seen that they can be readily distinguished from genuine horizon effects. A much more significant concern is that the behaviour-based estimation procedures are devoid of information on the sources of policy horizons. In this chapter, the horizon hypothesis is submitted to a testing process in which horizons are measured with direct reference to the constraints imposed on parties by their supporters, rather than indirectly via the coalitional consequences of those constraints.

The testing will be conducted on a data set derived from the expert survey of West European parliamentary democracies undertaken for this purpose and described in detail in the preceding chapter. The survey attempts to fill in many of the gaps in the measurement and testing procedures utilized earlier, including the aforementioned goal of measuring party horizons from their putative sources rather than their observed consequences. To achieve this goal, respondents were specifically directed to base their estimates of each party's compromise limits on the extent to which its members and supporters expect their leaders to abide by the party's policy commitments. It is easy to imagine that the request to keep these estimates independent of past coalition behaviour may have proven difficult to respect in many cases, but the available evidence, reported in Chapter 4, indicates that the respondents did manage to comply.

This does not mean that the estimates they provided are accurate, however. To ask respondents to estimate a novel entity like the location of individual parties' policy horizons is itself a difficult task; to rule out the guidance provided by their past coalition behaviour makes it all the more challenging. To some extent, deficiencies in measurement can be addressed with the use of simulations, but simulations can only do so much. This chapter will therefore undertake a detailed examination of the nature of the measurement error and introduce certain means of addressing it. Although these means have their limitations, clear and persuasive evidence of a horizon effect will nonetheless be uncovered.

Horizons versus distance

The testing of the horizon hypothesis will be conducted on government formation situations in the 13 post-War West European systems for which adequate survey data are available. The principal difference from the manifesto-based data set is that Luxembourg, the French Fourth Republic, and the Netherlands before 1977 are now missing (see Chapter 4 for details). As before, formation situations are excluded if a majority party was present or if they did not involve a real choice of government, such as when a prime minister died or retired and the government simply continued on in office with a new leader. For the remaining cases, the data are again considered sufficiently complete when positions and horizons are available for all parties holding 5 per cent or more of legislative seats.[1] These conditions and limitations leave us with 248 formation situations, only modestly less than the 273 formation situations in the manifesto-based data. Their distribution across countries is shown in Table 5.1.

The issue to be addressed in this section is, how well do the rival causal factors, policy distance and horizon intersections, account for which proto-coalitions formed the governments in these situations? This issue will be addressed using the original survey data as reported in Appendix 2. These data lack the manifesto-based data's variability over time, but they contain several features not available in the analyses already undertaken. The first new feature is country-specific policy dimensions, which allow us to define a separate ideological space for each system. In the analyses to follow, a system's ideological space will be defined by its three most important policy dimensions.[2] This focus on important dimensions is justified by the need to capture policy issues that have the potential to undermine the viability of proto-coalitions – after all, the less important a policy area is to a group of parties, the less likely it

Table 5.1   The survey-based data set coverage

	Period covered	Number of proto-coalitions	Number of formations
Austria	1949–1997	162	14
Belgium	1954–1999	1,993	23
Denmark	1953–1998	6,556	20
Finland	1946–1999	5,794	30
France	1967–1995	483	13
Germany	1961–1998	207	17
Iceland	1947–1995	525	19
Ireland	1961–1997	380	12
Italy	1958–1996	9,686	42
Netherlands	1977–1999	4,343	9
Norway	1961–1997	1,519	17
Portugal	1976–1999	645	11
Sweden	1948–1998	1,003	21
Total		33,296	248

is to prevent them from coalescing. But why a limit of three? Although this limit is primarily a consequence of computational considerations, we have seen that it is consistent with most previous analyses, which have seldom assumed more than three dimensions and often assumed less. Moreover, variations in the importance of dimensions in generating policy differences among parties can be addressed by weighting distances by party-specific dimension saliences, another element of the survey design. A system whose politics is dominated by two major policy dimensions, or perhaps just one, can thus be represented by the application of an appropriate set of dimensional weights.

Dimensional saliences are relevant not just to calculations of policy distance. Policy horizons, which are now defined by the mean locations of bounds on each of the three dimensions, also contain information on varying dimensional saliences. A party's bounds indicate not only where it draws the line on policy compromise on a given policy dimension but also, via the width spanned by the upper and lower bounds, the amount of salience the party attributes to that dimension. (Recall that the wider a party's horizon is on a dimension, the lower the salience of that dimension to it.) Since these are likely to vary across dimensions, horizons can be expected to lack the circular/spherical shape imposed in Chapter 3. The final novelty is that we have parameter-specific error estimates in the form of standard errors associated with each position and bound parameter; this allows simulations to be based on the error associated with each parameter rather than on some arbitrary global error specification.

These additional elaborations allow the capacities of the *Horizons 3D*© program to be put to full use. The construction of policy horizons on the basis of bounds estimates in all three dimensions (rather than simply with a single radius) makes it likely that they will take on a variety of irregular concave shapes. The existence of parameter-specific error estimates means that parameters about which there is a high level of disagreement among respondents will move about a good deal in the simulations, while those for which the consensus is much stronger will remain relatively immobile. While much is changed, however, the basic procedure remains the same: for each legislature, the parameters for the parties are entered into the *Horizons* program; calculations and simulations are performed; and the output for the various legislatures is concatenated so that data are available on all of the proto-coalitions for each of the 248 formation situations under scrutiny.

The analysis will begin with an examination of the effects of policy distance and horizon intersections on government formation under the assumption that all measurements are precise. We have seen that to estimate the policy distance effect adequately, it is necessary to distinguish between majority and minority proto-coalitions and, among the latter, to take account of how close they come to majority status. Both considerations are justified by the dependence of governments on parliamentary majorities, which encourages the formation of governments that achieve or approach majority status despite the greater distance costs that might be entailed.[3] Thus, the true test of the distance hypothesis is not whether more compact proto-coalitions are preferred to less compact ones in general, but whether this preference holds when the potentially offsetting issue of the government's legislative basis is controlled. The two variables that measure this issue are majority status and the size gap.

The impact of (salience weighted) policy distance with these two controls in place is given in the conditional logit analysis reported in Model 1 of Table 5.2. It shows that, conditional on being in the choice set, the odds of a proto-coalition emerging as the government are significantly enhanced if it is majoritarian, to the extent that it approaches majority status (for minority proto-coalitions), and to the extent that the policy distance it spans is small. Further testing (not shown) reveals that the policy distance effect is essentially the same for both majority and minority proto-coalitions; it just operates at a different level.

Table 5.2   Testing distance and horizon effects using the survey-based data

	Model 1	Model 2	Model 3
Majority status	0.42* (0.19)	0.43* (0.19)	0.47** (0.19)
Size gap	−0.12** (0.01)	−0.12** (0.01)	−0.11** (0.01)
Policy distance	−0.50** (0.03)	−0.48** (0.04)	−0.34** (0.05)
Horizon intersection dichotomy	–	0.17 (0.21)	–
Horizon intersection rate	–	–	1.35** (0.33)
Log-likelihood	−840.14	−839.82	−829.12

Note: Coefficients derive from conditional logit analyses covering 33,296 proto-coalitions in 248 formation situations. Standard errors are given in parentheses.
* $p < .05$ in a one-tailed test.
** $p < .01$ in a one-tailed test.

Policy distance as measured from the survey estimates of party positions and saliences thus appears to play a significant role in government formation. But how does this role compare with the distance effect produced with the CMP-based data and reported in Table 3.5? A comparison of the magnitudes of the effect coefficients cannot answer this question. The coefficient in Table 5.2 is clearly much smaller (−0.50 vs. −1.86), but this is due, in part at least, to the fact that distance is now measured on an 11-point scale rather than in standard deviation units (*z*-scores). Standardizing distance in both cases provides a truer comparison. With the policy distance variable standardized, the distance coefficients become very similar: −1.75 (manifesto-based data) vs. −1.93 (survey-based data).

This comparison gives us reasonable confidence that a policy distance relationship of similar magnitude is present in the survey-based data set, but what about the hypothesized horizon effect? The horizon hypothesis argues that the influence of policy distance is qualified by the operation of thresholds: whenever parties are so far apart that their horizons do not intersect, they cannot coalesce. Testing this proposition therefore requires evidence that the existence of a common horizon intersection affects a proto-coalition's odds of forming the government over and above the effect conveyed by policy distance. If the test utilizes the dichotomous horizon intersection variable, the results are disappointing: as Model 2 shows, the estimated effect of this variable has the predicted sign, but it falls well short of statistical significance. This is in marked contrast to the results of the corresponding analysis in Chapter 3 (see Model 4 of Table 3.5), and it suggests that policy horizons, as estimated by the experts, do not constrain the government formation process.

Such a conclusion would be premature, however. We have seen that one problem with the use of this measure of horizon intersections is that it takes no account of the existence of substantial uncertainty over where party horizons should be located. The appropriate corrective is to perform simulations in order to derive an intersection rate or probability that reflects this uncertainty. Each legislature was therefore subjected to 500 simulations in which party positions and bounds were randomly varied according to their individual levels of uncertainty as measured by their standard errors. In other words, in each simulation, every parameter was altered by drawing an error from a t-distribution with the standard error and degree of freedom associated with that parameter and adding that error to the parameter.

As noted in Chapter 3, the unbiased nature of the errors generated for the simulations results in a very close correspondence between the original distances and the mean distances produced in the simulations ($r = .996$). For the horizon intersections, however, the correspondence will not be so great. Indeed, the intersection dichotomy and the intersection rate may diverge much more than was the case in Chapter 3 since they are based on the standard errors of the survey means, which can be much larger than the relatively small global error specified in the earlier analysis.

The bar chart in Figure 5.1 illustrates the correspondence between the two. As in the corresponding figure for the CMP-based data set (Figure 3.2), the intersection rate has been grouped into ten equal-width categories and shading has been used to separate proto-coalitions with and without a common horizon intersection. Although the intersection rate is derived from parameter-specific errors rather than a global error specification, its relationship with the intersection dichotomy resembles that shown in Figure 3.2 to a surprisingly high degree. Not only do most proto-coalitions have intersection rates close to one extreme or the other (0 or 1), reflecting the horizon dichotomy very precisely, but the few cases in the middle also follow the dichotomy closely: non-intersecting proto-coalitions tend to have low intersection rates and intersecting ones higher rates. This close correspondence between the horizon intersection dichotomy and the intersection rate is reflected in a very high correlation between the two variables of .92, virtually identical to the correlations produced with the manifesto data.

The intersection rate clearly represents a more satisfactory rendering of the state of our knowledge about horizon intersections; moreover, it is achieved with only a modest increase in the degree of collinearity with policy distance (the correlation with policy distance rises from $r = -.60$

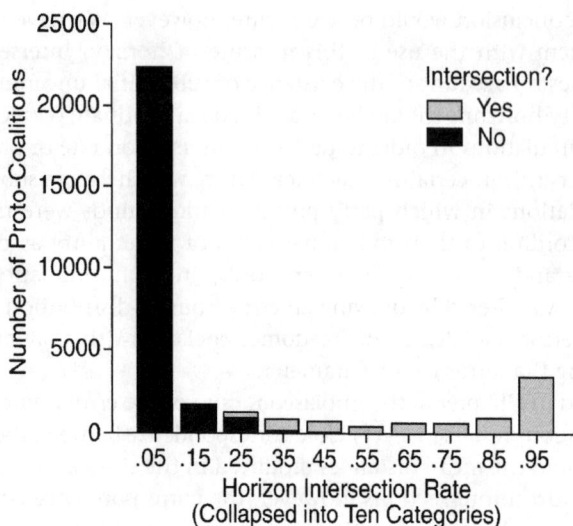

Figure 5.1   Survey-based intersections and intersection rates.

to $r=-.68$ when the intersection dichotomy is replaced by the intersection rate). But how much difference can it make, given that so little has changed? Model 3 in Table 5.2 shows that the modest changes to the measurement of intersections brought about via the simulations generate a substantial change in outcomes: the intersection rate shows a much larger and highly significant net impact on government formation. Correspondingly, the policy distance effect is reduced, indicating that some of the role previously attributed to policy distance actually reflects the role of horizons.

An examination of the anomalies

Although a significant horizon effect appears in Table 5.2, it is considerably weaker than the effect estimated with the behaviour-based horizons in Chapter 3. The natural temptation is to attribute this relative weakness to respondents' uncertainty over the locations of horizons; after all, the estimation task they were given is both unprecedented and daunting. Several respondents did indeed comment on how hard it was to make these estimates, especially for dimensions other than the left/right dimension, and how uncomfortable they felt with the estimates they came up with.

Another possible source of inaccuracy is the time factor: even if the respondents provided accurate measurements of horizon bounds at the time of the survey, one would expect these estimates to become increasingly less accurate the further back in time one goes. There is some indication that this is the case. For formations that took place in the 1980s and 1990s, for example, the net effect for the intersection rate in the four-variable model is a highly significant $\beta = 2.48$ ($SE = 0.51$), but it declines to an insignificant $\beta = 0.49$ ($SE = 0.44$) for formations that occurred before 1980.

A third possibility is that the weaker horizon effect is associated with certain specific parties. This could arise either because certain parties are prone to violate their horizons or because their horizons may have been especially poorly estimated for some reason. This avenue can be explored by examining the cases that violate the necessary condition that governments must come from the set of proto-coalitions with intersecting horizons. If these anomalous cases show no particular pattern, apart from perhaps a tendency to increase in frequency in the earlier time periods, it would suggest a generalized pattern of measurement error – hardly surprising given the circumstances. But if the errors were concentrated in certain types of situations, it might allow us to identify their nature and to determine whether the source lies with the experts making the judgements or with the parties they were judging.

The nature of the anomalies

In the present data set, the necessary condition is violated in about one-third (36.7 per cent) of government formations. What is striking about these cases is that they do display a high degree of patterning. In fact, of the 91 exceptions, fully 62 consist of governments in which the horizon of a Christian Democratic party does not intersect with those of one or more of its coalition partners (30 governments in Italy, 16 in Belgium, 6 in the Netherlands, and 10 in Germany). The other noticeable commonality is made up of 15 Finnish and 4 Swedish governments that lack an intersection between a Centre/Agrarian party and a Liberal party.[4] Further examination shows that the parties in question are separated primarily on the relevant dimensions (clerical/secular or rural/urban).

These exceptions clearly do not represent a random assortment of government formations; instead, they principally involve a tendency on the part of the survey respondents to establish a degree of separation for the Christian Democratic and Agrarian/Centre parties in certain countries that does not accord well with actual coalition behaviour. Figure 2.2 illustrates the nature of the problem in the case of Italy. Throughout the post-War era until its demise in the early 1990s, the Christian Democratic party was the major player in the Italian party system, the *sine qua non* of all governments formed in this period. Consistent with this role is the party's location at the centre of the left–right (horizontal) dimension in close proximity to a number of other parties. But the clerical–secular (vertical) dimension tells a very different story; here the Christian Democrats are located at the opposite end of the axis from most of these parties. As a result, the party's horizon intersects only with those of the extreme right-wing MSI and the tiny Social Democratic party (PSDI). This would suggest that its choice of coalition partners was severely limited, whereas in fact it appeared in coalition with parties such as the Liberals (PLI), the Republicans (PRI), and the Socialists (PSI) numerous times between the founding of the republic and the party's demise in the early 1990s.[5]

The fact that the anomalous cases fall largely into two particular patterns makes it possible to identify their source much more readily than might otherwise be the case. If that source lies with the parties themselves, there are several ways in which it might have occurred. The most basic alternative is that the hypothesized constraining effect of policy horizons is simply not operative for some of these parties; the horizon hypothesis, in other words, does not apply to them. A more nuanced view would be that, given the specialized nature of the issues in question, other parties may have been prepared to turn over prime responsibility to the parties most concerned with them. Thus, policy differences on issues that implicate religion, such as education or morality, may have been resolved by delegating decision-making power to the Christian Democratic parties; similarly, agricultural issues may have been delegated to the Agrarian/Centre parties in Nordic countries.[6] Finally, it may be that horizon violations were acceptable in these instances because the governments in question foreswore significant legislative initiatives in the areas of disagreement; clerical issues, for example, may simply have been put on the back burner so that governing coalitions could be formed.

The first interpretation, the one that argues that the six parties identified above are constrained little or not at all by policy horizons, is the least tenable. The fact that our respondents were willing to locate the parties well away from potential coalition partners and to give them fairly narrow horizons indicates that they saw policy on these dimensions as relatively constraining; to argue that the parties in question were not constrained at all flies in the face of such evaluations. It also sits poorly with other evidence that policy in the relevant areas mattered to these parties. The key source in this regard is Laver and Hunt's (1992) expert survey. Laver and Hunt asked their respondents to rate the importance for parties of the eight issues they identified as generally relevant in West European political systems. Two of these issues, as we have seen, are clericalism/secularism and rural/urban interests. The mean importance rating for the four deviant Christian Democratic parties on the former issue is 14.7 on a 20-point scale; the mean rating for the Swedish and Finnish Agrarian/Centre parties on the latter issue is 17.6. Such high ratings clearly suggest that, according to the experts polled by Laver and Hunt, achieving policy goals in these areas is important to these parties.

The possibility of a delegation of responsibility to the most affected parties, in contrast, does have some empirical support: Budge and Keman (1990, pp. 102–3) detected a strong tendency for Centre parties, when in government, to take agriculture portfolios and similarly for Christian Democratic parties to take education portfolios (clerical–secular disputes have often involved school policy). But why would their coalition partners defer to these parties on agricultural or clerical issues? Various possibilities can be suggested (see note 6), but the critical one for present purposes is the possibility that the issues do not matter very much to them. The reason this possibility is critical is that it would suggest that *their* horizons have been drawn too tightly on the relevant dimensions. Here, the Laver and Hunt data are also informative. They show that the coalition partners in question (e.g. the Republicans, Liberals and Socialists in Italy) place much less importance on these issues: their ratings average 8.7, which is less than half as great as the figures cited above. The salience levels provided by our respondents corroborate this pattern: on average, they indicate that the coalition partners attribute about three-quarters as much salience to the relevant dimensions as do the Christian Democratic and Agrarian/Centre parties. The substantially lesser importance these parties give to clerical or agrarian issues implies that their horizons ought to be considerably broader on the relevant dimensions, but this is not the case – in fact, they are slightly narrower, on average.[7] Thus, our respondents gave the coalition partners of these six Christian Democratic and Agrarian/ Centre parties much tighter horizons than either Laver and Hunt's importance ratings or their own salience ratings would lead one to expect, and the consequence is a set of anomalous non-intersections involving these parties.[8]

The impact of the anomalies

It would appear, then, that the survey respondents over-estimated the extent to which the clerical–secular and rural/urban cleavages produced incompatible coalition partners in these systems. These issues may not have been as highly charged for the coalition partners of Christian Democratic and Centre parties as our respondents believe them to have been. Why the respondents concluded otherwise cannot be answered with the data at hand, but the fact that the anomalies are patterned makes it possible to assess the extent to which they undermine the strength of the horizon hypothesis in the survey-based data set.

One simple means of gauging the negative impact of the anomalies is to observe what happens when the model is estimated without the formation situations that involved these combinations of parties. The result is a much stronger net horizon intersection effect, as shown in Model 1 of Table 5.3. This tactic, however, is very costly in terms of cases: more than half the formation situations in the data set are lost and several systems – Belgium, Iceland, Italy, the Netherlands, Sweden, and Germany – are eliminated entirely. It is far from inevitable that the removal of these cases distorts the picture; in fact, further testing suggests that the remaining formations are reasonably representative of the full set in other relevant respects.[9] Even so, it would be preferable to have a procedure for that does not require so great a sacrifice in data.

The loss of formation situations can be curtailed very considerably if we exclude just the anomalous non-intersections themselves, rather than the entire formation situations in which they appear. Under this tactic, formation situations are lost only when one of these combinations of parties actually formed the government. Excluding the anomalous non-intersections in other cases is premised on the assumption that the IIA condition is met, that is, that these exclusions do not bias the results, which appears to be the case (see pp. 107–8). Model 2 shows that the horizon effect remains of approximately the same strength and significance under this procedure.

Although the results reported in Models 1 and 2 are suggestive, it would clearly be much more valuable to have a viable procedure for estimating the dampening effect of the anomalous intersections that does not involve discarding them entirely. The most straightforward solution would be to recode the intersection rates for all the anomalous non-intersections to unity; this would convey the state of affairs under the assumption that there is total certainty that these proto-coalitions have common horizon intersections. The problem here is that it overstates the case: a suspicion, even a well-founded one, is not the same

Table 5.3 Taking account of the anomalous non-intersections

	Model 1 (Formation situations with anomalous non-intersections excluded)	Model 2 (Anomalous non-intersections excluded)	Model 3 (Imputed horizon intersection rates for anomalous non-intersections)	Model 4 (Horizons estimated by logit method)
Majority status	−0.32 (0.30)	0.28 (0.23)	0.39* (0.19)	0.42** (0.19)
Size gap	−0.12** (0.02)	−0.12** (0.01)	−0.11** (0.01)	−0.11** (0.01)
Policy distance	−0.23** (0.10)	−0.33** (0.07)	−0.15** (0.05)	−0.47** (0.04)
Horizon intersection rate	3.65** (0.67)	3.51** (0.53)	3.70** (0.53)	5.63** (0.45)
Log-likelihood	−242.7	−394.5	–	−615.8
N (formations)	92	162	248	235
N (proto-coalitions)	11,148	15,438	33,296	26,677

Note: Coefficients derive from conditional logit analyses (standard errors are given in parentheses). Model 3 is based on the analysis of five data sets with imputed values for the anomalous non-intersections.

$* p < .05$ in a one-tailed test.

$** p < .01$ in a one-tailed test.

thing as a certainty. A better way to proceed is to utilize multiple imputation to derive new values for these cases. The advantage of this tactic
is that it employs the data about which we have no particular concerns
to derive estimates of the data that do not inspire this level of confidence. It thus avoids the assignment of an arbitrary value for the anomalous non-intersections by allowing the data themselves to generate
more probable intersection rates for these proto-coalitions. In addition,
if a stronger horizon effect were to emerge, it would lend further
support to the conclusion that the respondents were off-track in their
estimates of the constraints affecting the small group of parties identified
above.

The multiple imputation approach was therefore invoked for this
purpose. For maximum effectiveness, it included not just the variables
in the standard model, but also the Martin and Stevenson variables and
variables such as the mean intersection size and the probability of an
EWM that will figure in the analyses of the next chapter. The first step
in this application of the procedure was to recode the intersection rates
for all suspicious non-intersections involving the six Christian Democratic
and Agrarian/Centre parties, as well as those involved in the Icelandic
anomaly (see note 4), to missing data.[10] Since inaccurate horizons also
affect estimates of intersection sizes and the possibility of an encompassed
weighted mean, the values of these variables for the proto-coalitions in
question were also re-set to missing data. This modified data set was
then submitted to Honaker et al's (2003) *Amelia* program to generate
five new data sets, each sporting imputed values for the missing data
and the original data elsewhere.[11]

How much difference does it make to assume the intersection rates
for this set of proto-coalitions are unknown and to impute new values?
Consider first the original data. The mean intersection rate for proto-
coalitions that are not judged to be anomalous and that did not form
governments is 0.261; the mean for those that did form governments is
0.853. This is very much as one would expect if having an intersection
is a requirement for forming a government. For the proto-coalitions
with anomalous non-intersections, in contrast, the corresponding rates
are just 0.028 and 0.175. These low rates – particularly the latter one –
reflect the basic problem with these cases. The imputed values generated for these cases are much closer to the mark, however: across the
five imputed data sets, they average 0.197 for proto-coalitions that did
not form governments and 0.547 for those that did. This gap is not as
great as it was for the non-anomalous cases, but it is clearly a good deal
larger than it was in the original data.

What matters more, of course, is whether the imputed intersection rates reveal a stronger horizon effect in a conditional logit analysis. The answer is contained in the third model of Table 5.3, which re-estimates the basic four-variable model using the imputed data sets. The consequence of imputing new values for the anomalous non-intersections is again to produce a large increase in the magnitude of the horizon intersection effect. Indeed, the estimated effect is very similar to those produced by the previous two tactics. Thus, whether we exclude formation situations involving the anomalous non-intersections, exclude just the anomalous non-intersections themselves, or impute new intersection rates for them, the size of horizon intersection coefficient increases by more than 250 per cent. The very large impact of this increase in magnitude is reflected in the odds ratios: in Model 3, a change in the intersection rate from zero to one now implies a 40-fold increase in the odds of a proto-coalition forming the government (as opposed to a 4-fold increase previously).

If we are willing to accept that the horizons of a relatively small group of parties were mis-estimated, the imputed data point to a horizon effect is a good deal stronger than that which was originally estimated. But is imputing new values for these cases enough to produce an accurate picture of the role of horizon intersections in the choice of a government? We have already seen evidence that the imputed data achieve only a partial correction of the problem, but we can gain some further purchase on the issue by comparing the results in Model 3 with those produced by a behaviour-based method. The defining feature of behaviour-based horizons is that they assume that parties generally or always respect their horizons when they decide to join or not to join governing coalitions. This means that the phenomenon of parties repeatedly violating their own horizons cannot occur: a party's limits of compromise are defined by what it does.

The method that will be used for the comparison is the logit method, since it still allows for occasional violations of the horizon principle. Recall that the logit method estimates circular/spherical horizons by means of a party-level logistic regression of government membership on distance from the government. Applied to the survey positions, this regression produces a strong distance effect ($\beta = -2.79$, $SE = 0.18$) and yields horizon estimates that satisfy the necessary condition in 96.6 per cent of government formations, a rate that compares very well with the rate of 85.3 per cent derived from CMP position estimates in Chapter 3. These new horizon estimates were entered into the *Horizons* legislature files, and the various simulations were performed. Since we no longer have parameter-specific standard errors for the horizons, the simulations were based on horizon errors drawn from a normal distribution with a standard error of 0.5.[12]

The output from these simulations was then concatenated to produce a new data set. The coverage of this data set differs only in that 24 formation situations are lost because of the requirement that five appearances in formation situations are needed to estimate a party horizon. Fortunately, testing shows that the loss of these cases is not consequential.[13] The results of re-estimating the standard four-variable model using this data set are shown in the final model of Table 5.3. It reveals a horizon effect that is a good deal larger than that produced with the imputed data sets. The highly significant effect coefficient of $\beta = 5.63$ ($SE = 0.45$) implies that moving from an intersection rate of zero to a rate of one brings with it an increase in the odds of forming the government by about 200-fold.

While the increase in the horizon effect has been dramatic as we have moved from taking the original data at face value to adjusting intersection rates for questionable non-intersections to estimating horizons on the basis of coalition behaviour, there is no reason to believe that the effect has been fully captured. There are bound to be plenty of other inaccuracies in the survey data, including other estimation errors on the part of survey respondents and inaccuracies that stem from aspects of the measurement enterprise that are beyond their control, such as its inability to capture changes in parameters over time. For example, even if all formation situations with anomalous non-intersections are excluded, one can still detect a very noticeable difference in the net strength of the intersection rate effect between the pre-1980 and post-1979 periods (the effect is $\beta = 4.71$, $SE = 0.91$ in the four-variable model for the latter period, vs. just $\beta = 2.01$, $SE = 1.05$ for the earlier period). Although we cannot capture its full impact, however, it is clear enough that the horizon effect is very strong – stronger than the effect originally estimated with the survey data and stronger than the effect estimated with the imputed data.

Adjusting for the anomalies

The much more powerful horizon effect that merges when logit horizons are used makes it clear that this initial attempt to estimate horizons by the survey method should be considered a qualified success at best. If the predictive errors had been scattered more or less randomly throughout the original data set, we would have little recourse but to accept this fact and rely on the still-significant horizon effect shown in Table 5.2

(Model 3) as evidence for the hypothesis. But the concentration of predictive anomalies in the horizons of certain parties, together with the inconsistency of these horizon estimates with corresponding salience ratings in both this survey and another expert survey, allow us to take a more interventionist approach.

The most appropriate means of intervention is to substitute imputed intersection rates for the anomalous non-intersections. The advantage of this approach is not just that it preserves cases, but that it does so in a particularly appealing way: by using the other information provided by our respondents to impute values for those areas where their estimation errors are concentrated. It cannot go beyond the level of accuracy that the survey respondents were able to achieve elsewhere, to be sure, but it can go some distance to bringing greater uniformity to the accuracy level of those estimates. The five partially imputed data sets will therefore serve as our main survey-based resource in the remainder of this study.

Model assumptions

The conclusion that a reasonably powerful horizon effect is in evidence in the survey-based data depends, to be sure, on the credibility of the assumptions that underpin it. The assumption that there are certain anomalies in the intersection data that should be replaced with imputed values has already been examined. But there are two other important assumptions that have not yet been assessed: the independence from IIA assumption and the ceteris paribus assumption. This section examines these assumptions in turn.

The IIA assumption

The IIA assumption states that the relative probabilities of any two choices in a choice set emerging as the outcome do not depend on what other choices are available. In Chapter 3, both a general test and a more specialized test were utilized to assess the viability of this assumption. The general test consisted of removing choices randomly from the various choice sets and determining the impact on the estimated horizon effect; the specialized test focussed on the consequences of removing proto-coalitions containing very small parties. In each test, the expectation is that the estimated coefficients will not be affected in any noteworthy way by the exclusions.

The tests will be conducted on Model 3 of Table 5.3, which estimates the standard four-variable model using the imputed data sets. The first application of the general test consists of removing a random 10 per cent of proto-coalitions from each formation situation; the second application increases that percentage to 20 per cent. These sampling procedures bypass the proto-coalition that went on to form the government, since its removal would cause the entire formation situation to be eliminated from the analysis.

The fact that we are dealing with five data sets means that the testing procedure must be altered somewhat. Rather than running 20 trials on a single data set, four trials were performed on each of the five imputed data sets. In the majority of the trials based on 90 per cent samples, the generalized Hausman test included in *Stata: Release 8* (StataCorp 2003) again showed that the intersection rate coefficient is altered significantly. However, as before, the substantive inconsequence of the changes is also in evidence. As the second column of Table 5.4 shows, the intersection rate coefficients in the reduced sample scarcely differ from that produced by the full sample (the mean difference in coefficients is just −0.016) and the standard error of 0.012 indicates that there is relatively little fluctuation in these differences across the trials. The third column reveals that removing a random 20 per cent of choices from each choice set actually produced smaller differences, averaging 0.006 ($SE = 0.008$). Clearly, the exclusion of randomly chosen sets of proto-coalitions has no substantive impact on the magnitude of the horizon effect estimated from the partially imputed survey data.

Table 5.4 also reports the mean intersection rate effect in the five partially imputed data sets when proto-coalitions containing a party with less than 2 per cent of legislative seats are removed (column 4). Although these exclusions amount to more than one-half of the original data, the mean horizon intersection rate effect shows only a very modest decrease in magnitude. Moreover, none of the five imputed data sets produces a difference between the two estimates of the horizon effect that is statistically significant in a generalized Hausman test. This basic continuity suggests that the estimates produced here are not dependent on how broadly or narrowly one wishes to define the relevant choice set.

The ceteris paribus condition

We have seen that the Martin and Stevenson (2001) study, at the time of writing the most thorough investigation of the factors affecting the choice of a government in parliamentary systems, found significant effects for nine factors, eight of which are not included in the four-variable model developed here. The common factor is, of course, policy

Table 5.4 Testing the IIA assumption

	All proto-coalitions (from Table 5.3)	Random 10% of proto-coalitions per choice set removed	Random 20% of proto-coalitions per choice set removed	Proto-coalitions containing a party with 2% or fewer seats excluded
Mean intersection rate effect	3.70	3.71	3.69	3.53
Mean difference from full-sample coefficient	–	−0.016	0.006	0.169
Standard error of difference	–	0.012	0.008	0.039
N (proto-coalitions)	33,296	29,966	26,637	17,937

Note: Coefficients are from conditional logit analyses with majority status, the size gap and policy distance also included in the specification. The means for analyses with randomly removed proto-coalitions are based on four trials in each of five partially imputed data sets; the other means are averaged across the five data sets.

distance. The eight unique ones consist of seven dichotomous attributes – whether or not the proto-coalition is minimal winning, is minoritarian in a system that requires investiture, contains the largest party in the legislature, contains a VSP, is composed solely of a VSP, is based on a pre-electoral pact, and is the outgoing government – and one continuous variable, the degree of anti-system presence in the proto-coalition. In Chapter 3, the continuous variable was replaced by another dichotomy, extremist party presence, which proved to have a much stronger influence on government formation.

All the nine Martin–Stevenson variables showed significant net effects on government formation in the CMP-based data set and, as Model 1 of Table 5.5 reveals, the same holds for the survey-based data, despite the fact that they do not cover precisely the same formation

Table 5.5 Testing survey-based horizons effects in the Martin–Stevenson model

	Model 1	Model 2 (Original survey horizons)	Model 3 (Imputed horizon intersection rates for anomalous non-intersections)
Minimum winning status	0.98**(0.18)	0.73**(0.22)	0.39* (0.23)
Proto-coalition has largest party	1.29**(0.20)	0.40* (0.22)	0.28 (0.22)
Minority proto-coalition in investiture system	−0.66**(0.28)	−0.88**(0.31)	−0.54* (0.32)
Anti-system presence	−1.82**(0.28)	−2.03**(0.29)	−2.00** (0.29)
Pre-electoral pact	2.84**(0.68)	2.70**(0.63)	2.70** (0.67)
Proto-coalition has VSP	0.69* (0.36)	0.63* (0.37)	0.71* (0.39)
Proto-coalition consists of VSP	1.28**(0.36)	0.95**(0.38)	0.84* (0.38)
Incumbent government	2.32**(0.18)	2.08**(0.19)	1.94** (0.19)
Majority status	–	−0.55* (0.28)	−0.23 (0.29)
Size gap	–	−0.09**(0.01)	−0.09** (0.01)
Policy distance	−0.20**(0.03)	−0.23**(0.05)	−0.07 (0.05)
Horizon intersection rate	–	0.65* (0.39)	2.89** (0.57)
N (proto-coalitions)	33,296	33,296	33,296

Note: Coefficients derive from conditional logit analyses of five partially imputed data sets. Standard errors are given in parentheses.
* $p < .05$ in a one-tailed test.
** $p < .01$ in a one-tailed test.

situations and proto-coalitions.[14] But Chapter 3 also demonstrated that the horizon effect as estimated from the CMP data was able to survive the presence of these variables. Can the same be said when horizons are measured by our expert respondents?

This would seem to be unlikely if we utilize their original estimates because of the measurement anomalies discussed earlier, although the effect is marginally significant ($p = .049$), as the second model in Table 5.5 indicates.[15] The situation may be quite different when imputed intersection rates values are substituted for the anomalous ones, however, since the imputed data clearly go some distance towards eradicating the anomalies. This possibility is addressed in Model 3. It reveals that the horizon effect in the partially imputed data sets survives very well the introduction of those additional variables: the estimated effect declines somewhat from $\beta = 3.70$ to $\beta = 2.89$, but remains large and highly significant. Provided we are willing to accept that the imputed values come closer to the truth for the anomalous non-intersections, we can conclude that a strong horizon effect is present even when these other variables are introduced.[16]

The same cannot be said, however, for the distance effect. In Model 2, it survives reasonably well but this may be due to the under-estimation of the horizon effect in these data. In Model 3, it has become not only much weaker but also statistically insignificant as well. This finding brings into question an effect that has been so central to contemporary understandings of the coalition formation process. The reader may recall that the parallel analysis in Chapter 3 also raised doubts about the viability of the distance effect. We shall come back to this question again as other causal factors related to the horizon hypothesis are introduced in the next chapter.

This comment serves as a useful reminder that there may be other relevant factors not present in these models. Nevertheless, we should not discount the value of the 'ceteris paribus' tests reported in Table 5.5. The Martin and Stevenson study did examine a large number of potential influences on government formation and, with the exception of horizon-related variables, the set they ended up with would seem to stand a good chance of constituting a reasonably comprehensive list. If this is the case and provided also that some corrective step is introduced to deal with the anomalous non-intersections, the horizon effect based on the survey data appears to be as capable of meeting the 'ceteris paribus' condition as are the effects estimated solely from the CMP data. All in all, this result lends substantial support to the credibility of the policy horizon hypothesis.

Discussion

In Chapter 3, the logit and MJD methods of deriving policy horizons yielded estimates that reveal a powerful constraining force on government formation in coalition situations, even when other relevant factors are taken into account. The question this chapter has addressed is whether expert judgements can yield estimates of horizon bounds that show a comparable effect. In other words, can the influence of horizons on government formation be detected when the horizons of parties are estimated from beliefs concerning the expectations of supporters rather than from government membership records?

It is tempting, but incorrect, to answer this challenge by arguing that the willingness of almost all respondents to estimate reasonably narrow horizons is proof in itself that horizons play a role in government formation.[17] The problem with such an inference is that we cannot be certain that there is a consensus of expert opinion on this matter: some who received questionnaires may have decided not to participate because they reject the very concept of policy horizons. What is needed is evidence that the horizons identified by those who did respond have a net influence on the choice of government.

Demonstrating a horizon effect with survey estimates of horizon positions is thus an important step in establishing the overall validity of the policy horizon hypothesis, but there are plenty of reasons – apart from the possibility that the hypothesis itself is false – why it might not succeed. The expert respondents were asked for a type of information that is unprecedented in surveys of this type and, indeed, may never have occurred to them. Moreover, the survey instrument seeks these estimates for several policy dimensions, not just the familiar left–right one. Finally, the experts provided a single estimate for each parameter, even though the data analysis applies those parameters to formation situations that occurred over a time span of as much as half a century.

The initial results using the mean expert estimates of party horizons gave some credence to these fears: they imply that the estimates were too inaccurate to reveal the role of horizons in structuring government formation behaviour, or else that there is no such role. Further analysis, however, allayed these concerns. Simply replacing the horizon intersection dichotomy with an estimate of the probability that an intersection exists, a change which mainly implicates the small minority of cases where uncertainty is high (the near-hits and near-misses), was sufficient to reveal a significant horizon effect. This effect was strengthened very considerably when a set of anomalous non-intersections, mainly involving some Christian Democratic and Agrarian/Centre parties and certain of their coalition partners, was identified and a multiple imputation procedure was used to provide alternative estimates of the probability of horizon intersections in these cases. It held up, moreover, even when the eight other variables identified as significant influences on government formation in Martin and Stevenson's (2001) recent investigation were entered into the analysis. The results thus appear to be robust with respect to other influences that have been identified as relevant to the choice of a government.

Why these anomalies should have appeared is uncertain at this point. Our expert respondents, as well as those surveyed by Laver and Hunt (1992), clearly regard the parties as policy-driven, which suggests that they are unlikely to be free to violate policy commitments at will. Both sets of experts, moreover, agree that clerical issues are a good deal more important or salient to the Christian Democratic parties, and agrarian issues to the Agrarian/Centre parties, than these issues are to their coalition partners. But our respondents, in the aggregate, chose to give the coalition partners narrower horizons on the relevant dimensions, which implies the reverse. The result of this inconsistency is that the coalition partners appear to be so unyielding in their policy positions on these issues that they could not possibly agree to coalesce with the Christian Democratic and Agrarian/Centre parties, which is, of course, belied by what actually happened. In quantitative terms, the result is a set of anomalous non-intersections that greatly diminish the overall horizon effect.

Despite the large impact of these anomalies, it is clear that they are the exceptions rather than the rule. In general, the evidence of the expert surveys, like that produced with the manifesto data, supports the contention that coalition behaviour is structured not just by a distaste for policy compromise but a definite limit on the amount of policy compromise that can be tolerated. The fact that the magnitude of the horizon effect increases further when logit-based horizons are used suggests that the survey estimates of horizons, even with imputed values for the anomalous cases, under-estimate the true strength of the effect, but it remains very apparent nonetheless. In fact, the predictive success rate – the rate at which the proto-coalition with the highest formation probability actually does form the government – of the standard four-variable model is 20.3 per cent (averaged across the five imputed data sets), which is on a rough par with the rates reported in Chapter 3.

The analyses presented in this chapter conclude the basic testing of the policy horizon hypothesis. If the central finding that the horizon hypothesis has been sustained is valid, however, certain other things may follow. For instance, government formation may be affected not just by the existence of horizon intersections but by their relative sizes and by whether they would allow member-parties to implement their weighted mean position; in addition, horizon intersections may go some distance towards explaining a puzzle of European parliamentary life, the frequent formation of minority governments. In the next chapter, we turn our attention to these and other implications of the policy horizon approach.

6
Elaborating the Horizon Framework

We have seen that the horizon effect is relatively weak when horizons are estimated by our expert respondents, a consequence of the formation of governments by certain combinations of parties whose horizons, in the collective judgement of the respondents, do not intersect. What caused these exceptions is open to debate. It cannot be definitively proven that they result from over-estimates of the extent to which policy differences create incompatible bedfellows in these instances, rather than from a failure of certain parties to abide by the policy constraints imposed by their supporters; it is simply the most plausible interpretation of the available evidence. Had horizon ranges provided by our experts been more consistent with their own estimates of the salience of the relevant issues, or with those provided by the experts surveyed by Laver and Hunt (1992), the situation would have been a good deal less clear. As it is, the grounds for concluding that our expert respondents have missed the mark – a very difficult mark to hit, it should be emphasized – in a handful of instances are reasonably solid.

If this conclusion is valid, it follows that we would be well advised to pursue the other ramifications of the policy horizon hypothesis using the logit and MJD horizons estimated from the manifesto data; then, if certain effects become evident, to determine if they can also be detected using the survey estimates of horizons. It also follows that the version of the survey-based data that we should use is the one that substitutes imputed values for variables affected by the anomalous non-intersections. This is the course that will be followed in this chapter. To simplify the presentation of the results, the terms 'logit data' and 'MJD data' (collectively, the 'manifesto-based data') will refer to the government formation data sets that utilize the first two horizon measurement strategies, while the term 'survey data' will refer to the formation data set that incorporates the last-mentioned approach.

What are these other ramifications of the horizon hypothesis? They consist, first, of other influences on government formation implied by, or consonant with, policy horizon framework. For example, if governments are selected from among the proto-coalitions that have intersecting horizons, might a preference be given to those that have larger intersection sizes? Or perhaps those whose intersections enclose their member-parties' weighted mean position? The second type of ramification relates to the majority status of the government that is ultimately formed. A natural extension of the horizon approach would be to hypothesize that minority governments are formed when no majority intersection exists. This is in fact almost always the case, but they also form when there are majority intersections. In fact, most minority governments were formed despite the existence of at least one majority intersection. Can the horizon approach provide any insight on these formations, or does the phenomenon escape the analytical grasp of the horizon approach? A final ramification concerns the policy distance hypothesis, the mainstay of virtually every policy-based model of coalition government. The evidence thus far suggests that at least some of the explanatory effect that might be attributed to policy distance actually belongs to horizon intersections; could the remaining distance effect be spurious as well?

Auxiliary effects in the manifesto-based data

Subsets of majority intersections

The first ramification of the horizon hypothesis that we shall examine concerns minority governments. These governments present a challenge because they depend on the support of external parties whose identities may not be known to observers. Some leverage on this issue may be gained, however, by determining which minority proto-coalitions are subsets of majority intersections. A subset of a majority intersection, or SMI, is a minority proto-coalition that has a common horizon intersection some part of which falls within the common intersection of a majority proto-coalition. When this condition is present, it means that the parties participating in the minority proto-coalition could form a majority government by adding one or more other parties without violating the horizon constraint. But knowing that you can form such a government does not mean that you need to do so. Why add these other parties to a governing coalition if, by adopting a policy stance that satisfies their horizons as well as yours, you can form a government that garners their support without having to give them a share of the spoils of office?

An illustration of how this situation might arise is shown in Figure 6.1. The figure portrays a hypothetical legislature with five parties, any three of which can form a majority government. Suppose party C is chosen as formateur. It participates in a majority intersection with parties A and B and another majority intersection with parties D and E; either one would be a viable majority government under the horizon hypothesis. In this situation, C might decide to form a government based on its intersection with A and B but without coalescing with one or both of those parties. The excluded party or parties would not be pleased, but there is not much that either could do to undermine the government since C has another alternative that would be much less satisfactory for both A and B: forming a government based on its horizon intersection with D and E (again, either or both of these two parties could be held captive in the same way).

The basic idea, then, is that a minority proto-coalition might be more likely to form the government if it is a subset of a majority intersection and is therefore in a position to elicit the support of other compatible parties without offering them membership in the cabinet. In a sense, it may be able to have all the benefits of majority status without paying all of the costs. There are initial signs that this incentive may be operative: although relatively few minority proto-coalitions are SMI (26.6 per cent based on logit horizons and 38.8 per cent based on MJD horizons), the vast majority of minority governments (78.0 per cent in the former case, 82.6 per cent in the latter) have this property.

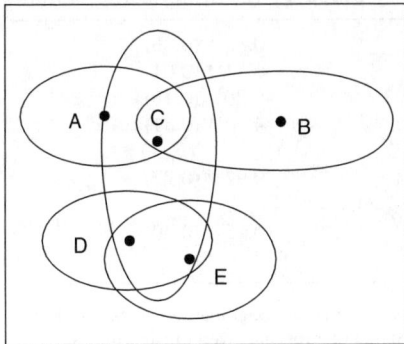

Figure 6.1   A hypothetical five-party legislature.

These figures assume, however, that intersections are accurately measured by the two intersection dichotomies and that no other factors are relevant. Obviously, neither assumption is safe. To address the issue of accuracy, we shall rely, as before, on simulations. When simulations are specified, *Horizons 3D*© counts the number of times the proto-coalition is a subset of a majority intersection, from which a rate can be calculated. This '*SMI rate*' will be taken to measure the probability that the proto-coalition meets the SMI condition.

Addressing the second or ceteris paribus assumption means, in the first instance, examining the role of the SMI rate when the four variables of the standard model are also included in the model specification. There is another consideration that must be included, however. Single-party proto-coalitions are much more likely to meet the SMI condition than other minority proto-coalitions, primarily because each of the parties that participates in a majority intersection automatically provides a single-party SMI proto-coalition to the choice set.[1] If it should be the case that single-party proto-coalitions are also more likely to form governments than other types of minority proto-coalitions, a spurious association between the SMI rate and government formation may emerge. Establishing the presence of a net advantage for a minority proto-coalition that is a subset of a majority intersection therefore requires that we also control for whether the proto-coalition is composed of a single party.

Models 1 (logit horizons) and 2 (MJD horizons) of Table 6.1 contain the results of testing the hypothesis that subsets of majority proto-coalitions have a net formation advantage. A dichotomous variable, *Single-party*

Table 6.1 Subsets of majority intersections (manifesto-based data)

	Model 1 (Logit horizons)	Model 2 (MJD horizons)
Majority status	0.85** (0.36)	1.60** (0.44)
Size gap	−0.11** (0.01)	−0.11** (0.01)
Policy distance	−0.20 (0.15)	−0.42** (0.16)
Horizon intersection rate	4.64** (0.31)	5.14** (0.39)
Single-party proto-coalition	0.97** (0.27)	0.92** (0.27)
SMI rate	−0.15 (0.40)	0.53 (0.46)
Log-likelihood	−812.1	−817.8

Note: Coefficients derive from conditional logit analyses covering 52,271 coalitions in 273 formation situations. Standard errors are given in parentheses.
* $p < .05$ in a one-tailed test.
** $p < .01$ in a one-tailed test.

Proto-coalition (coded '1' if a proto-coalition consists of a single party and '0' otherwise) identifies single-party proto-coalitions. With it and the other controls in place, the SMI rate shows no significant net effect on the odds of formation.[2] This evidence suggests that proto-coalitions that are subsets of majority intersections are not able to exploit this apparent advantage with any regularity.

The weighted mean position

The second consideration that we shall evaluate is not an implication or extension of the horizon hypothesis so much as it is a factor that might work in conjunction with it. This factor is the weighted mean position of the proto-coalition. In previous research (Warwick 2001b), I found that the policy that coalition governments declare they will implement corresponds very closely with the mean position of the parties in the coalition, weighted by their legislative seat contributions to the coalition. This may represent a further manifestation of the proportionality principle that appears to govern closely the allocation of cabinet portfolios in coalition governments (Browne and Franklin 1973; Warwick and Druckman 2001, 2005). Whatever its source, however, it suggests another hypothesis nested within the policy horizon hypothesis: governments will tend to be chosen from the set of proto-coalitions with horizon intersections that encompass the (legislative) size-weighted mean positions of their member-parties.

Horizons 3D© calculates a dichotomous variable, the encompassed weighted mean (EWM), that registers whether or not each proto-coalition's weighted mean position is encompassed within the bounds of its horizon intersection, provided it has one (i.e. the variable is receives a score of '1' if the proto-coalition has a common horizon intersection and the weighted mean lies inside that intersection, and '0' otherwise). Here, too, there is some prima facie evidence to suggest that this is indeed a relevant consideration. Of those proto-coalitions that have logit horizon intersections but do not go on to form the government, less than half (45.6 per cent) encompass their weighted mean positions. But for those that do form the government, their intersections encompass the weighted mean more than four-fifths (81.1 per cent) of the time. Using MJD horizons, the corresponding percentages are 53.5 per cent and 77.3 per cent. It would seem that having an intersection that encompasses the weighted mean gives an added boost to the odds of forming the government.

As with other variables that are dependent on the measurement of policy horizons, there is always some uncertainty over whether a proto-coalition has an encompassed weighted mean. In the multivariate analysis, we shall again resort to the rate at which this condition is met in the simulations, rather than the dichotomous version of the variable. The variable will be called the *EWM rate*. Needless to say, a proto-coalition's EWM rate will always be less than its intersection rate, since an intersection is a necessary but not a sufficient condition for having an encompassed weighted mean.

The net contribution of the EWM rate is evaluated in Model 1 (logit horizons) and Model 2 (MJD horizons) of Table 6.2. The control variables again include the four of the standard model plus the single-party indicator. This indicator variable is included because single-party proto-coalitions have a formation advantage (Table 6.1) and they always satisfy the EWM condition (a party's policy ideal must, by definition, lie within its horizon); without controlling for single-party status, a spurious linkage between the EWM rate and government formation could emerge as a result. The findings in Table 6.2 paint a different picture: even with this and the other controls in place, the EWM rate displays an effect that is both correctly signed and highly significant.[3]

Intersection size

The final ramification of the horizon approach to be examined concerns the size (area or volume) of the horizon intersection. Proto-coalitions with larger intersection sizes may appear more credible or viable because they have more policy options that are acceptable to all their members. Other things being equal, this should make it easier for them to arrive at a coalition policy agreement in the first instance and

Table 6.2   Encompassing the weighted mean (manifesto-based data)

	Model 1 (Logit horizons)	Model 2 (MJD horizons)
Majority status	0.95** (0.20)	1.17** (0.21)
Size gap	–0.11** (0.01)	–0.12** (0.01)
Policy distance	–0.25 (0.15)	–0.38** (0.16)
Horizon intersection rate	3.38** (0.38)	4.42** (0.47)
Single-party proto-coalition	0.19 (0.28)	0.79** (0.27)
EWM rate	1.72** (0.31)	0.88** (0.38)
Log-likelihood	–795.6	–815.8

Note: Coefficients derive from conditional logit analyses covering 52,271 coalitions in 273 formation situations. Standard errors are given in parentheses.
* $p < .05$ in a one-tailed test.
** $p < .01$ in a one-tailed test.

easier to make adjustments to that policy stance as conditions change during the government's tenure in office.

Horizons 3D© calculates the area (two dimensions) or volume (three dimensions) of each horizon intersection and, when simulations are specified, reports the mean intersection size in the simulations. This mean is calculated across just those simulations in which an intersection occurred; if none of the simulations produce an intersection, a size of zero is returned. The equivalent concept for single-party proto-coalitions, which have no intersections as such, is the area or volume of the region enclosed by the party's horizon. It, too, will be referred to as an intersection size. For simulations, the mean size of this region is calculated.

The objective for both single- and multi-party proto-coalitions is to measure the magnitude of the region that contains policies consistent with the horizon hypothesis. But there is clearly a problem of scale here: unless there is a high degree of horizon overlap, these regions are bound to be a lot smaller for multiparty proto-coalitions than for single-party proto-coalitions. The data bear this out. The mean logit-based intersection size is 3.23 for single-party proto-coalitions but just 0.16 for multiparty proto-coalitions; MJD and survey horizons produce similar discrepancies. Moreover, even among multiparty proto-coalitions, the degree of skewness can be substantial. Consider logit horizons again. Although the average size of multiparty proto-coalitions is just 0.16, about 0.5 per cent of them have intersection sizes of at least 5.[4]

The nature of the problem can be understood more readily with the aid of an example. Figure 6.2 shows the MJD horizons of parties in 1988 Danish legislature. The parties are laid out in an appropriate order on the horizontal or left–right axis, with the Conservatives (KFP) at one end and the Left Socialists (SFP) and Social Democrats (SD) at the other. The ideal points of the Radical Liberals (RV) and the Christian People's Party (KrFP) are located somewhere between these extremes. But note the size of the RV-KrFP intersection: both parties have very large horizons that overlap almost totally, producing an intersection size of 12.67. Intersections of this magnitude occur only rarely, but they clearly will have a disproportionate effect on the role estimated for this variable.

The problem is compounded if expected values are taken. The *expected value of a horizon intersection* is the product of the probability that it exists and its size if it did exist, that is the product of the intersection rate and the mean intersection size. This concept represents the intersection size that the parties in a proto-coalition can expect to have

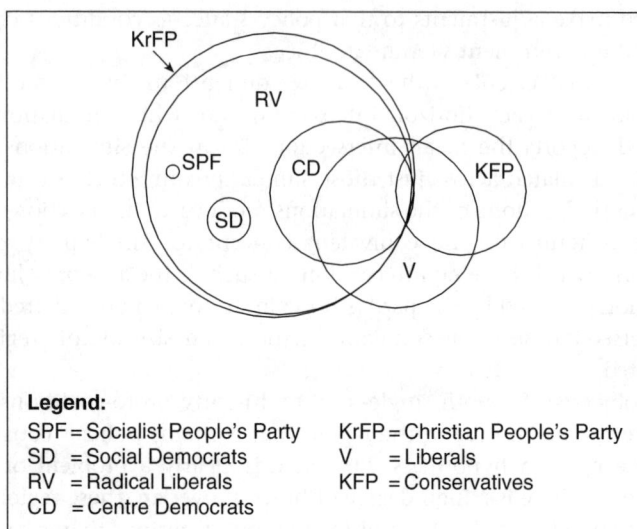

Figure 6.2   Denmark 1988 (MJD horizons).

if they were to form the government. It is clearly a more meaningful way to introduce intersection size than simply to treat it as an additional independent variable, totally separate from the intersection rate. But consider the way in which the intersection size relates to the intersection rate. It stands to reason that the more often horizons intersect in the simulations, the larger will be the mean intersection size. This is because intersections occur more often when the original horizons cut heavily into one another and, when they do, the mean intersection size will tend to be large as well. As a result, taking the product of the two will cause the skewness of the intersection size variable to be magnified.

The scatterplot in Figure 6.3a illustrates the problem as it manifests itself with logit horizons. It shows that the expected value gradually increases with the intersection rate through most of the latter's range, but then explodes when the intersection rate gets very close to 1.0. Although single-party intersection sizes contribute disproportionately to this explosion, the pattern is very much the same for multiparty proto-coalitions.

The standard practice for highly skewed variables is to implement some transformation, such as a log transformation, that reduces the influence of the outliers. Substantively speaking, this is often justifiable on the grounds of diminishing marginal utility, and such a justification

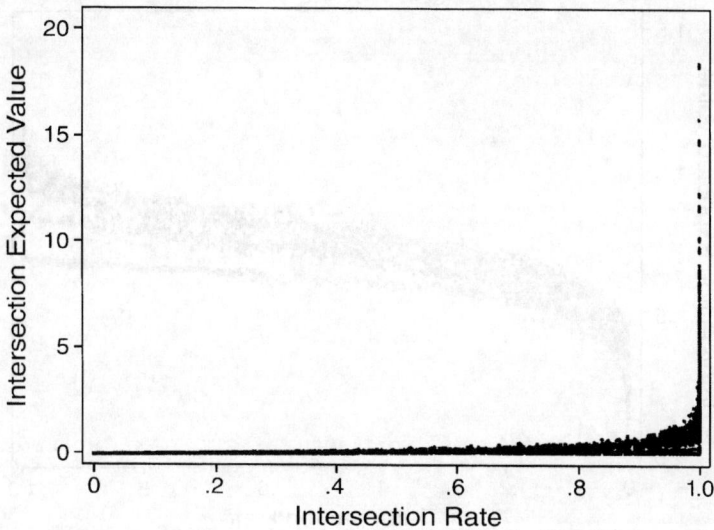

Figure 6.3a Scatterplot of logit horizon intersection rates and expected values. *Note*: The horizon expected value is the product of the intersection rate and the intersection size.

would seem to be pertinent here. If the Danish Radical Liberals and the Christians had formed a two-party government in 1988, for instance, it is very unlikely that all of the region jointly enclosed by their horizons in Figure 6.2 would have been useful to them. Since the parties together did not command a parliamentary majority, one may anticipate that their usable ideological space would have been considerably reduced by the expectations or demands of one or more parties providing external support in the legislature. Even if they had been majoritarian, the amount of space enclosed by their horizons represents far more compromise room than they are likely to have needed, no matter what the circumstances.

While the notion of capturing the diminishing marginal value of very large intersection sizes is a sensible one, the issue cannot be tackled by the common remedy of taking logarithms because so many proto-coalitions have mean expected values of zero, for which there is no logarithm. Changing these values to some extremely small positive number will not solve the problem either, since logarithms plummet to negative infinity as numbers become very small. A better transformation would be to take roots (i.e. raising the expression to some value less than one). While this may be applied either to the intersection size

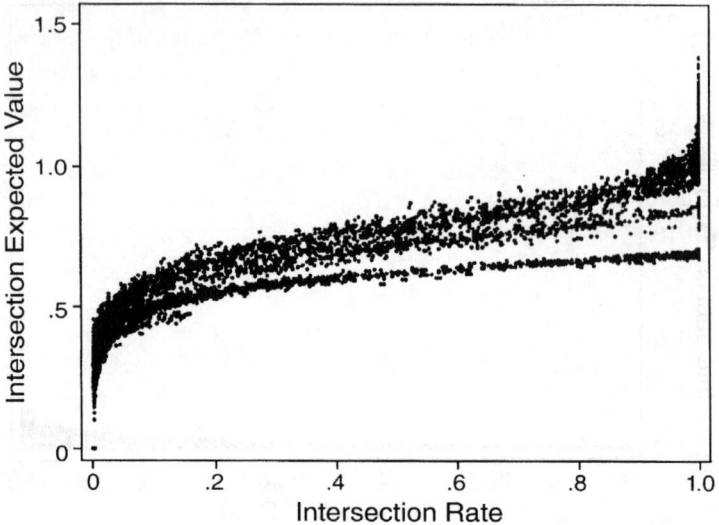

Figure 6.3b   Scatterplot of logit horizon intersection rates and expected values (raised to the one-ninth power). *Note*: The horizon expected value is the product of the intersection rate and the intersection size.

component of the expected value expression or to the entire expression, it turns out that the latter brings to the transformation an additional feature of some value, as Figure 6.3b shows.

Figure 6.3b plots the relationship between the intersection rate and the ninth root of the intersection expected value. Taking the ninth root has no theoretical justification – we have no way of knowing in advance how heavily to discount intersection sizes. It is chosen simply because it produces particularly strong results in the logit data.[5] One reason why this is the case is that the extreme inflation in expected values when intersection rates approach 1.0 has been dampened very considerably. There is still an inflation in expected values in this region of Figure 6.3b, but it is clearly far less than in Figure 6.3a.

Taking an appropriate root of just the intersection size component would have produced a similar effect, but the approach adopted here has the added advantage of expanding expected values on the extreme left of the graph. The reason why this matters has to do, in part at least, with the way behaviour-based horizons are estimated. The radii of these horizons depend on the frequency with which parties enter governments, which means that parties that never participate in governments receive horizon radii of zero (this was set to 0.001 in *Horizons 3D*© since the program requires some positive value). Occasionally, even a party that has participated in government will receive a zero horizon. Yet these are certainly under-estimates; just because a party has seldom or never participated in government in the observation period does not mean that it has no flexibility in policy matters. Total inflexibility is, in fact, an improbable situation, even for the most doctrinaire of parliamentary parties. The transformation shown in the figure, by expanding expected values at this end of the scatterplot, counter-acts these estimation errors.

Let us now turn to the impact of this version of the expected value of the horizon intersection. We shall begin by looking exclusively at majority proto-coalitions; minority cases represent more ambiguous situations since we do not know how much of their intersections contain policy points acceptable to their 'external support' parties. Model 1 of Table 6.3 shows the effects of adding the intersection expected value to policy distance and the intersection rate (the size variables are excluded since they are only relevant to minority proto-coalitions). Regardless of whether horizons are estimated on the basis of the logit method (Panel A) or the MJD method (Panel B), the intersection expected value entirely eliminates the significant role formerly played by the intersection rate.

The next step is to expand the analysis to include minority proto-coalitions. The inclusion of minority proto-coalitions introduces two possible complications, both related to the possibility that their intersection sizes are less informative because they take no account of the expectations of external support parties. The first concerns the likely inflation in the intersection sizes of single-party proto-coalitions. These proto-coalitions all have unit intersection rates and they also have by far the largest – and probably the most exaggerated – intersection expected values. This suggests that they will distinguish themselves from other proto-coalitions, a possibility that can be captured by adding to the model specification the single-party indicator variable and the interaction between it and the intersection expected value. The second complication is that other minority proto-coalitions may also deviate from the general relationship, since their intersection expected values, which are generally larger than those for majority proto-coalitions, may also be exaggerated. This possibility can be assessed by adding the interaction between the intersection expected value and the majority status.

Model 2 shows the effects of including the minority proto-coalitions and adding these variables to capture any deviations they might bring

Table 6.3   The expected value of the horizon intersection (manifesto-based data)

	Model 1 (majority proto-coalitions)		Model 2 (all proto-coalitions)		Model 3 (all proto-coalitions)	
Panel A (logit horizons)						
Majority status	–		–0.32	(0.67)	–	
Size gap	–		–0.10**	(0.01)	–0.10**	(0.01)
Policy distance	–0.32	(0.23)	0.16	(0.17)	0.14	(0.17)
Intersection rate	0.22	(0.63)	0.42	(0.54)	–	
Intersection expected value	6.37**	(0.90)	5.47**	(0.91)	6.23**	(0.47)
Intersection expected value×majority status	–		1.41*	(0.73)	1.09**	(0.21)
Single-party proto-coalition	–		3.43*	(1.68)	4.23**	(1.45)
Intersection expected value×single-party proto-coalition	–		–2.26	(1.53)	–3.05**	(1.29)
Log-likelihood	–381.6		–762.9		–763.3	
Number of proto-coalitions	14,864		52,271		52,271	
Panel B (MJD horizons)						
Majority status	–		–0.51	(0.94)	–	
Size gap	–		–0.12**	(0.01)	–0.12**	(0.01)
Policy distance	–0.38*	(0.23)	–0.31*	(0.16)	–0.31*	(0.15)
Intersection rate	–0.14	(0.88)	0.05	(0.68)	–	
Intersection expected value	9.77**	(1.50)	6.70**	(1.21)	7.18**	(0.62)
Intersection expected value×majority status	–		1.86*	(1.00)	1.34**	(0.22)
Single-party proto-coalition	–		7.33**	(1.39)	7.81**	(0.98)
Intersection expected value×single-party proto-coalition	–		–6.09**	(1.39)	–6.56**	(0.98)
Log-likelihood	–383.8		–780.6		–780.7	
Number of proto-coalitions	14,864		52,271		52,271	

Note: Coefficients derive from conditional logit analyses. Standard errors are given in parentheses.
* $p < .05$ in a one-tailed test.
** $p < .01$ in a one-tailed test.

to the pattern for majority proto-coalitions. Consider first the results for logit horizons (Panel A). The first and most important point to note about this model is that the intersection rate continues to be displaced by the intersection expected value; clearly, there is considerable added value in taking intersection sizes into account. Beyond this, we see some indication that the effect is different for single-party proto-coalitions and for other minority proto-coalitions. Single-party proto-coalitions appear to have better formation prospects than other proto-coalitions, although the role played by the intersection expected value in those prospects does not differ significantly. In addition, the expected value plays a stronger role for majority than minority proto-coalitions, accounting entirely for the advantage formerly attributed to majority status itself.

With MJD horizons (Panel B), the dominance of the intersection expected value over the intersection rate persists. The degree to which minority proto-coalitions deviate from the overall pattern is more pronounced, however. Single-party proto-coalitions as a group clearly show better formation chances and there does not appear to be much differentiation among them. Other minority proto-coalitions again show a weaker expected value effect, the consequence of which is to eliminate entirely the role played by majority status.

Model 3 removes the two variables whose influence has clearly been displaced, the intersection rate and majority status. The roles of the two interaction terms and the single-party indicator are now more clearly significant in both panels. They indicate that the intersection expected value, despite its transformation to accommodate better the highly skewed nature of intersection sizes, cannot totally capture the situation of minority and especially single-party proto-coalitions. This should come as no surprise: the intersection sizes of minority proto-coalitions tend to be both larger than those of majority proto-coalitions and based on incomplete information, since they take no account of external constraints that minority governments have to deal with. Despite these imperfections, however, the results provide strong evidence that what matters is not just whether an intersection exists, but how large it is.

Overall effects

The preceding analyses have isolated two factors that may increase the odds that a proto-coalition with an common horizon intersection emerges as the government. These are the expected value of the horizon intersection (transformed and with adjustments for single-party and other minority proto-coalitions) and whether it encompasses the proto-coalition's weighted mean position. The question now is, do both kinds of influence play independent roles relative to each other? Models 1 (logit horizons) and 3 (MJD horizons) of Table 6.4 address this question by adding the EWM rate to the final model of Table 6.3. They reveal that when the intersection size variables and the EWM rate are included, the former continue to play a statistically significant role in

Table 6.4   Overall effects in the manifesto-based data

	Logit horizons		MJD horizons	
	Model 1	Model 2	Model 3	Model 4
Size gap	−0.10** (0.10)	−0.09** (0.01)	−0.12** (0.01)	−0.10** (0.01)
Policy distance	0.13 (0.17)	−0.01 (0.19)	−0.37* (0.17)	−0.34* (0.19)
Intersection expected value	5.01** (0.60)	4.38** (0.67)	8.15** (1.04)	7.54** (1.16)
Intersection expected value × majority status	1.09** (0.21)	1.17** (0.30)	1.35** (0.22)	1.16** (0.30)
Single-party proto-coalition	2.67* (1.54)	2.93 (1.79)	8.83** (1.31)	7.97** (1.50)
Intersection expected value × single-party proto-coalition	−1.89 (1.34)	−2.06 (1.53)	−7.48** (1.26)	−6.64** (1.40)
EWM rate	1.03** (0.34)	0.43 (0.37)	−0.62 (0.52)	−1.02 (0.55)
Minimum winning status	–	−0.30 (0.21)	–	−0.07 (0.21)
Proto-coalition has largest party	–	−0.37* (0.22)	–	0.13 (0.21)
Minority proto-coalition in investiture system	–	−0.22 (0.31)	–	−0.12 (0.31)
Anti-system presence	–	−0.88** (0.29)	–	−1.33** (0.28)
Pre-electoral pact	–	3.44** (0.78)	–	3.09** (0.75)
Proto-coalition has VSP	–	0.63* (0.34)	–	0.70* (0.33)
Proto-coalition consists of VSP	–	0.25 (0.40)	–	0.17 (0.42)
Incumbent government	–	1.57** (0.18)	–	1.68** (0.18)
Log-likelihood	−758.8	–	−779.9	–

Note: Coefficients derive from conditional logit analyses covering 52,271 coalitions in 273 formation situations. Models 2 and 4 are based on analyses of five data sets, with imputed data for missing Martin–Stevenson scores. Standard errors are given in parentheses.
* $p < .05$ in a one-tailed test.
** $p < .01$ in a one-tailed test.

both versions but the EWM rate shows a significant effect only in the logit-based version.

The results based on MJD and logit horizons thus appear to deviate from each other in a substantive way. Before reaching any conclusions, however, it would be useful to see which effects hold up when other relevant factors are introduced. Throughout his study, we have used eight other causal factors identified by Martin and Stevenson (2001) to test the ceteris paribus condition. These factors may not make all things equal, to be sure, but they represent the best available list of candidates. In order to preserve cases, missing values for the Martin–Stevenson variables have been replaced by imputed values; this means that the results are calculated over five imputed data sets (see Chapter 5 for details).

Models 2 and 4 show what happens when the Martin–Stevenson variables are added to the model specification. In Model 2 (logit horizons), the EWM rate is now highly insignificant, as are the variables distinguishing single-party proto-coalitions. If majority status and the intersection rate had been included, they would have been highly insignificant as well. Thus, of the effects that have concerned us, the only ones to remain significant are the size gap and the horizon intersection expected value, particularly for majority proto-coalitions. With MJD horizons (Model 4), these effects are also in evidence but single-party proto-coalitions continue to distinguish themselves. It is also notable that policy distance is now highly insignificant in both data sets.[6]

The fact that single-party proto-coalitions are differentiated only when MJD horizons are used should not be interpreted as an inconsistency between the two versions of the model. We know that the intersection expected value, even transformed as it is, cannot compensate completely for our relative lack of information concerning the relevant intersection sizes of minority governments. The logit horizons and their (transformed) expected values may have been more adept at filling this void, but only better knowledge than is currently available can accomplish the job completely. The basic message of both models is clear despite the measurement limitations: government formation is a function of the expected values of horizon intersections, not just of their existence.

Auxiliary effects in the survey data

Let us turn now to the data set built with the survey estimates of policy horizons. As noted earlier, the version that we shall be examining is the one that uses imputed values to adjust for the anomalous non-intersections identified in the previous chapter. Although these imputations go some distance towards relieving the problem, it is worth remembering that they do not completely remedy it: in each of the five imputed data sets, there still remain plenty of anomalous non-intersections.

Despite this limitation, it turns out that the previous findings carry over to these data reasonably well. The first instance of consistency concerns the influence of the SMI rate, the probability of being a subset of a majority intersection. It shows no significant net influence when added to the standard model, provided the tendency for single-party proto-coalitions to be subsets of majority intersections is taken into account by means of the single-party indicator. The consistency in results continues when the role played by the EWM rate is examined. Even though there is a stronger connection between the EWM rate and single-party status (the weighted mean is always encompassed in a single-party proto-coalition), the EWM rate again manages to survive the presence of the single-party indicator in the model. (For brevity's sake, these results are not presented here but are available on request.)

The effect of replacing the intersection rate with the intersection expected value variables is shown in Model 1 of Table 6.5. Majority

Table 6.5 Intersection expected value and overall effects in the survey data

	Model 1	Model 2	Model 3
Majority status	−0.50 (0.73)	–	–
Size gap	−0.13** (0.01)	−0.13** (0.01)	−0.10** (0.01)
Policy distance	−0.22** (0.05)	−0.22** (0.05)	−0.07 (0.06)
Intersection expected value	1.53* (0.77)	1.86** (0.55)	1.64** (0.53)
Intersection expected value × majority status	1.01 (0.71)	0.58** (0.21)	−0.22 (0.31)
Single-party proto-coalition	−19.50** (5.12)	−18.99** (5.06)	−8.77 (6.07)
Intersection expected value × single-party proto-coalition	13.51** (3.37)	13.08** (3.31)	6.22 (3.94)
EWM rate	–	–	0.59 (0.60)
Minimum winning status	–	–	0.81** (0.24)
Proto-coalition has largest party	–	–	0.14 (0.23)
Minority proto-coalition in investiture system	–	–	−0.44 (0.33)
Anti-system presence	–	–	−1.97** (0.29)
Pre-electoral pact	–	–	2.56** (0.65)
Proto-coalition has VSP	–	–	0.71* (0.38)
Proto-coalition consists of VSP	–	–	0.18 (0.43)
Incumbent government	–	–	1.91** (0.20)

Note: Coefficients derive from conditional logit analyses of five data sets, each covering 33,296 coalitions in 248 formation situations with imputed data for missing scores. Standard errors are given in parentheses.

* $p < .05$ in a one-tailed test.

** $p < .01$ in a one-tailed test.

status and its interaction with the intersection expected value are both insignificant, although it is clear that the weaker influence of the two is the majority status effect (it is also perversely signed). Its removal produces Model 2, which corresponds to Model 3 of Table 6.3. The results are fairly similar, although it is noticeable that the impact of the intersection expected value, although till highly significant, is a good deal weaker than in Table 6.3. Further investigation indicates that this is a consequence of imputing intersection rates and sizes for the anomalous non-intersections. In fact, without them, the estimated coefficient for the intersection expected value would rise to $\beta = 6.55$ (SE$=0.86$), which is very similar to its estimated impact in Table 6.3.

The capacity of the EWM rate and the intersection expected value to survive the introduction of the Martin–Stevenson variables is examined in Model 3. As in the corresponding analysis using the behaviour-based horizons (Table 6.4), the EWM rate does not survive this test. Nor does the policy distance effect, despite its strength in Model 2. The intersection expected value, in contrast, does remain significant, although the addition of the Martin–Stevenson variables does raise doubts concerning whether the adjustments for minority and single-party proto-coalitions matter. If the proto-coalitions with anomalous non-intersections were removed, however, the variables involving single-party proto-coalitions would become significant, suggesting that, at least for this type of minority proto-coalition, some degree of adjustment to the intersection expected value effect is probably appropriate.

In sum, the survey-based data reveal patterns of influence on coalition formation that resemble closely those identified earlier using the behaviour-based data. With imputed values for the variables affected by the existence of a set of anomalous non-intersections, we have found no support, other things being equal, for the hypotheses that the formation prospects of minority proto-coalitions are affected by the probability of being a subset of a majority intersection or for the hypothesis that the prospects for all proto-coalitions are influenced by the probability that their horizon intersections encompass their weighted mean positions. Support remains, however, for the hypothesis that the probability of forming the government is affected by the intersection expected value. Although it appears that the use of imputed values for the anomalous non-intersections causes this effect to be under-estimated, the effect is still powerful enough to survive the introduction of the Martin–Stevenson variables. This is not the case for the policy distance effect, however, a finding that again raises doubt about the causal efficacy of this concept.

Model assumptions

The conclusion that the intersection expected value is an important factor in the selection of a government rests, as always, on certain assumptions. We have already seen that the ceteris paribus assumption is met, at least to the extent that the other relevant influences are represented in the variables identified by Martin and Stevenson (2001). But it is also necessary to examine whether the effect can satisfy the IIA assumption that underpins the conditional logit method, including independence with respect to the inclusion or exclusion of very small parties. In addition, it would be valuable at this point to examine whether its presence is evident on a country-by-country basis. In this section, the effect will be subjected to both of these tests.

The issue of irrelevant alternatives

The first IIA test consists of removing proto-coalitions randomly from the various choice sets and determining whether estimated coefficients change appreciably. Our focus will be on the major variable of interest, the intersection expected value. As before, the independence of its estimated effect from alterations in the choice set will be tested by deleting a random 10 per cent and a random 20 per cent of proto-coalitions from each choice set. None of these reductions involves the proto-coalition that formed the government, however, since the loss of this choice would entail the loss of the entire formation situation in which it figures.

The first column of Table 6.6 shows the estimated effect coefficient for the intersection expected value based on logit horizons (Panel A), MJD horizons (Panel B), and survey horizons (Panel C). The effect shown in each case is taken from the six-variable model that also includes the size gap, policy distance, and the variables that capture the ways in which the expected value effect differs for minority proto-coalitions (i.e. Model 3 of Table 6.3 and Model 2 of Table 6.5).

The consequences of removing 10 per cent and 20 per cent of proto-coalitions are shown in the next two columns in the table. The first row in each panel contains the mean coefficients across 20 reduced-sample trials.[7] Below this value is the mean difference between the full-sample and reduced-sample estimates and, below that, the standard error of this difference. As we found in Chapters 3 and 5, the reduced-sample coefficients deviate significantly from the full-sample coefficient in the majority of the trials. However, these differences are relatively trivial in substantive terms, since the reduced-sample coefficients are generally within 1 per cent of the full-sample values and the small standard errors

Table 6.6 Testing the IIA assumption

	All proto-coalitions	Random 10% of proto-coalitions per choice set removed	Random 20% of proto-coalitions per choice set removed	Proto-coalitions containing a party with 2% or fewer seats excluded
Panel A (logit horizons)				
Intersection expected value	6.23 (0.47)	6.21	6.17	6.09 (0.51)
Mean difference from full-sample coefficient	–	0.021	0.056	–
Standard error of difference	–	0.013	0.014	–
N (proto-coalitions)	52,271	47,044	41,817	33,838
Panel B (MID horizons)				
Intersection expected value	7.18 (0.62)	7.24	7.27	6.52 (0.64)
Mean difference from full-sample coefficient	–	-0.063	-0.094	–
Standard error of difference	–	0.015	0.017	–
N (proto-coalitions)	52,271	47,044	41,817	33,838
Panel C (survey horizons)				
Intersection expected value	1.86 (0.55)	1.85	1.84	2.21
Mean difference from full-sample coefficient	–	0.011	0.021	-0.340
Standard error of difference	–	0.007	0.008	0.024
N (proto-coalitions)	33,296	29,966	26,637	17,937

Note: Coefficients are from conditional logit analyses with the size gap, policy distance, and the other intersection expected value variables also included in the specification. Standard errors are given in parentheses. The means for analyses with randomly removed proto-coalitions are based on 20 trials.

associated with the differences between the two suggest a high degree of consistency across the trials.

The final step is to determine whether the results hold up when small parties are excluded. There are two rationales for testing the effect of excluding small parties, defined here as parties with 2 per cent or less of parliamentary seats. The first is that policy data are often unavailable for these parties and many analyses, including this one, exclude at least some of them for this reason. It would be disturbing indeed if the basic import of the present analysis were dependent on whether or not these parties were included. The second reason is a more substantive one: very small parties are usually irrelevant to the process of forming governments and, if our analyses are valid, they should reflect that irrelevance.

The final column of Table 6.6 shows the expected value effect in the three data sets when parties with a 2 per cent seat share or less are excluded.[8] Although the differences now appear more substantial, the generalized Hausman test indicates that they are statistically insignificant in each instance. Overall, these results support the conclusion that the intersection expected value plays a role that is not dependent on whether or not small parties are included in the set of relevant actors.

Country effects

Throughout this investigation, data from more than a dozen countries have been pooled in the quest for signs that policy horizons are an important structuring feature of government formation processes. This practice is motivated by the need to have a healthy number of formation situations for statistical analysis, but it is also justified by the premise that the policy horizons hypothesis, if valid, should make its presence felt across the board. Like other premises, however, it ought to be examined empirically to the extent that this is possible.

Country differences are usually examined by introducing into the model a set of country dummy variables, typically by themselves and perhaps also in interaction with other covariates. More elaborate mixed models are also becoming increasingly common. This type of approach cannot be applied in conditional logit analyses, however, because of the requirement that covariates vary *within* choice sets. This leaves us with two options: removing countries one at a time to see if estimated effects change noticeably and re-estimating the models on individual countries. The six-variable model developed in this chapter easily passes the first type of test in all three data sets, indicating that none of the results is being driven by just one country. But this test is relatively undemanding; the tougher test is clearly to show that the results hold up in each country. Unfortunately, this test can become very problematic for countries with few cases. In fact, the full six-variable model is not estimable in countries that have relatively low numbers of formations and proto-coalitions.[9]

We can, however, examine a pared-down version of the model in all countries and for all data sets. This reduced specification eliminates both the adjustments to the intersection expected value for single-party and other minority proto-coalitions and the distance effect, which, as we have seen, does not appear to have an independent role in government formation once other relevant factors are controlled. What remains, then, is majority status, the size gap, and the effect we are concerned with, the intersection expected value.[10]

Table 6.7 shows the effect for that covariate when this three-variable model is estimated, by data set and by country. In every instance, the effect has the correct sign, and in 37 of the 41 analyses, the effect is statistically significant. No country is exceptional in more than one of the three data sets. With parliamentary size controlled, it is evident that the existence and size of a horizon intersection plays a role in a proto-coalition's chances of forming the government in all of these countries.

A closer look at minority governments

In this section, we look more closely at the formation of minority governments. Table 6.1 revealed that there is no net tendency for minority proto-coalitions to form governments when they are subsets of majority proto-coalitions and may therefore be in a position to advance policies acceptable to other parties without compensating them with cabinet portfolios. Why, then, do minority governments form?

Within the context of the horizon hypothesis, the most obvious explanation is that minority governments emerge in situations that lack majority proto-coalitions with common horizon intersections. There is a measure of truth to this assertion. There are no majority intersections, based on logit horizons, in 7 per cent of the formation situations under scrutiny here, and in 16 of these 19 cases, a minority government was formed. MJD horizons tend to be broader, so there are fewer formation situations that lack a majority intersection (just 14), but in every case the government that emerged was minoritarian.

The problem with these figures is what they leave out: while minority governments are almost always formed in the absence of majority intersections, they are also formed in their presence as well. In fact, in excess of four-fifths of all minority governments in the manifesto-based data

Table 6.7 Country-by-country analyses of the effects

	N (cases)	N (proto-coalitions)	Logit horizons	MJD horizons	N (cases)	N (proto-coalitions)	Survey horizons
Austria	12	100	7.29** (2.21)	1.29 (1.93)	14	162	4.44** (1.83)
Belgium	24	9640	6.42** (0.91)	10.69** (1.82)	23	1993	3.83* (1.85)
Denmark	25	8775	6.53** (0.93)	6.81** (1.29)	20	6556	5.87** (1.19)
Finland	34	6430	5.58** (0.82)	10.40** (1.75)	30	5794	1.16 (0.84)
France	34	10,894	8.50** (1.42)	6.21** (1.20)	13	483	8.01** (2.03)
Germany	13	91	13.94** (5.44)	10.09** (4.32)	17	207	2.69* (1.59)
Iceland	14	226	10.91** (3.16)	13.40** (4.32)	19	525	4.14 (3.27)
Ireland	11	189	4.66* (2.33)	22.95 (19.91)	12	380	7.27** (2.65)
Italy	34	12,894	7.32** (0.80)	11.45** (1.94)	42	9686	2.20* (0.83)
Luxembourg	12	180	4.40** (1.71)	6.57* (3.11)	–	–	–
Netherlands	15	561	7.56** (2.31)	7.19** (2.45)	9	4343	3.79** (1.00)
Norway	17	1391	5.82** (1.37)	6.76** (1.91)	17	1519	3.84** (0.82)
Portugal	9	215	6.69** (2.17)	5.08** (1.77)	11	645	5.97** (1.66)
Sweden	19	685	6.00** (1.54)	5.58** (1.65)	21	1003	7.76** (2.79)
All countries	273	52,271	6.97** (0.35)	8.15** (0.50)	248	33,296	3.55** (0.41)

Note: Coefficients are estimated effects for the intersection expected value (ninth root), with majority status and the size gap also in the model specification. Standard errors are given in parentheses.
* $p < .05$ in a one-tailed test.
** $p < .01$ in a one-tailed test.

sets emerged in situations where majority intersections also existed. How was it possible for minority proto-coalitions to succeed in these instances?

This question cannot be answered precisely without a fully elaborated model of parliamentary government, but we can gain some insight into this problem by looking at predicted values. The predicted values in question are the predicted probabilities of forming the government derived from the six-variable conditional logit model. For behaviour-based horizons, these analyses were reported as Model 3 in Table 6.3 (both panels).

Since majority governments occur more often than minority governments, it is not surprising that the mean predicted probability for majority proto-coalitions exceeds that of minority proto-coalitions by a substantial margin (e.g. 63.3 per cent using logit horizons). But in situations where a minority government is formed, a different picture emerges. In nearly half of these situations, the minority proto-coalition that formed the government actually has a higher predicted probability than any of the majority proto-coalitions in the choice set.[11] This indicates that the disadvantages of minority status can be overcome by the presence of other traits, most notably the expectation of a sizeable horizon intersection.

Minority proto-coalitions have another intriguing horizon-related feature: if they have intersecting horizons, it is very likely that they will be subsets of majority intersections as well. In other words, the two traits overlap heavily. For example, 86.0 per cent of the minority proto-coalitions that have intersecting logit horizons are also subsets of majority logit intersections. In some cases, intersecting proto-coalitions lack this property simply because no majority intersections exist; excluding these cases raises the percentage to 88.8 per cent. With MJD horizons, the rates are virtually identical (86.0 per cent and 88.4 per cent, respectively).

This high degree of collinearity between the intersection rate and the SMI rate undoubtedly contributes to the failure of the latter to show a significant net effect in Table 6.1. But that does not mean that being a subset of a majority intersection is irrelevant to the formation of minority governments. Consider the following. Almost all minority governments (95.4 per cent) have intersecting logit horizons; most, as we have seen, are formed in situations where there is at least one majority intersection. If this is the case, fully 93.4 per cent (i.e. 85 out of 91 minority governments) are subsets of at least one of those majority intersections. With MJD horizons, the rate for minority governments is higher still: 94.7 per cent are subsets of majority intersections, provided majority intersections exist. In other words, if a minority government forms, it is virtually certain that it will not only have a common horizon intersection but also be a subset of a majority intersection (if any exist) and therefore have readily available support to survive in office. Given that this conclusion is based on the intersection dichotomies, with all the measurement imperfections that they possess, the apparent strength of this tendency is remarkable.

Thus, what we find with minority governments is that they are almost always formed of either a single party or a coalition of parties whose horizons intersect. If there are no majority intersections in the formation situation, then there cannot be any subsets of those intersections and the source of its support in the legislature will be unclear. But the government will not be especially disadvantaged relative to any majority government that might have been formed, since the absence of majority intersections means that no majority government could have arrived at a policy that fits the horizons of all its member-parties. For the remainder of minority government formations, we can say a good deal more about their likely external support since they almost always can find a policy stance that fits within the horizons of a parliamentary majority. The decision to form a government that has no built-in parliamentary majority is thus less of a gamble that it might seem; these governments generally have the potential to be as policy-viable, in the sense of the horizon hypothesis, as any majority government.

The same pattern holds when horizons are estimated by the expert survey respondents. About 84 per cent of minority governments have intersecting horizons, a figure that is lower than those reported for behaviour-based horizons but still quite impressive, given that it makes no allowance for the anomalous non-intersections. Eleven per cent of these formations can be explained by the absence of a majority intersection, and in 85.3 per cent of the remaining cases, the minority coalition that took office was a subset of a majority intersection. Moreover, in half (50.9 per cent) of the cases in which a minority government formed, its predicted probability of formation (based on the six-variable model) exceeds those of all majority proto-coalitions.[12]

The explanatory impact of horizons

The evidence of this chapter suggests that the intersection expected value, duly transformed and with appropriate adjustments for single-party and other minority proto-coalitions, plays a considerable more important role in determining which proto-coalition will emerge as the government than does just the intersection rate alone. This finding naturally raises the question, how much additional explanatory power is contributed by this change in specification? The indicator used in earlier chapters to assess explanatory power is the rate at which the proto-coalition with the highest predicted probability actually formed the government. This sets the bar very high, since it would count a government formed by a proto-coalition whose predicted probability is only marginally lower than the maximum in the choice set as a predictive failure; nevertheless, it serves reasonably well as a rough guide.

According to this standard, a substantial increase in predictive power occurs in the logit data. I noted in Chapter 3 that the standard model has a predictive success rate of 22.3 per cent. The move to the six-variable model that incorporates the intersection expected value (Model 3 of Table 6.3) causes that rate to rise to 37.8 per cent. Using MJD horizons, the same changes produce an increase in the predictive success rate from 20.5 per cent to 32.8 per cent. This lower predictive success rate is a further indication that the MJD method of estimating horizons may be less accurate than the logit method. Too much weight should not be placed on this observation, however, since the method is clearly good enough to reveal all of the covariate effects that the logit horizons convey. The corresponding survey-based model (Model 2 of Table 6.5) yields a predictive success rate of 31.6 per cent, only marginally lower than the rates produced using the behaviour-based horizons.[13]

Another way to gauge the impact of the horizon format is to consider its effect on previous explanations. The key previous work is, of course, Martin and Stevenson's (2001) conditional logit analyses of government formation, which examined a host of potential influences and came up with a set of nine that play significant net roles in the choice of a government. They consist of the eight that were added in Tables 6.4 and 6.5, plus policy distance which has been included in the models tested here from the beginning.

We have seen that Martin and Stevenson's explanatory model holds up very well in both the manifesto and the survey data (see Model 1 of Tables 3.7 and 5.5). Once the size gap and the intersection expected value variables are introduced, however, a different picture emerges. Of the nine Martin–Stevenson variables, the only ones that survive the introduction of the logit and MJD horizon variables in Table 6.4 are the indicator variables for the existence of a pre-electoral pact, for the incumbent government, for the presence of an extremist party, and for the presence of a VSP. The survey data yield results (Table 6.5) that deviate only in adding minimal winning status. Thus, the set of explanatory factors proposed by Martin and Stevenson is reduced very considerably by the variables introduced here.

A consideration of the theoretical foundations of the survivors is also instructive. The 'previous government' and 'pre-electoral pact' variables do not appear to be theory-driven in any strong sense. Both of them may simply signal a proto-coalition's viability as a government, the former by virtue of its past experience and the latter by virtue of prior policy commitments on the part of all the member-parties. Alternatively, the advantages may stem from the fact that many of the bargaining costs of forming a government have already been incurred by previous governments or formally allied partners. In any case, these considerations would probably be consistent with any theoretical approach to parliamentary government.

The VSP indicator variable, in contrast, is clearly theory-driven; it emerges from Laver and Shepsle's (1996) portfolio allocation model. In that model, a VSP is a party whose size and position place it in a dominant bargaining position, allowing it to form a government on its own or to anchor a coalition government of its choosing. Although this model and the policy horizon approach are incompatible in key respects, however, the idea that a centrally placed party could dominate the formation process and assure itself a place in government also fits with the policy horizon approach. In fact, this is precisely the role played by party C in the hypothetical scenario portrayed in Figure 6.1.

The situation with respect to the extremist party presence is less clear. The antipathy to coalescing with extremist parties may be simply an idiosyncratic consequence of the Cold War context of most of the post-War era, or it may represent an additional systematic factor in the government formation process. Even if it is the latter, however, it would not violate the horizon hypothesis. The status of the minimal winning condition is also ambiguous but for a different reason: it appears significantly only when the survey-based data are used. Nevertheless, even if it turns out to be a significant net factor in government formation, the horizon hypothesis would not be compromised. Nothing in the hypothesis prevents parties from preferring to form governments with no surplus members.

Thus, of the variables proposed by Martin and Stevenson (2001), only about half survive the introduction of considerations related to the operation of policy horizons and nothing that does survive is incompatible with the policy horizon approach. This outcome may change as our knowledge of formation processes increases, to be sure. But for the time being, it would appear that the policy horizon framework can sit very nicely with what remains of our previous knowledge of government formation in coalition situations.

Discussion

The principal positive finding of this chapter has been that the expected value of a horizon intersection, rather than just its possible presence, matters in determining which proto-coalition emerges as the government. That the added information provided by intersection size can be an important one is illustrated in the following comparison. The comparison involves Austria and (West) Germany, two systems that have displayed the classic three-party configuration in which any two parties can form a majority government. In the formation situations that occurred in West Germany between 1961 and 1980, all three parties had intersecting logit horizons and hence any of the seven potential governments could have formed under the horizon hypothesis. The coalitions that did assume power generally had less policy distance (and higher intersection rates), however, and the original four-variable model therefore predicts the government most of the time.

Austria, too, experienced a substantial period in which all three parties had intersecting horizons (1949–1961), but the successful proto-coalition was not the most compact majority coalition and often not the one with the highest intersection rate; as a result, the standard model predicts none of the five governments that formed in this period correctly. Once the intersection expected value is taken into account, however, the picture changes drastically. Among majority proto-coalitions, the successful proto-coalition (a Social Democratic–People's Party coalition) is invariably the one with the largest intersection expected value. As a result, the expanded model that incorporates this variable correctly predicts the formation of this government in every instance.

A second finding of note concerns minority governments. In situations where none of the majority proto-coalitions has a common horizon intersection, the result is almost always the formation of an (intersecting) minority government, as one would expect. But most minority governments are not formed in this circumstance; they are formed despite the existence of at least one majority intersection. What appears to make this palatable, apart from any other features the minority coalition may possess, is that the government is highly likely to be a subset of a majority intersection. This means that it can find policies within its horizon intersection that would also meet the horizon requirements of enough other parties to provide it with a parliamentary majority.[14]

A third notable finding of this chapter is that policy distance as such no longer seems to matter. In Chapters 3 and 5, we saw that much of the effect that might have been attributed to policy distance more properly belongs to the probability of a horizon intersection. It was also suggested that the remaining distance effect would be consistent with the idea that policy distance operates within policy horizons, rather than in an across-the-board fashion. This view of the horizon hypothesis as, in effect, a qualification of the policy distance hypothesis does not receive support in the data analyses of this chapter. Replacing the intersection rate with the intersection expected value variables weakens it considerably in both the logit and the MJD data sets and adding the Martin–Stevenson variables eliminates it totally in all three data sets. A similar conclusion emerges if the analysis is confined to proto-coalitions that meet the horizon constraint: distance appears to play no role in determining which intersecting proto-coalition will emerge as the government.[15]

The findings of this chapter leave many issues undetermined. Is being a subset of a majority intersection a necessary condition for forming a minority government, or does it just appear so because intersecting minority proto-coalitions almost always have this property? Is it really true that policy distance plays no net role at all in the choice of a government in coalition contexts? Finally, do single-party proto-coalitions show a heightened propensity to form governments because they tend to have very large intersection sizes? Since we do not know what constraints might be placed on these governments by the demands of their external support parties, we do not know the effective intersection size under which they operate. It may be that their advantages are due to entirely different factors.

These remaining questions should not, however, distract us from what has been learned. It is reasonably clear from the evidence of this and previous chapters that a proto-coalition's chances of forming the government depend on whether, and how extensively, the policy horizons of its member-parties intersect. It is also reasonably clear that a proto-coalition's policy diversity does not play the role usually assumed for it in quantitative models. Finally, it is evident that the policy horizon approach can provide insight into the formation of minority governments, a relatively common occurrence in West European parliamentary systems. It was never the purpose of the approach to provide a complete explanation of government formation and there is nothing in the results reported in this chapter to revise that position, but they do strengthen the case for fundamental changes in how that explanation is conceived.

7
Policy Horizons and Government Survival

From a formal theoretical perspective, it might seem strange to raise the question of government survival at all. Formal models of the government formation process generally seek to identify equilibrium outcomes, that is outcomes from which no participating party has an incentive to defect. If a formation process yields a government that embodies some such equilibrium – and for many theorists, this must be the case – the government should survive as long as the conditions that create the equilibrium remain in place (or until the government's mandate has run out). Parties whose interests are not well served by the incumbent government might seek to change some of those conditions; they might, for example, alter their policy positions so as to upset the equilibrium. But the same ontological position implies that the configuration of party positions also represents an equilibrium outcome from which there is no incentive for any party to deviate. The only thing that could bring down the government is a change in external conditions that erodes some aspect of this double equilibrium.

The idea that government survival depends on changes in the extra-parliamentary environment is most closely associated with a group of scholars that became known as the 'events theorists' (Browne *et al.* 1984a). The gist of their approach is that, since the events that topple parliamentary governments are likely to originate from outside the parliamentary field of play, they will occur in a fashion that appears to be random. This is not to say that they are uncaused in some fundamental sense, just that their causes are unlikely to form part of any theory or model of parliamentary government. From the perspective of the theorist of parliamentary government, and perhaps also of the players in the parliamentary game, they just happen.

The events theorists argued that these government-toppling occurrences are best modelled by a Poisson process, which yields an exponential distribution of government duration records (Browne *et al.* 1986). As we shall see, there is justification for modelling government survival with an exponential distribution. But there are also grounds for introducing systematic causal factors. Consider, for example, the issue of whether the government is the first to form after an election. Previous research (e.g. King *et al.* 1990; Warwick 1994) has shown that post-election governments, as they are known, tend to survive longer than other governments (and not just because there is more time available to them in the parliamentary term). But this factor is common to all proto-coalitions in any formation situation and therefore is unlikely to figure in any model of the government formation process.[1]

It is not just theoretically extraneous factors that may cause government survival to vary across cases in a systematic fashion. Suppose that formation is determined almost exclusively by seat size and intersection size (heroic assumptions, to be sure) and that the current government has the most advantageous combination of these traits, including a parliamentary majority. Being the best of the available choices may still not guarantee longevity, however, if changing economic, social, political or international conditions require a change in government policy that is larger than the government's horizon intersection can accommodate. Since governments based on smaller intersections are more likely to find themselves in this situation, survival prospects may tend to reflect intersection sizes.

What makes this outcome more likely than it might seem at first glance is that the government may not embody the most favourable combination of formation traits to begin with. We saw in the previous chapter that many of the governments under scrutiny here fall into this category, that is they are not formed by the proto-coalition with the highest predicted probability of formation. This need not be the result of the omission of important causal factors in the formation process. Nor would such outcomes necessarily reflect some element of irrationality or miscalculation on the part of players in the formation game. Even if size and compliance with the horizon hypothesis were the predominant considerations for potential governments and they operated in the fashion modelled here, outcomes that appear to be suboptimal could result from perfectly rational behaviour. To see this, let us return to the five-party scenario shown in Figure 6.1.

The parliamentary set-up portrayed in this figure consists of five parties of roughly similar sizes. Although any three parties comprise a majority, party C is in a particularly privileged position from a policy horizon standpoint, since it is the only common element in the two proto-coalitions ({ABC} and {CDE}) that have majority intersections. In view of the findings of the previous chapter, a {CDE} government would appear to be the more likely outcome of the two, since it has a larger horizon intersection than {ABC}. But C would probably prefer to form {ABC} because the latter's intersection defines a relatively small area that includes C's ideal point.[2] As long as the members of {ABC} respect their horizon constraints, its policy in government would have to be very close to C's preferences.

Whether an {ABC} government can survive its full parliamentary term is another matter, however. One reason why its survival prospects might be poor is that the size of its horizon intersection is relatively small, which means that it has little room to manoeuvre. But the fact that there is another majority government that could replace it, one with considerably more policy options, might accelerate its demise.

Indeed, this may have figured in C's choice of government all along. These two potential governments represent different trade-offs for C: the {ABC} government promises a better policy payoff, but a greater risk of premature collapse, than a {CDE} government. But C may have calculated that it can have the best of both worlds by forming an {ABC} government and reaping the policy benefits for as long as possible, then switching to a {CDE} government if problems arise that make the {ABC} government no longer viable. In other words, in making its choice, C is evaluating not just expected policy outcomes but expected durations as well, and in some situations the better choice may be to opt for the inherently less stable government.

The fact that governments may be created whose compliance with the horizon hypothesis is weak, either in absolute terms or relative to that of other proto-coalitions, clearly creates a risk that government survival may be abbreviated. It is therefore plausible that the existence and size of horizon intersections may play a significant role in government survival. It is important to recognize, however, that this role may be under-estimated. This is because survival analyses are different from formation analyses in one very basic respect: they are estimated not on the basis of all governments that might be formed, but only on the basis of the small subset of proto-coalitions that actually went on to become governments.

The problem is not that other possibilities cannot be taken into account. Survival in office must depend, in part at least, on how well the government compares with other alternatives that might replace it, and we can use the information that we have on these alternatives to assess the government in these terms. Rather, the problem is one of selection bias. Selection bias occurs when the unmeasured factors that affect the selection of cases are correlated with the unmeasured factors that affect the relationship estimated from those cases; in this application, when the error in the formation model is correlated with the error in the survival model. It is easy to imagine that selection bias might be present here.

Suppose, for example, government formation is influenced by the degree of personal compatibility between party leaders: some leaders just do not like each other and are reluctant to work together. This is at present (and probably will remain) an unmeasured factor, but it may mean that proto-coalitions that would otherwise be unlikely candidates to form governments are able to do so because the leaders involved get along very well together. Since it is the combination of traits that determines which proto-coalitions become governments, one can expect many of those that do so to have high scores on leader compatibility and lower scores on the other factors, or vice versa, generating a negative correlation between the two in the sample of governments.[3] If survival is also influenced by the same factors, the fact that one of them, leader compatibility, is unmeasured means that there will be a negative relationship between the independent variable(s) and the error in the survival equation. This will tend to bias downward the estimated effect(s) of the independent variable(s). The same would happen if some of the variables in the formation model contained measurement error, which is certainly the case with respect to horizon intersections.

At present, there are no available statistical means for dealing with this problem. The only effort to tackle it that I am aware of is Boehmke *et al.*'s model (forthcoming), but their model does not (yet) have the capacity to deal with a conditional logit selection model. While we can estimate survival models and would expect, for the reasons given above, to see some effects of horizons on survival, we should always bear in mind that we may not be observing the full impact that would exist if, say, governments were selected randomly from the various choice sets.

Modelling survival

Although we cannot change the reality that observed governments are unlikely to constitute a representative sample of all governments that might be formed, nor correct for it statistically, existing modelling techniques do allow us to address a number of other issues that present themselves in the analysis of government survival. These issues require some attention if the most appropriate modelling choices are to be made, and this section addresses that task.

The first choice concerns the statistical model. Unlike the case for formation studies, where just one model (the conditional logit model) is currently the gold standard, there are a plethora of potentially viable options for examining government survival. These can be classified into two basic types: fully parametric models, which require an assumption about the nature of the underlying risk of government collapse, or the semi-parametric or partial likelihood model developed by Cox (1972, 1975). The normal criterion is to use the Cox model if the underlying risk of termination, known as the *baseline hazard*, is not of particular interest in the investigation. Such is the case here, since our concern is with how horizon intersections (and other factors) might affect the underlying risk, rather than with the nature of that risk itself. The Cox partial likelihood model will therefore serve as our principal estimating device. A parametric specification will also be tested, however, to ensure that nothing is lost or distorted in bypassing this aspect of the explanandum.

Although the Cox model makes no assumption about the shape of the baseline hazard, it does assume that all cases follow the same shape and that the various covariates (independent variables) affect the baseline hazard multiplicatively. Since the hazard rate cannot be negative (one cannot have a negative risk of collapse), this is typically parameterized as:

$$h_i(t) = h_0(t) \exp(X_i' \beta_x)$$

where $h_0(t)$ is the baseline hazard and X represents a vector of covariates with associated effect coefficients, β. The fact that the hazard for any government i is proportional to a baseline hazard shared by all cases makes this a *proportional hazards* model. Proportionality is a fundamental assumption of the model and various tests will be utilized to assess its viability.

There are two features in particular that recommend survival models to researchers: the ability to assess the impact of variables that change in value over the lifetimes of individual cases and the ability to adjust for terminations that are not theoretically relevant. In previous research (Warwick 1994), I found that the inflation rate and changes in the unemployment rate, both measured on a monthly basis, affect the odds of government survival (and that the impact of these variables depends on the length of time the government has been in power). I also found, however, that these factors work independently of the 'fixed' or time-independent variables in the model. This is a useful finding because it suggests that we can ignore these time-varying factors and concentrate on the much more tractable fixed effects, including those that are of prime concern here, the horizon variables. (As far as I am aware, this practice has been followed in all subsequent work on government survival.)

While we can avoid specifying a baseline hazard and introducing time-varying covariates, we cannot bypass the issue of theoretically irrelevant terminations. The need to address this issue is indicated by the fact that governments often end due to the legal necessity of holding parliamentary elections. In most cases, their actual durations will be less than what they would have been in the absence of this legal requirement. Another type of termination that has little bearing on our theoretical understanding of parliamentary government is that caused by the death or retirement (for non-political reasons such as illness or old age) of the prime minister. These situations are handled in survival analysis by (right) *censoring*, which amounts to treating the termination dates of these cases as marking their minimum, rather than their actual, durations. Thus, a government that survives up to the point at which it is legally obliged to hold an election is treated statistically as having a duration that is at least as long as its actual period in office, but potentially longer.[4]

The ability to adjust for irrelevant terminations by means of censoring feeds into the definition of a termination. What if the same government remained in office after an election – should it be treated as a new government or simply as a continuation of the old one? The fact that the parliamentary bargaining structure, and thus the survival prospects of the government, may have been changed by the election suggests that we ought to treat the post-election situation as new; on the other hand, it may be the same government to all appearances. This question also arises if an incumbent prime minister dies – should the government that survives him or her be considered as a new government even if the only changes that occur are that a few cabinet posts are shuffled? After all, cabinet reshuffles by themselves are not normally considered as marking the birth of new governments.

The censoring mechanism provides a cogent solution to this dilemma: treat the initial government as having an unknown duration of at least as long as its actual duration at the point at which the event in question occurred, and then define a new government as starting in its aftermath.[5] But it would be misleading to treat censoring simply as a means of dealing with technical issues such as these, since censoring also provides a handle on the less transparent issue of causal heterogeneity.

There is ample reason to believe that such heterogeneity characterizes government terminations. In testing implications of a formal model developed by Lupia and Strøm (1995), Diermeier and Stevenson (1999) demonstrated that the causal process governing whether or not a government will be replaced (without an election occurring) is fundamentally different from the process governing whether the government will end in a premature parliamentary dissolution and new elections. In essence, dissolution terminations were found to be affected by the government's majority status and whether or not it was formed immediately after an election; they also become more likely as duration time increases (a condition known as positive *duration dependency*). This latter finding is consistent with Lupia and Strøm's expectation that governments become increasingly likely to seize upon favourable opportunities to call elections as their terms run out. Replacement terminations, in contrast, lack any duration dependency, but are more likely to be affected by the other variables in my 1994 model, most notably the degree of ideological diversity in the government. Thus, it appears that governments face *competing risks* of termination driven by very different causal processes.

Separating these two processes turns out to be very straightforward with censoring: to estimate a model for one type of risk, one censors all terminations occasioned by the other type(s) of risk and vice versa. Since we are interested in the risk of a government collapsing and being replaced, not in the risk that the government may seize the opportunity to hold an early election, this means censoring all terminations that ended in elections. These terminations, plus the various kinds of technical terminations (which include not just the deaths of prime ministers but also technical circumstances such as the requirement in Finland for a government to resign when a new president is elected) constitute the set of censored terminations in the analyses that follow.

There is, to be sure, an assumption built in here: that all early elections are opportunistic. This is a central feature of the Lupia–Strøm model, but it may not be a central feature of reality. One can readily imagine an election following a coalition breakdown, not because a coalition party saw an opportunity to increase its legislative size but because the head of state decided to see if a more workable configuration of forces might be obtained from the electorate. As a robustness check, the final models produced in the analysis will also be estimated using a censoring scheme that isolates (i.e. does not censor) all terminations due to political difficulties.

Regardless of which censoring scheme is used, competing risks models embed the assumption that, conditional on the independent variables, the various types of risk are independent of one other. There are grounds for suspecting that this assumption is not met here, at least in an unconditional sense: it stands to reason that governments that are vulnerable to collapse and replacement during the legislative term are unlikely to survive until it nears or reaches its end and vice versa. Gordon (2002) has shown, however, that the inter-correlation of these risks is a relatively unimportant factor in my previous model of government survival. This may indicate that the model is reasonably well specified (since the assumption is conditional on the covariates), but in any case it suggests that the assumption can be made with some confidence, provided we start the analysis with that model, which is the intention here.

Researchers are agreed that the occurrence of elections or a change in prime minister should be considered as marking the end of a government, even if no formal change in government has taken place. The same holds when a party joins or leaves the governing coalition; the government may see itself, and/or be seen in political and media circles, as continuing on in office, but the event is invariably defined in studies as marking the end of one government and the beginning of another. (Researchers are also agreed that censoring should be applied to the former situations – since the government's viability was not at issue – but not to the latter.) Agreement on what constitutes a government termination is not total, however. The controversial situation involves governments whose resignation is rejected by the head of state. When this occurs, should we assume that a new government identical to the original government has been formed, or should we just ignore the resignation?

Most observers take the latter position; they regard only those resignations that are accepted by a head of state as marking the end of a government. This position has the virtue of consistency with the official reckoning, but it can stretch reality quite a bit if a government that resigned but had its resignation refused some time later, perhaps because no viable alternative government could be found, is considered to have continued in office without a hitch. It is at least plausible that the government, having failed once and been obliged to soldier on in office, is now in a much more precarious situation. Indeed, higher hazard rates may characterize other repeat governments, such as those that are re-formed or simply continue on after a technical termination, since they already have had time to use up some of the goodwill with which they began.

Here, too, survival analysis can come to the rescue by distinguishing between new governments and those that are repeats or continuations of outgoing governments. Repeat governments are defined here as governments that have the same party composition as their predecessors and are in the same legislature (those that follow an election are exempted because they are deemed to have had their right to govern renewed). The possibility that they differ in their survival prospects can be handled in three ways: (1) include in the model a covariate that registers whether or not the government is a repeat or not (perhaps distinguishing a first repeat from subsequent repeats); (2) include a covariate that records the amount of time the government has already occupied power at the time of its current formation, to capture the amount of initial goodwill that may have dissipated; or (3) *stratify* the analysis by the repeat status covariate. The first two solutions assume that the same baseline hazard characterizes the survival prospects of all governments, while the third allows the shape of their baseline hazards to differ according to their repeat status.

An initial indication of whether or not these distinctions matter can be garnered by examining the survivor functions for these different types of government. Figure 7.1 shows the Kaplan-Meier survivor estimates for new governments, governments that are repeats of their immediate predecessors ('first repeats'), and governments that repeat two or more of their immediate predecessors ('subsequent repeats'), based on the manifesto data set.[6] If repeat governments face a higher risk of collapse, their survivor functions should decline more steeply with time in office. This appears to be somewhat true for both second and subsequent repeat governments, but the differences are not great. In fact, various tests for the equality of survivor functions (specifically, the log-rank, Wilcoxon, Peto-Peto-Prentice, and Tarone-Ware tests) show that these survivor functions are not significantly different from one another. Figure 7.1 also makes it clear, however, that it may be inappropriate to distinguish between second and subsequent repeat governments; their estimated survivor functions are very close to each other. Repeating the tests based on just a dichotomous distinction between new and repeat governments reveals that, while the survivor functions are not different from each other at the 0.05 level, they are at the 0.10 level. Thus, there is some, albeit weak, evidence that governments

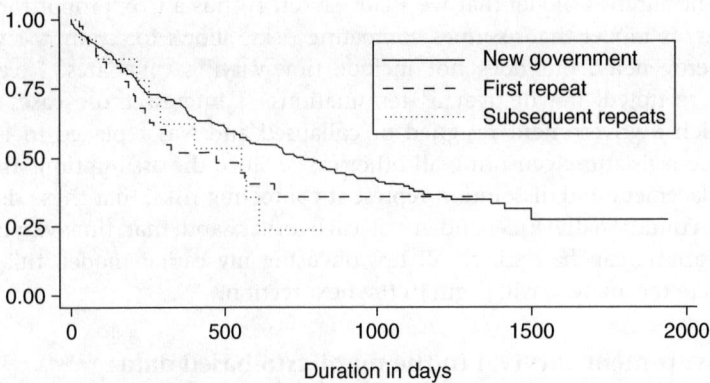

Figure 7.1 Kaplan-Meier survival estimates, by repeat status.

that re-form or continue on in the same legislature following a collapse, resignation, or technical termination have lower survival prospects. These will be treated as terminations, but the possibility that their survival prospects differ significantly will be fully explored.

The final modelling option that needs to be addressed concerns heterogeneity across countries. This is usually handled by introducing a set of country dummy variables into the analysis, but a much better option would be to use a *shared frailty* model. The vulnerability or frailty of governments in one country may differ from that in another country because of various unmeasured factors; a shared frailty model introduces a random coefficient to account for the variance associated with such factors. Since it captures unobserved heterogeneity, the introduction of shared frailty assists competing risks models to meet the assumption that the risks are conditionally independent; taking account of shared frailties also prevents attenuation in the estimates of the other covariate effects and preserves the proportional hazards property (Box-Steffensmeier and Jones 2002, pp. 147–8). Unlike models that treat country differences as fixed effects (i.e. a model with country dummies), a model that accounts for country-level frailty can also include country-level covariates. It does, however, require the choice of a distribution for the group-level frailties (a gamma distribution is usually chosen) and entails the assumption that this distribution is independent of the covariates in the model. The risk inherent in choosing an inappropriate distribution can be assessed by comparing results produced using different distribution specifications.

The survival model that we shall rely on is thus a Cox proportional hazards model that assumes competing risks, allows for country-level heterogeneity, but does not include time-varying covariates. Except where noted, it will treat as terminations of interest those cases in which a government resigned or collapsed and was replaced in the same legislature, censoring all other cases. Since the assumptions that replacement and dissolution represent competing risks, that these risks are conditionally independent of each other, and that time-varying covariates can be omitted all rest on using my earlier model, this is where the analysis will begin in the next section.

Government survival in the manifesto-based data

The investigation of government survival will be pursued in this section using a data set that is derived largely from the data utilized in Chapter 3. This implies that the same set of governments is covered (except for a very few cases with missing data, as discussed below), that party positions are estimated from the first two principal components of the CMP data, and that horizons are calculated by applying the logit and MJD methods to these data.

My previous study of government survival (Warwick 1994) produced a model with seven fixed (time independent) covariates. Three of these are dichotomous indicators of whether or not the government is majoritarian (*majority status*), was the first government to form after an election (*post-election status*), and had to undergo a formal investiture vote (*investiture*). Another three are measures of the amount of *ideological diversity* spanned by the government on left/right, clerical/secular, and regime support dimensions. The final fixed covariate is *returnability*, a system-level measure of the probability that a government party will return to power following a government collapse or early termination. The purpose of this covariate was to capture the possibility that a government party may be less reluctant to bring about the demise of the government if it knows that its chances of returning to power in the next government are good.

For the present investigation, both the measurement of ideological diversity and the measurement of returnability have been altered. The government's ideological diversity is now measured by the policy distance it spans in the two-dimensional ideological space, as in Chapter 3, rather than by the three separate measures noted above.[7] Returnability, too, deviates from its original version. That version measured each system's returnability with the average rate at which parties return to power in the entire observation period (which ran from the start of normal democratic government following 1945 until 1989). This meant that the returnability scores for most governments that held office in this period were based in part on events that occurred after their demise. The new version of returnability removes this *ex post* element by utilizing only information available to parties at the time they enter a government to calculate the returnability rate that prevails during the government's lifetime. More specifically, returnability is now operationalized as the average rate of return based on the composition of the present government plus the four that preceded it.[8] This means that the returnability variable now varies across governments within each system, rather than assuming just one value per system.

The results of re-estimating this five-covariate version of the 1994 model are shown in Model 1 of Table 7.1. Each coefficient, when exponentiated, gives the effect on the hazard rate of a one-unit change in its associated covariate. Thus, the coefficient of 0.32 estimated for policy distance indicates that each additional unit of distance increases a government's risk of termination by 41.9 per cent ($\exp(0.35) = 1.419$). Similarly, the majority status coefficient of -1.18 implies that the risk of collapse for majority governments is just 30.7 per cent of that for minority governments ($\exp(-1.18) = 0.307$). Both of these effects are in the expected direction, as are the remaining three effects: post-election governments are more durable but an investiture requirement and high returnability undermine government survival.

Apart from the changes to the measurement of two concepts, Model 1 differs from its predecessor in containing a frailty variance term. This measures the degree of correlation that exists within systems, and the fact that it is significant indicates that there is unmeasured system-level heterogeneity. The most noticeable consequence of including this type of frailty is to lower the significance level of the investiture effect (without the frailty specification, investiture would be significant at the $p = .002$ level in a one-tailed test); thus, once unmeasured cross-system heterogeneity is taken onto account, it is less than clear that the existence of an investiture requirement shortens government durations.

This is an interesting finding because it addresses an earlier puzzle in the literature. In their study of government survival, King *et al.* (1990) interpreted the investiture effect as a result of the fact that an investiture requirement imposes an early test that governments may not survive. I found, however, that the effect survives even when governments that fell in investiture votes were excluded from the sample (Warwick 1994, p. 44), which implies that it must stand in for some

Table 7.1 Policy distance and government survival (manifesto data)

	Model 1	Model 2	Model 3	Model 4	Model 5
Majority status	-1.18** (0.27)	-1.50** (0.30)	-1.40** (0.29)	-1.46** (0.27)	-1.60** (0.28)
Post-election status	-0.60** (0.19)	-0.61** (0.19)	-0.60** (0.19)	-0.63** (0.19)	-0.64** (0.19)
Investiture	0.60* (0.35)	–	–	–	–
Returnability	4.60** (1.14)	4.16** (1.09)	4.11** (1.07)	3.97** (1.02)	3.84** (1.02)
Policy distance	0.32** (0.12)	0.17 (0.14)	–	–	–
Number of cabinet parties	–	0.28** (0.11)	0.25** (0.09)	0.21** (0.09)	0.19* (0.09)
Effective number of parliamentary parties	–	-0.09 (0.11)	–	–	–
Relative government diversity I[a]	–	–	0.14 (0.16)	–	–
Relative government diversity II[a]	–	–	–	0.24* (0.11)	0.39** (0.16)
Relative government diversity II × majority status	–	–	–	–	-0.26† (0.19)
Frailty variance	0.37**	0.26**	0.25**	0.21**	0.20**
Log-likelihood	-664.5	-662.6	-663.4	-661.4	-660.5
N	264	264	264	264	264

Note: Coefficients are estimated from Cox partial likelihood models (standard errors in parentheses).

[a] Version I of the relative government diversity variable calculates the difference between the policy distance spanned by the government and the policy distance spanned by the most compact alternative majority proto-coalition regardless of its composition. Version II excludes from the alternatives any proto-coalition containing the formateur party.

† Significant at .10 level in one-tailed test.

* Significant at .05 level in one-tailed test.

** Significant at .01 level in one-tailed test.

other factor or factors that curtail survival in the systems that have it.[9] We still do not know what these factors are, but the marginal significance level of the effect in Model 1, together with the fact that its theoretical basis has evaporated, suggests that the matter is better handled by means of the frailty specification. This solution is certainly preferable to leaving a spurious covariate effect in the model.

All other covariate effects in Model 1 are highly significant, so we may take it that my earlier findings have survived reasonably well. But this may be the case only because of what the model does not include. The most notable challenge in this regard comes from Saalfeld (2001), who finds that the ideological distance effect cannot survive the presence of certain other variables in the model. Nyblade (2004) confirms that two variables in particular, the *number of cabinet parties* and the *effective number of parliamentary parties*, render the policy distance effect insignificant, at least in the data set they both use.

The effects of including these two covariates in the present data set are shown in Model 2 of Table 7.1. The analysis that yields Model 2 differs in many respects from both the Saalfeld and Nyblade analyses; not only are the coverage of countries, the censoring regime, and the definition of government terminations all different, but system frailties have been taken into account. Nevertheless, the results point in the same direction. While the effective number of parliamentary parties is a negligible factor, the number of cabinet parties variable not only has a highly significant effect, but its presence renders the policy distance effect statistically insignificant. Saalfeld's basic conclusion that the ideological diversity or policy distance factor lacks robustness is thus sustained.[10]

This is a puzzling finding since it seems to indicate that how far apart a coalition government's members are in terms of their policy preferences makes no difference for the government's survival; all that matters is how many members there are. To put it differently, a governing coalition of, say, three parties whose policy positions are very similar should not expect to survive longer than a governing coalition of three parties with serious policy differences. There is, however, another interpretation. Nyblade suggests that policy distance fails to show a significant net effect, not because of its causal irrelevance but because of the way in which it has been conceived. Specifically, he argues that it is not the absolute level of policy distance spanned by the government that matters, but rather the relative level. Thus, a diverse government may survive for a long time provided there are no other more compact alternatives available; if such an alternative does exist, however, it could mean that the government's days are numbered.

To capture this effect, Nyblade proposes two measures. The first is *relative government proximity*, operationalized as the government's left/right policy distance minus the distance between the government's position (presumably the mean or weighted mean position of its members) and that of the closest opposition party. The second is *relative government diversity*, the difference between the government's left/right policy distance and the distance spanned by the most compact majority coalition that excludes the largest coalition party.

The first measure is the less intuitively appealing for a couple of reasons. First, the closest opposition party may, in fact, be a relatively minor player in the system; its size or bargaining power may never enter the picture. Second, the measure takes no account of the coalition that might replace the incumbent government. Presumably, the idea is that a close opposition party may be well placed to tempt some of the member-parties to defect from the government, but in fact we do not know what kind of alternative it could put together. The second measure directly addresses this issue of what the best available alternative is. Consistent with this reasoning, Nyblade's findings indicate that virtually all of the explanatory power of the concept is borne by this latter measure.

The analysis that follows therefore concentrates on relative government diversity. Nyblade's operationalization of this concept rests upon an assumption that may not be warranted, however. This is the assumption that the best available alternative must be one that excludes the largest government party. The rationale for this assumption may be that the largest party is the one that is most likely to get what it wants in the present government and is therefore very unlikely to be tempted to join or form a different coalition government. It seems more plausible, however, that the principal beneficiary of any government would be the formateur party (which is usually but not always the largest party), since it is the one that put the governing coalition together. Alternatively, it may be that all parties should be considered as potential defectors.

The variable has therefore been constructed in two versions. The first calculates the difference between the policy distance spanned by the government and the policy distance spanned by the most compact alternative majority proto-coalition, regardless of its composition. The second excludes from the alternatives any proto-coalition containing the formateur party.[11] In each case, negative scores occur when there is at least one alternative majority government that is more policy-compact; positive scores indicate the absence of any such alternative. Note that the policy distances of the various proto-coalitions are those utilized in Chapter 3, that is, they are calculated from the CMP-based two-dimensional policy positions, not from Nyblade's single left/right scale.

Models 3 and 4 of Table 7.1 show the effects of adding each version of relative government diversity to the model specification. The version that treats all alternative majority proto-coalitions as potential alternatives does not appear to play a significant net role in government survival (Model 3). But a different story emerges for the other version, which excludes alternatives containing the formateur party: it has a significant net impact on survival (Model 4). Nyblade's intuition that the set of alternatives needs to be limited in this way is thus supported.[12]

Although these results re-establish a role for policy distance, there is another refinement that needs to be taken into consideration. This is the distinction between majority and minority governments. It is possible that the availability of compact majority alternatives would be especially pertinent for minority governments, since their hold on power may be substantially less secure than that of majority governments. This possibility can be captured by introducing the interaction between majority status and relative government diversity. As the final model of Table 7.1 shows, it does appear that majority governments are a good deal less susceptible to the presence of viable alternatives. The effect is not especially significant by conventional standards, but to the extent that it is credible, its magnitude indicates that relative diversity plays a significant role only for minority governments.

The relative diversity of the government, that is its diversity relative to potential majority alternatives, does appear to rescue a causative role for ideological diversity in government survival, at least for minority governments. But we have not yet considered the possible impact of policy horizons. Chapter 6 developed a six-variable formation model that included the intersection expected value, operationalized as the ninth root of the product of the horizon intersection rate and the intersection size (Model 3 of Table 6.3). Together with adjustments for single-party and other minority governments, this variable proved to be an important predictor of government formation. But can these variables, and in particular the horizon-related ones, also account for the survival records of the governments that actually were formed?

If policy horizons play a role in survival, one would expect that governments that have a high probability of formation, based on this six-variable model, would tend to survive longer than governments that are less well endowed in this respect. This possibility can be tested by means of the predicted probabilities that are generated by the model. As Nyblade observes, however, what ought to matter more than the government's level itself is how that level compares with those of its potential rivals. A government with what would appear to have a high predicted value may not be especially secure in its hold on office if the choice set contains another proto-coalition with an equal or greater predicted value. The contribution of policy horizons to government survival will therefore be assessed by calculating a *relative predicted value* for each government.[13] Paralleling the construction of relative government diversity, the government's predicted value is made relative by subtracting from it the maximum predicted value among majority alternatives to the government (excluding those that contain the formateur party).[14] Since the manifesto data provided two estimates of horizon radii, two sets of predicted values will be calculated, the first based on logit horizons and the second on MJD horizons.

Model 1 in Panel A of Table 7.2 shows the consequences of adding the logit version of this variable, together with its interaction with majority status, to the model specification. The two variables totally dislodge the two relative government diversity variables. Model 1, which removes the insignificant relative diversity variables, makes it clear that this effect, like that for relative diversity, is mainly concentrated among minority governments. That is, a minority government can expect to be short lived to the extent that a majority alternative exists with a relatively high probability of formation. The corresponding models in Panel B, which are based on MJD horizons, show essentially the same pattern.

Models 1 and 2 reveal a role for the relative predicted probability of formation in government survival, but they do not establish that this emanates from the existence and size of horizon intersections. This is because the relative predicted values are based on formation models that combine horizon variables with other variables, including policy distance itself. An alternative version of each of the relative predicted value variables was therefore created, based exclusively on the covariates conveying the effects of horizon intersections, that is, the intersection expected value, its interaction with the single-party indicator, and its interaction with majority status. These versions will be referred to as

Table 7.2 The effect of formation predicted values on survival (manifesto data)

	Model 1	Model 2	Model 3
Panel A (logit horizons)			
Majority status	−1.37** (0.30)	−1.35** (0.26)	−1.17** (0.27)
Post-election status	−0.59** (0.19)	−0.59** (0.19)	−0.57** (0.19)
Returnability	3.70** (1.05)	3.71** (1.05)	4.12** (1.07)
No. of cabinet parties	0.20* (0.09)	0.20** (0.08)	0.23** (0.08)
Relative government diversity	0.02 (0.20)	–	–
Relative government Diversity × majority status	0.08 (0.25)	–	–
Relative predicted value	−2.88** (1.02)	−2.93** (0.79)	–
Relative predicted value × majority status	2.59** (1.39)	2.37* (1.09)	–
Relative intersection predicted value	–	–	−4.89** (1.23)
Relative intersection predicted value × majority status	–	–	4.50** (1.42)
Frailty variance	0.20**	0.20**	0.22**
Log-likelihood	−657.1	−657.3	−658.1
N	264	264	264
Panel B (MJD horizons)			
Majority status	−1.58** (0.29)	−1.40** (0.26)	−1.18** (0.28)
Post-election status	−0.63** (0.19)	−0.62** (0.19)	−0.60** (0.19)
Returnability	3.85** (1.02)	3.54** (1.00)	4.03** (1.05)
No. of cabinet parties	0.18* (0.09)	0.25** (0.08)	0.29** (0.08)
Relative government diversity	0.23 (0.21)	–	–
Relative government diversity × majority status	0.04 (0.26)	–	–
Relative predicted value	−1.85† (1.24)	−2.66** (0.94)	–
Relative predicted value × majority status	−3.28* (1.65)	3.01** (1.26)	–
Relative intersection predicted value	–	–	−4.19* (1.85)
Relative intersection predicted value × majority status	–	–	4.80* (2.11)
Frailty variance	0.19**	0.20**	0.25**
Log-likelihood	−657.8	−659.3	−661.5
N	264	264	264

Note: Coefficients are estimated from Cox partial likelihood models (standard errors in parentheses).
† Significant at .10 level in one-tailed test.
* Significant at .05 level in one-tailed test.
** Significant at .01 level in one-tailed test.

the *relative intersection predicted value.* Model 3 shows that, regardless of whether intersections are estimated from logit horizons (Panel A) or MJD horizons (Panel B), the same general effect persists: a minority governments tends to be short lived to the extent that its intersection expected value compares unfavourably with that of at least one majority alternative (excluding alternatives that contain the government's formateur).[15]

The finding that horizon intersections play a role in the survival of minority governments depends, to be sure, on the assumption that other things are equal. One means of inferring the satisfaction of this condition is to evaluate the goodness of fit of the models, which will be undertaken in the next section. Following the logic that the factors affecting formation and survival may be very similar, however, we can also examine this assumption by introducing the Martin–Stevenson variables into the picture.[16]

Model 1 of Table 7.3 shows the results when the Martin–Stevenson variables are added to the model based on logit horizons; Model 3 has the corresponding results when MJD horizons are used. The results are again very consistent across the two models. They indicate that only one of the Martin–Stevenson variables conveys a significant net impact, minimal winning status. In fact, not only does it play a significant net role, but further investigation shows that its presence is the crucial factor in eliminating any significant role for the number of cabinet parties. The independent causal role conveyed by this latter variable is thus not sustained in the present analysis; apparently, the key issue is not the number of cabinet parties, but whether or not there are more parties than are needed to command a parliamentary majority. For present purposes, however, the key point is that the presence of these additional eight covariates does not eliminate the highly significant roles played by the relative predicted value and its interaction with majority status. This also turns out to be the case when the relative predicted values are replaced by relative intersection predicted values (i.e. predicted values based just on the three intersection expected value variables).[17]

Models 2 and 4 show these effects with the insignificant covariates removed. They will be taken as the final models from this analysis. This is not to say that no other potential causal factors exist; after all, the Martin–Stevenson variables were not even proposed with government survival in mind. But it must be remembered that the model we began with emerged through an analysis of a wide variety of other potential causal variables. Taken together, therefore, considerable weight may be

Table 7.3 Adding the Martin–Stevenson variables (manifesto data)

	Logit horizons		MJD horizons	
	Model 1	Model 2	Model 3	Model 4
Majority status	-0.59** (0.41)	-0.47* (0.23)	-0.52 (0.41)	-0.64** (0.23)
Post-election status	-0.65** (0.22)	-0.52** (0.19)	-0.71** (0.21)	-0.56** (0.19)
Returnability	3.51** (1.11)	4.52** (1.11)	3.52** (1.05)	3.87** (1.04)
Number of cabinet parties	0.11 (0.30)	–	0.13 (0.10)	–
Relative predicted value	-2.95** (1.08)	-5.30** (1.14)	-2.30* (1.22)	-3.23** (0.91)
Relative predicted value×majority status	2.82* (1.32)	4.93** (1.38)	2.96* (1.54)	3.90** (1.28)
Minimal winning status	-0.96** (0.32)	-0.84** (0.27)	-0.99** (0.31)	-0.96** (0.26)
Government has largest party	-0.10 (0.31)	–	-0.24 (0.29)	–
Minority coalition in investiture system	0.45 (0.41)	–	0.55 (0.40)	–
Anti-system presence	-0.46 (0.44)	–	-0.47 (0.44)	–
Pre-electoral pact	0.43 (0.48)	–	0.38 (0.48)	–
Coalition has VSP	0.08 (0.23)	–	0.04 (0.23)	–
Coalition consists of VSP	-0.16 (0.52)	–	-0.34 (0.54)	–
Repeat government	-0.22 (0.25)	–	-0.26 (0.25)	–
Frailty variance	0.22**	0.30**	0.20**	0.26**
Log-likelihood	-651.4	-655.7	-652.7	-656.4
N	264	264	264	264

Note: Coefficients are estimated from Cox partial likelihood models (standard errors in parentheses). Predicted values are from formation models that use logit horizons.

* Significant at .05 level in one-tailed test.

** Significant at .01 level in one-tailed test.

attached to the conclusion that policy horizons, as estimated by the behaviour-based methods, play an independent causal role in government survival.

Model adequacy

This conclusion rests on a host of assumptions in addition to the ceteris paribus assumption, as we have seen. Fortunately, tests exist to assess the appropriateness of most of them. Since Models 2 and 4 convey the full impact of formation probabilities on government survival, this section will concentrate on the results of applying the tests to those models. Additional research indicates, however, that the conclusions are also valid for versions of the model that use the relative intersection predicted values. The presentation will be fairly abbreviated; interested readers are referred to Cleves *et al.* (2004) and Box-Steffensmeier and Jones (2002) for a more detailed discussion of the nature of the tests.

The first assumption to be evaluated is the proportional hazards assumption. One means of doing so is the link test which assesses whether the coefficient on the square of the linear predictor is insignificant. Cleves *et al.* (2004, p. 176) note that this is a reasonably powerful test for errors in specifying $X'\beta$, provided one has the right set of covariates (which is tested below). The application of the test reveals that the squared linear predictor is insignificant in both models. In addition, an analysis of the Schoenfeld residuals indicates that none of the covariate effects in either model appears to change significantly over time, which would have indicated a violation of proportionality.[18] We may thus be reasonably confident that the two models meet the proportional hazards assumption.

The functional form of the model covariates can be assessed with the aid of Martingale residuals, which measure the difference between observed and predicted numbers of terminations. The method followed here was proposed by Klein and Moeschberger (1997). In this method, each covariate is tested by estimating the model without it, calculating the Martingale residuals and plotting them against the omitted covariate. A linear relationship would be indicative that the covariate has an appropriate functional form. Visual inspection of these plots for both models indicates that linearity is not noticeably absent in any of them.

A third type of residual, the Cox-Snell residual, is used to assess the overall goodness of fit of the model.[19] If the model fits the data, these residuals will have an exponential distribution whose hazard rate is 1; systematic deviations from this value may indicate an inappropriate functional form or the omission of an important covariate (Box-Steffensmeier and Jones 2002, pp. 120–5). Visual inspection of the residual plots based on Models 2 and 4 indicates that this condition is well satisfied.

Another diagnostic test consists of determining whether the estimated covariate effects are driven by certain influential cases. This possibility can be evaluated by constructing a matrix, known as an 'influence matrix', whose elements indicate how much each case influences the value of each parameter in the model in standard deviation terms. An examination of these estimates based on Model 2 reveals 15 cases that have an effect on any parameter of at least 0.2 standard deviations. Certain cases are thus quite influential, but the key issue is whether they distort the overall picture. Estimating the model without these cases shows that their overall effect is negligible: all covariates show effects that remain correctly signed, highly significant, and of approximately the same magnitude as in the full model. The same holds true when Model 4 is re-estimated without its influential cases.

Earlier, I noted that the analysis needs to ascertain whether new and repeat governments need to be distinguished and, if so, how this should be done. The intuition is that the political capital of repeat governments may already been partly used up by their predecessors (except where it has been renewed in an intervening election). We saw some indication that this might be a relevant consideration in Figure 7.1, although the differences in survivor functions did not prove to be especially significant. Another contraindication is provided by the analysis of the roles played by the Martin–Stevenson variables (Table 7.3); one of the variables that did not show a significant net effect is 'repeat government'. This negative finding is also supported if this dichotomous indicator is replaced by a variable that records the length of time in which the government was preceded by governments with the same party composition; in neither model does it play a significant role.

These findings assume that the hazard has the same shape for new and repeat governments. An indication of whether this assumption should be relaxed can be garnered by re-examining the survivor functions for new, first repeat, and subsequent repeat governments after adjustments have been made for the six covariates of the survival model. Figure 7.2, which plots these functions with adjustments for the covariates in Model 2, makes it very clear that these adjustments eliminate all traces of the differentiation between these types of government

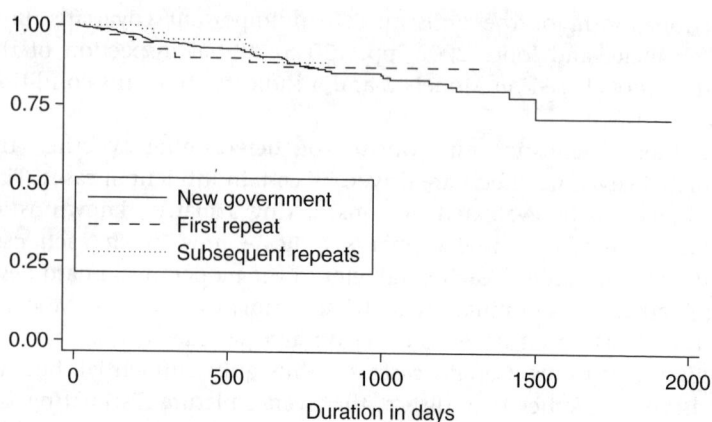

Figure 7.2   Kaplan-Meier survival estimates, adjusted for covariates, by repeat status. *Note*: These estimates are adjusted for covariates in Model 2 of Table 7.3.

that were evident in Figure 7.1 (the same holds for Model 4). In other words, once differences in covariate values are taken into account, repeat governments do not distinguish themselves from new governments in their survival prospects. All of the evidence thus points to the conclusion that differences between new and repeat governments do not need to be taken into account in any way.

The censoring scheme also deserves some scrutiny. As noted earlier, the decision to censor all electoral terminations rests in part on the assumption that early elections are invariably due to opportunism on the part of one or more coalition partners. It may be, however, that they are the result instead of deadlocked political configurations, which would imply that they should be treated as real collapses (i.e. not censored). To test this possibility, a new censoring scheme was created that leaves uncensored all terminations that were the result of political circumstances, regardless of whether they were followed by a new government or a premature election.[20] Re-estimating the models based on this censoring scheme produces the results shown in Table 7.4. The estimated coefficients are somewhat altered, as one would expect, but the basic pattern of the results remains intact. Other censoring schemes might yield different conclusions, to be sure, but at least these two schemes produce highly consistent results.

Finally, there is the issue of the frailty term. The assumption that the frailty is gamma-distributed is fairly standard in the literature, but it may not be entirely appropriate. *Stata: Release 8* (StataCorp 2003) does

Table 7.4 Government survival with all non-political terminations censored

	Model 1 (Logit horizons)	Model 2 (MJD horizons)
Majority status	−0.73** (0.23)	−0.70** (0.23)
Post-election status	−0.56** (0.18)	−0.58** (0.18)
Returnability	3.27** (0.93)	3.46** (0.89)
Minimal winning status	−1.07** (0.26)	−1.12** (0.25)
Relative predicted value	−2.93** (0.67)	−2.70** (0.77)
Relative predicted value × majority status	2.65** (1.02)	3.77** (1.18)
Frailty variance	0.17**	0.18**
Log-likelihood	−723.8	−725.4
N	264	264

Note: Coefficients are estimated from Cox partial likelihood models (standard errors in parentheses). Predicted values are from formation models that use MJD horizons.
** Significant at .01 level in one-tailed test.

not allow any other specification in Cox models, but in fully parametric models, there is the option of specifying a negative Gaussian distribution. We can therefore assess the suitability of the gamma specification that we have been using by re-estimating the models using a fully parametric specification and both gamma and negative Gaussian frailty distributions.

The parametric model that will be used is the Weibull model, which allows the baseline hazard to display monotonic duration dependency (i.e. it may either rise or decline with duration time, but not change direction). The issue of the nature of the underlying duration dependency ought not to be a significant factor for terminations that end in replacements; as noted earlier, the Lupia–Strøm (1995) model anticipates no duration dependency in these situations and Diermeier and Stevenson (1999) found that this was indeed the case. This also turns out to be the case here regardless of which frailty distribution and which horizon measurement method (logit or MJD) is used.[21] In fact, the covariate effects using a Weibull specification turn out to be virtually identical to those produced with the semi-parametric Cox model, indicating that no harm was done in performing the basic analysis with the latter. More to the point, it turns out not to matter at all whether a gamma or a negative Gaussian frailty specification is specified; the results remain essentially identical in both models.

Government survival in the survey data

Let us now examine whether and in what manner policy horizons, as estimated by the expert respondents to the surveys, influence government survival. We saw in Chapter 5 that this set of estimated horizons appears to structure government formation to a significant degree, but that the relationship is weakened by the presence of anomalous non-intersections involving Christian Democratic or Centre/Agrarian parties and their coalition partners. The remedy proposed there was to impute new horizon intersection rates for these cases. Although this remedy did not completely resolve the problem, the use of these imputed values nevertheless led to a large increase in the estimated impact of that variable on government formation. The five imputed data sets were also used to examine the role of auxiliary factors in Chapter 6. We shall continue to use these data sets in the present investigation, but because multiple imputation is not implemented for survival analysis in *Stata*, the procedure will be different: instead of estimating models in each of five data sets and combining the results, the five data sets will be combined first to produce a single data set for estimation purposes.[22]

The resulting survival data set covers some 272 governments, of which 252 have valid data for the returnability variable.[23] If the findings of the previous section are valid, one would expect this data set to yield similar patterns of causal influence. The first sign of continuity appears when my earlier model (Warwick 1994) is re-tested. In this instance, the three ideological diversity variables of the original model have been replaced by the government's salience-weighted policy distance in three dimensions. As Model 1 of Table 7.5 shows, this variable plus the other three (investiture is left out because of the shared country frailty) show significant effects in the expected direction at the .05 level (one-tailed tests).

The policy distance effect is not particularly strong in Model 1 and it is no surprise that adding minimal winning status to the model results in its elimination as a significant influence on government survival. This result is shown in Model 2. Unlike the earlier finding, however, replacing policy distance with the relative government diversity fails to restore a significant role for ideological diversity, either by itself or when supplemented by its interaction with majority status (Model 3). Nevertheless, significant causal roles do appear for relative predicted value and its interaction with majority status (albeit only at $p = .084$), as shown in Model 4. If these variables are based on relative intersection predicted values (i.e. predicted values based solely on intersection

Table 7.5 Government survival in the survey-based data set

	Model 1	Model 2	Model 3	Model 4	Model 5
Majority status	-0.92** (0.28)	-0.57* (0.32)	-0.53* (0.29)	-0.62** (0.27)	-0.35† (0.26)
Post-election status	-0.68** (0.20)	-0.63** (0.20)	-0.64** (0.20)	-0.64** (0.20)	-0.65* (0.20)
Returnability	4.01** (1.14)	4.04** (1.10)	4.07** (1.14)	4.05** (1.13)	4.21** (1.16)
Policy distance	0.07* (0.04)	0.05 (0.04)	–	–	–
Minimal winning status	–	-0.65** (0.28)	-0.70** (0.27)	-0.73** (.27)	-0.67** (0.27)
Relative government diversity	–	–	0.04 (0.04)	–	–
Relative government diversity × majority status	–	–	-0.01 (0.06)	–	–
Relative predicted value	–	–	–	-3.01** (0.93)	–
Relative predicted value × majority status	–	–	–	2.10† (1.52)	–
Relative intersection predicted value	–	–	–	–	-8.67** (3.22)
Relative intersection predicted value × majority status	–	–	–	–	8.17** (3.57)
Frailty variance	0.28**	0.23**	0.28**	0.26**	0.29**
Log-likelihood	-598.2	-595.3	-595.2	-590.2	-592.2
N	252	252	252	252	252

Note: Coefficients are estimated from Cox partial likelihood models (standard errors in parentheses).
† Significant at .10 level in one-tailed test.
* Significant at .05 level in one-tailed test.
** Significant at .01 level in one-tailed test.

expected values), however, much stronger and more significant effects emerge (Model 5). Moreover, both Model 4 and Model 5 survive well the battery of diagnostic tests described earlier.[24] The analysis of the survey data thus points to the same conclusion as before, namely that minority governments whose formation predicted values compare unfavourably with those of alternative majority proto-coalitions (excluding those containing the government formateur) have significantly reduced life expectancies.

Discussion

The analysis of government survival is inherently challenging because of the potential for selection bias inherent in the fact that the durations of only a small proportion of possible governments are ever observed. This consideration provides ample reason for anticipating that the effects of the intersection expected value have been under-estimated in the analyses undertaken in this chapter. It would therefore be risky to conclude from the results presented here that the formation traits encapsulated in the relative predicted value variables are irrelevant to the survival of majority governments.

Another reason why the role of horizon intersection in government survival may not be apparent in the survival analyses is that most majority governments face no competitors whose predicted values exceed theirs. In fact, excluding alternatives containing the government formateur, this condition holds for 71.7 per cent of majority governments when logit horizons are employed to generate the predicted values, 57.2 per cent when MJD horizons are used, and 50.0 per cent when survey horizons are used.[25] I noted earlier that the survival records of these governments might reflect intersection sizes if some of those sizes are small enough to constrain policy manoeuvrability in a significant way. But this may seldom be the case. If the survival of these governments appears to depend on other factors, or to be somewhat random, it may be because most of them are not vulnerable in this domain.

But what of minority governments? Like majority governments, they are usually formed by proto-coalitions with unsurpassed predicted values. In fact, regardless of whether horizons are measured by the logit, MJD, or survey methods (with imputations for anomalous non-intersections), about two-thirds of minority governments do not face a majority alternative that has a predicted value that is at least as great as theirs. But unlike majority governments, the present analysis indicates that the availability of viable majority alternatives powerfully reduces their survival prospects. We can only speculate as to why this is the case. Large intersection sizes may matter more for minority governments because they depend on external parliamentary support and require greater flexibility in order to maintain it. When difficulties emerge for a minority government, attention may shift to potential majority alternatives much more readily than would be the case if the government itself were majoritarian. The evidence of this chapter suggests that if the minority government has a substantial advantage over its majority rivals to begin with, the minority government will probably not be threatened, but if that advantage is less pronounced or non-existent, its days may well be numbered.

8
Conclusion

In order to understand parliamentary politics, one must be able to understand the motivations of parties. The early literature on coalition government possessed the simple elegance of seeing parties as nothing more than office-seekers, willing to make any compromise to gain or increase their share of cabinet portfolios. This simplicity diminished, however, as policy-seeking increasingly assumed a major role in accounts of coalition behaviour. A further loss came with the proposal that a third type, vote-seeking, be added to the repertoire of party motivations (Strøm 1990a). Since vote-seekers may value future electoral prospects over current rewards, this category not only increases the possibilities but also adds a time dimension to the understanding of party behaviour.

From identifying the types, it is a straightforward step to see them as leading to 'independent and mutually conflicting forms of behaviour' (Strøm 1990a, pp. 570–1). This implies that trade-offs must be made, and clearly they are. It is difficult to imagine, for example, that there are many parties in West European parliamentary democracies that would be unwilling to make at least some policy concessions in order to gain a place in a coalition government. Strøm portrays the range of possible trade-offs by means of a triangle whose vertices are the three ideal-type behaviours; any point on or inside the triangle, that is any mix of types, represents some feasible behaviour in this framework. He then identifies various factors that influence the nature of the trade-off that parties adopt. For instance, office-seeking will be encouraged, he suggests, if elections are competitive and the electoral system accurately translates votes into legislative seats (or bargaining weights), while policy-seeking flourishes to the extent that party decision-making is decentralized, recruitment to leadership positions is 'impermeable' (i.e. confined to the party membership), and leaders are held accountable for their actions.

The policy horizon hypothesis may be understood as a departure from this framework: it is consistent with much of it, but it slices through certain key assumptions. Take the issue of policy-seeking behaviour. Strøm (1990a) identifies two reasons why parties might emphasize their fidelity to stated policy goals and perhaps reinforce that commitment with the devices of intraparty decentralization, impermeability, and accountability noted above. The first is Downs' (1957, pp. 103–9) suggestion that voters prefer parties that have stable policy goals and stick to them when in office because it reduces uncertainty over future outcomes. The second is that 'labour-intensive' parties, that is parties that rely heavily on the unpaid efforts of their activists, need some means of making credible policy commitments to those activists (Strøm 1990a, p. 576).[1] The non-simultaneous nature of both types of exchange clearly provides a strong incentive for parties to develop reputations for fidelity to stated commitments, even at some short-term cost in terms of offices or perhaps even of votes.

There are other reasons why a party might abide by its commitments; as noted in Chapter 2, there may be considerable advantage in establishing a 'brand label'. Parties may seek not merely to prove the credibility of their promises to the attentive party voter or activist, but also to package and sell a particular vision of political reality. To be convincing in this effort and achieve the kind of non-reflective brand loyalty that would lead supporters to stick to the party through thick and thin, party leaders must appear to act as if they believe in the vision they have promulgated. In many cases, of course, they actually do.

Where the policy horizon approach departs from Strøm's framework is in pushing these arguments somewhat further than it would allow. If there are powerful incentives for parties to establish and conform to particular political positions, then it may no longer make much sense to conceive of party behaviour in terms of a three-way trade-off among policy, office, and votes. While policy may be compromised to gain office, and office may be kept even at the costs of future votes, perhaps there are limits to how much trading can occur, at least when it involves policy. Perhaps policy is not totally fungible.

The concept of policy horizons translates this doubt into the notion that there is an absolute limit on the policy trade-offs that parties can undertake. By 'absolute', I do not mean that these limits or bounds can never be changed; if parties create something akin to brand loyalties in the minds of their supporters, they should be able to 're-position' that brand as the need arises. But in the normal course of events this can only happen gradually, since all of the objectives noted above – reducing voter uncertainty, maintaining activist commitment, fostering brand loyalty – might be undermined if a party were to move opportunistically to avail itself of cabinet posts or to scoop up new electoral support at the expense of prior commitments. Not only would the current supporters have no reason to trust the party, the targeted new ones would not, either.

Thus, in the short term, the existence of policy horizons implies relatively fixed limits on the trade-offs that parties can undertake. The available options for a party no longer include all of Strøm's triangle but only that portion of it that stretches from the policy vertex to some boundary in the triangle. This portion, moreover, must be relatively small since the explanatory capacity of the concept would be eviscerated if the boundary encompasses most or all of the area of the triangle. The horizon hypothesis becomes an significant consideration in parliamentary politics only if the policy options that horizons allow are fairly limited.

An important consequence of the policy horizon hypothesis is therefore to simplify the analysis of coalition behaviour in parliamentary systems. The range of options is no longer as great as it seemed; a good deal of what might have been possible is ruled out – essentially because of a constraint imposed from outside the parliamentary arena. In other words, bringing the interests of voters and activists into the picture helps to reduce the apparent complexity of the parliamentary bargaining arena by excluding many of its possible outcomes. If we no longer conceive of a legislature as a 'house without windows', we no longer need to see its operations as a free-for-all.

The virtue of simplification is not that it makes life easier for the student of parliamentary politics; after all, any reduction in complexity at a theoretical level may be offset by the empirical challenges of measuring horizons. Rather, the virtue is that, if horizons do structure behaviour in the way envisaged, it becomes a lot easier to understand how political leaders can make decisions concerning whether to join, oppose, tolerate, or quit governments. No longer are they assumed to perform elaborate utility calculations involving complex trade-offs of votes, policies, and offices for all potential governing coalitions in their parliamentary arena; instead, they apply a rough sense of how far they and other parties can move on policy in order to eliminate most possibilities at a stroke. For instance, it would not take a lot of time for conservatives to realize that a coalition with an extreme left party would not meet their policy requirements. As for the other possibilities, the horizon hypothesis does not tell us precisely how they proceed – intersection size appears to be a factor, but factors unrelated to the horizon approach may be involved as well – but it need not require elaborate calculations. If the horizon constraint has cleared out most of the options, the remaining decisions may follow relatively easily.

In a nutshell, then, the advantage of the policy horizon hypothesis lies with its capacity to simplify the tasks of government formation and survival in multiparty legislatures and thereby to bring them more in line with what we know about the limits of human rationality, while at the same time expanding the range of relevant considerations to include the external environment of voters and/or party activists. But these gains can only be realized if there really are relatively fixed limits on the capacity of parties to compromise on policy commitments. This study consists of a sustained effort to show that these limits exist, but no one effort can be conclusive – especially when it involves the search for so intangible a concept. It is therefore appropriate to conclude this study with a re-assessment of the strength of the evidence for the hypothesis, an examination of what we would need to know to flesh out the policy horizon framework more fully, and an evaluation of whether the effort to do so would be worthwhile.

What has been found

The fundamental paradox of this study is that the policy horizon hypothesis is so simple to state and yet so difficult to test. Effecting a valid test requires two new elements: computer software capable of handling the calculation of horizon intersections and related concepts, and some means of measuring the main raw ingredient, the horizons themselves. The second is by far the greater challenge, and three measurement strategies have been employed in this study to address it.

The first two strategies – the logit method and the MJD method – estimate party horizons from coalition behaviour. Their basic approach is to use the available data to derive some guess of where the horizon for each party, if it exists, is likely to be located and then to determine if those suppositions carry some net explanatory power. The operation is akin to likelihood estimation, in which the data are scanned to produce a best estimate of the effect of some covariate. Since this approach utilizes information on policy distances to estimate horizons, there is a risk that any horizon effect it yields could simply reflect the impact of distance on government formation. Experimentation with a simulated data set showed, however, that a horizon effect that is merely circumstantial – the result, say, of parties never joining governments located more than a certain distance away because more compact alternatives are always available – stands a very high chance of being revealed for what it is. In addition, the analysis of formations in West European systems in the post-War era revealed that horizon intersections and policy distance lack the close association that was induced in the simulated data, which facilitates even further the separation of the two effects.

Valid measurement need not mean accurate measurement, however. For the purposes of establishing the horizon hypothesis, the critical issue is not how accurately horizons are measured in some absolute sense, but how accurate they are relative to the measurement of policy distances. Since both distance and horizons are calculated from the same estimates of party positions, it is reasonable to conclude that the method of calculating positions used here – party scores from the first two principal components of the CMP data – does not favour one hypothesis over the other. But the two behaviour-based methods assume that horizons can be estimated from as few as five appearances in formation situations, that the horizons are circular, which implies equal dimension and directional saliences, and that they are fixed over the entire observation period, which spans up to half a century. None of these assumptions is especially compelling. The MJD method assumes, moreover, that the maximum joining distance displayed by each party is its horizon bound, while the logit method allows for occasional violations of the horizon principle, but at the cost of stipulating an arbitrary threshold (the distance at which the odds of joining the government reach 50 per cent).

Given these limitations, it is striking how well the horizon hypothesis fares in Chapter 3 against its natural foil, the policy distance hypothesis. This conclusion becomes especially compelling when allowance is made for error in the measurement of horizon bounds, and perhaps some degree of fuzziness in their actual location, through the use of simulations. The horizon effect also fares impressively well when a substantial array of other factors is also taken into account. It appears that the designation of bounds on the extent to which each party can compromise for the purposes of joining governments, based both on its record of coalition behaviour and the assumption that governments implement the weighted mean position of their member-parties, goes some considerable distance to accounting for what actually occurred in these situations.

The discovery of a pattern in the data that is consistent with the existence of horizons is an important step, but it is still valuable to establish a link to the putative cause, the need to satisfy the policy expectations of voters and activists. There is no easy measurement strategy here. The one adopted in this study consists of eliciting estimates of the limits of compromise for the parties of each country from academics who are knowledgeable about the country's politics. This is a high risk strategy: it asks volunteers to donate considerable time and effort to provide estimates for parties on a trait most have never heard of before, without reference to its most obvious indicator, the parties' actual records of compromise.

Cast in this light, it is surprising that anyone responded, yet respond they did – not in great numbers, but in enough to proceed with a test of the hypothesis. It is perhaps also surprising that the horizon effect again revealed itself from the information they provided. Granted, the effect was a good deal weaker than that previously demonstrated, but this turned out to be traceable in large measure to certain specific situations. These situations involved a failure of the estimated horizons of some Christian Democratic and Agrarian/Centre parties to intersect with those of certain other parties with which they frequently formed coalition governments. This in itself might indicate that some of these parties felt free to violate their horizons at will, but apart from raising the question of what a horizon might mean in this circumstance, this interpretation runs afoul of evidence, from both this survey and another expert survey, which suggests that the compromise bounds for the coalition partners in question were drawn too tightly by our respondents.

The remedy adopted here was neither to assume that the relevant horizons must intersect, nor to discard the cases as hopelessly contaminated with measurement error. Either alternative would greatly strengthen the horizon effect, as would replacing all the survey estimates of horizons with behaviour-based estimates. Instead, the remedy was to treat the anomalous non-intersections as missing data and impute new values for the intersection variables. This goes some distance towards correcting the problem, but it still leaves many of the suspicious non-intersections with very low intersection rates. Nevertheless, the amount of change is sufficient to produce a very sizeable increase in the magnitude of the horizon effect. Provided one is willing to believe that our survey respondents collectively missed the mark on the two types of situation noted above, the survey data also yield compelling evidence for the horizon hypothesis.

The remainder of the study was concerned with fleshing out the role of horizons by exploring some other implications of the hypothesis and by examining the role of horizons in government survival. In the former category, the principal finding is that the intersection expected value, which combines the intersection rate with its mean size, is a more important explanatory factor than is the rate itself. As one might expect, the effect of this variable is subject to diminishing returns: marginal increases become less important as the expected value gets larger. It is also necessary to adjust for minority proto-coalitions and especially for single-party proto-coalitions, since the failure to take account of the external support on which they rely means that their true expected values, that is the expected values under which they would actually have to operate, are very likely to be smaller than their measured values. All three formation data sets – those based on logit and MJD horizons (calculated from the manifesto data) and that based on survey data (with imputed values) – yield consistent results in this regard, and those results stand the test of introducing a host of other potential influences on government formation.

The analysis of government survival differs from that of formation because we can directly include only those proto-coalitions that formed governments, a small subset of all possible proto-coalitions. Given that governments are under risk of replacement at almost any time, it clearly would make a lot of sense to consider not just the government itself, but also what stands in the wings. Fortunately, information on these other possibilities may be introduced indirectly by utilizing variables that measure the government's traits relative to those of other proto-coalitions. The alternatives considered here encompass all proto-coalitions that do not contain the government formateur, and what we find is that half or more of governments have predicted values, based on the six-variable formation model, that match or exceed those of all such alternatives.

Does this mean that those governments with relatively high predicted values survive longer than those with lower relative scores? If we look only at majority governments, this is not the case. The effect of relative predicted values may be under-estimated because of selection bias, but as far as we can tell now, having a higher value does not seem to lead to greater longevity in office. Presumably, the other factors that caused proto-coalitions with lower relative predicted values to succeed in forming governments continue to favour them while they are in office, but it would require some adequate statistical means of adjusting for this possibility to establish whether the relative predicted values convey some net impact.

An impact for this variable does appear, however, for minority governments. Why this is the case cannot be answered with any confidence at the present time. It may simply be that their more precarious state makes comparisons with majority alternatives especially relevant, but a more adequate understanding of these matters will probably require the ability to take account of support parties in measuring intersection sizes as well as some means of handling selection bias when the selection model is a conditional logit. What we can say is that the existence and size of a horizon intersection seems to be strongly related to the odds that a proto-coalition will emerge as the government and, at least in the case of minority governments, the extent to which the government is advantaged in these respects over its competitors significantly influences its survival prospects as well. Apart from the full effect of horizons on survival, however, there remains much to be learned about horizons and their impact on parliamentary governance. In the next section, we examine some of these gaps.

What we do not know

The purpose of this study has been to determine if credible evidence can be found for the proposition that the behaviour of parties in parliamentary systems is constrained by policy horizons. The data analysis undertaken here has uncovered such evidence, but there are limits on how much more it can tell us. Consider, for example, the formation of minority governments, a fairly frequent occurrence in West European parliamentary systems. Although a minority government is very likely to be formed when the choice set does not contain any majority intersections, most of these governments are formed despite the existence of at least one such intersection. At first glance, this seems puzzling from a policy horizon standpoint, but it turns out that the minority proto-coalitions that form governments are almost always subsets of majority intersections, which means that they can govern on the basis of policy positions that fit the horizon constraints of a legislative majority.

If we could take it that minority governments can only be formed under this circumstance, it would provide a clear direction as to how to incorporate the horizon concept into a larger model or theory of government formation. But we cannot. The problem is that the vast majority of all minority proto-coalitions that have intersecting horizons are also subsets of majority intersections – regardless of whether they assumed office. Thus, we cannot tell if being a SMI is a necessary condition for forming a minority government, or if it is merely circumstantial to that outcome.

The uncertainty that this creates can be illustrated by referring again to Figure 6.1. Recall that there are two majority intersections {ABC} and {CDE} and that party C, the common element in both, is in a position to choose between them. But C need not choose to form a majority government at all; it could govern with the external support of A and/ or B or with the external support of D and/or E. Now, alter the scenario slightly by shifting E's position so that its horizon no longer intersects the horizons of parties D and C. This would eliminate the {CDE} option and thereby put A and B in a position to insist on a place in government – but only if parties are limited to supporting governments that implement policies within their horizons. If parties were free to lend external support whenever it would lower their own policy costs, then all options save a {CDE} majority government remain open.

This notion that external support is unbounded may seem inconsistent with the concept of policy horizons, but there is no inconsistency in supposing that parties can offer support to governments located at least some distance beyond their horizons. In other words, it is perfectly plausible that parties have 'support horizons' that encompass more, perhaps much more, of the ideological space than do their policy horizons. This too would tend to expand the range of possible outcomes, although not as much as would a total lack of limits on external support. The present data analysis is mute on this issue, but a careful investigation of the sources of support for minority governments may yield consistent evidence on how far it can be extended.

A second area of uncertainty concerns the impact of policy distance on government formation. Since horizon intersection rates tend to decline with policy distance (other things being equal), one would expect that the emergence of a sizeable intersection effect would be accompanied by a weakening of the role played by policy distance, which is indeed the case. But policy distance should still have a part to play. There is nothing in the horizon hypothesis that prevents parties from seeking to minimize policy costs within the horizon constraint. In addition, the fact that horizons are inherently more difficult to locate than party positions should help the policy distance hypothesis. Any estimation bias due to measurement error ought to favour distance over horizons.

Despite its theoretical plausibility and its measurement advantages, the three formation data sets used in this study do not provide credible evidence for a distance effect operating within the horizon constraint.

It also disappears in the survival analyses, even in its relative form.[2] Yet, a conclusion that parties are indifferent to policy costs, provided policy outcomes fall within their horizons, may not be warranted. Consider once more the hypothetical five-party scenario depicted in Figure 6.1. If we confine the choice to majority outcomes, there are just two possibilities that fit the horizon hypothesis: an {ABC} government or a {CDE} government. The former alternative represents a much better choice for C, since the government's policy stance would have to be located very close to, if not at, its own ideal point. But it would span a much greater policy distance than would an {CDE} coalition. Thus, although A, B, and C would all be minimizing their policy costs by forming {ABC}, the end result would be the emergence of a relatively diverse government.

This example shows that the formation of relatively policy-compact governments is not an inevitable consequence of policy-seeking behaviour by political parties. Nor would a preference for large intersection sizes inevitably lead to the formation of governments with this property; in Figure 6.1, it is evident that not only does C's preferred coalition, {ABC}, have a relatively large policy distance, but it also has a relatively small intersection size. As noted in Chapter 6, C might still be willing to form {ABC} in order to get the maximum policy benefit because it knows that, if circumstances arise that cannot be adequately addressed within the scope of its small intersection, there remains the option of forming a government with D and E. It follows that the formation of governments that have relatively high policy distance and/or relatively small intersection sizes is perfectly compatible with the notion that parties seek to minimize policy costs and maximize manoeuvrability in government.

Thus, the data analysis undertaken here, because it does not capture the exact process by which governments are formed, cannot provide foolproof evidence of which factors are involved and in which ways. This is especially evident in the case of minority governments. It is very difficult to estimate the effects of variables like policy distance and intersection sizes for these governments because we do not know their true values: these depend in part on constraints that may be imposed by their external support parties. And which parties can act as external supporters depends on whether and how far support can extend beyond horizons.

These considerations imply that the ultimate determination of the causal role of policy distance and policy horizons in the formation (and survival) of governments will require the elaboration and testing of fully developed models. These models, ideally, would generate precise predictions of what ought to emerge in any given formation situation, and the relative accuracy of their predictions should resolve many of the uncertainties that this investigation has raised. But any such testing would only be effective if we are very sure that horizons have been measured accurately. How confident can we be in the measurement methods developed and utilized here?

A good indicator of a problem in measurement precision would be a lack of agreement across the three measurement methods. In Chapter 3, we saw that the logit and MJD methods agree very often on the existence of a horizon intersection, despite the fact that the MJD method generally produces larger horizon radii. Specifically, if intersection rates of 0.5 and above are taken as indicating the probable existence of an intersection and intersection rates below 0.5 as indicating its likely absence, then logit and MJD horizons reach the same verdict for 84.5 per cent of the proto-coalitions in the manifesto-based data set. But how consistent are estimates derived from coalition behaviour with estimates provided by expert respondents? The most effective way of addressing this question is to compare survey-based intersections with those produced when the logit method was applied to the same survey-based data set. The application of the logit method to these data takes no account of the horizon estimates themselves; the only survey information it utilizes is the respondents' estimates of party positions. Nevertheless, the rate of agreement, based on the same dichotomization of intersection rates, is 86.9 per cent. If we exclude the anomalous non-intersections, this rate rises to an even more impressive 90.7 per cent.[3]

The three measurement methods thus appear to be capable of producing reasonably consistent results. Nevertheless, they all share the limitation of producing just one horizon per party for the entire observation period. While the concept of policy horizons requires a substantial degree of fixedness, there is no reason why the degree of ideological rigidity to which parties adhere cannot evolve over half a century, just as the actual positions they espouse can change over the same period. Repeated survey efforts, of course, could capture such changes. Moreover, as familiarity with the concept of horizons increases among political scientists, it is likely that the appearance of anomalies such as those encountered in the survey administered for this study will diminish. Finally, survey estimates have the advantage of providing for the possibility of non-circular horizons, and they also yield parameter-specific estimates of measurement uncertainty. These observations suggest that, although the survey method has yielded the weakest results in the present investigation, there is every reason to expect that it could prove its superiority over the behaviour-based methods if carried forward on a regular basis.

A final lacuna in the present study is some means of tracing horizons to their sources. The expert survey asked respondents to estimate horizons on the basis of the extent to which party members and supporters are willing to tolerate compromise for the purpose of joining coalition governments, and tests reported in Chapter 4 indicate that they succeeded, at least to the extent of not letting the parties' coalition behaviour influence their judgements. But more precise information on the sources of horizons would certainly be desirable, and for this we may have to resort to different tools.

One such tool is population surveys. If horizons are consequences of the expectations of party voters, this should be detectable by means of suitably designed questions in population surveys. Indeed, it should be possible to find out not only whether respondents expect all parties, or at least the parties they support, to respect policy commitments, but also how closely they expect these commitments to be respected; in other words, to gain some idea of the constraints parties face relative to one another. To implement this strategy, all that would be required is the addition of a small number of relevant questions to regular survey efforts such as the Eurobarometer series. While this approach would provide valuable corroborating information, however, one should not expect it to yield precise estimates of horizons. It is leaders who ultimately make coalition choices and, as noted earlier, they cannot be expected to have precise knowledge of voter expectations or to perform complex calculations to derive optimal locations for their horizons from that information.

It seems more likely that leaders locate their compromise limits at any one time from their own informal impressions of what their voters or activists expect. If so, the horizons they come up with may not accurately reflect these expectations. Leaders may tend, for example, to exaggerate the level of voter or activist attention to, or concern about, their coalition decisions, and thus to over-estimate the potential for dissension or alienation on the part of these groups. This suggests that the best way of tracing horizons to their sources might be to interview the leaders themselves; the problem here is that, even if enough leaders were willing to be interviewed, the incentive they have to exaggerate their obligation to respect party commitments would render their responses suspect. In these circumstances, the optimal tool for understanding the sources of horizons and measuring their sizes would probably be surveys of party elites, which would provide the anonymity and sample size to foster candidness. Unlike population surveys, there is no regular series of party elite surveys, but they have been conducted on a cross-national basis in the past and might profitably be revived for this and other purposes in the future.

Is it worth it?

The preceding discussion indicates that the further investigation of the policy horizon framework would benefit considerably from a fairly regular series of party elite surveys, with perhaps the inclusion of relevant questions in existing series of population surveys, such as the Eurobarometer series. At the very least, it would call for a continuing series of expert surveys, whose value as a measurement instrument would presumably increase with usage. On the theoretical side, it would require the elaboration of models based on the horizon hypothesis – perhaps several models to encompass the various uncertainties surrounding the approach, such as the different ways in which external support may manifest itself. The third key ingredient, the computing software, has already been created, but it may require changes. For instance, if evidence is produced that external support has its own bounds, *Horizons 3D$^{©}$* would have to be able to calculate intersections and intersection sizes for minority proto-coalitions based on the combination of both policy and support horizons.

These are fairly significant undertakings and they naturally raise the question of whether the effort involved would be worthwhile. In large measure, this depends on the degree to which the evidence presented here is persuasive. But 'persuasive' need not mean 'convincing'. One does not have to believe that policy horizons constrain coalition behaviour to undertake further investigations; one simply has to believe that it has some reasonable possibility of being true. Substantial plausibility based on systematic evidence should be the test, and I would argue that the present investigation has established at least that level of credibility.

This may seem a rather low standard to meet, but it has not always been respected in the investigation of parliamentary governance. Granted, the assumptions about what parties want are usually quite plausible; these often consist of nothing more than the most beneficial combination of office benefits and policy costs (with perhaps some consideration of the trade-off between the present and the future).

It is very difficult not to believe that most parties in parliamentary systems seek these things. Indeed, some might argue that the assumption of policy distance minimization is a good deal more plausible than the assumption that policy calculations are subject to bounds. Bounds imply a rigidity to decision-making that may seem at odds with human nature.

Where plausibility suffers is in the consequences of the assumptions. Researchers who adopt simple assumptions often end up with complex models. Some models require politicians to have not only full and exact information on key parameters such as the preferences of their voters, but also sophisticated knowledge of game theory and calculus in order to determine their optimal strategies. There may be relatively straight-forward rules of thumb that would allow them to arrive consistently at the correct decisions without doing the computations, but it never seems to be a priority to indicate what these rules might be. Without some such indication, it can become virtually impossible to believe that the model in question describes actual behaviour.

The policy horizon approach takes the opposite approach: by stipulating greater limits on what can be done by parties, it rules out the vast bulk of possible outcomes. In fact, based on the dichotomization of intersection rates described above, the logit horizons calculated from the manifesto data eliminate four-fifths of all proto-coalitions and the MJD horizons eliminate two-thirds; the survey horizons rule out about four-fifths if all cases are included, three-quarters if the anomalous non-intersections are removed.[4] As noted earlier, it is also a lot easier to imagine how leaders would identify which possibilities can be eliminated. Many of them would be automatic. Less obvious judgements would emerge through prior experience in coalition negotiations, leaving few, if any, cases where two parties are genuinely uncertain about whether they share any common policy ground.

Among the parties with which they do share common ground, it is not difficult to imagine that a reasonably accurate sense of how large that common ground is would also emerge over time. Much of this information would be subject to regular updating through informal day-to-day interactions, but periods of coalition formation would certainly be occasions when more precise information would become available. Through these processes, parties would come to possess a good sense of how to rank order their coalition possibilities in terms of the size of their intersections and, to the extent that intersection size matters, this information would provide further guidance in making coalition decisions.

It should be clear from these remarks that the ontological position I defend is far removed from the 'as if' view famously advanced by Milton Friedman (1953). That is, I maintain that the ultimate goal of the study of parliamentary government is to understand how outcomes are actually produced; a model that does not describe behaviour correctly is of little value, regardless of the accuracy of its predictions. This provides an important rationale for taking the policy horizon hypothesis seriously: although it may have seemed at first glance a mere footnote to the idea that parties seek to minimize policy distance costs, the image it presents of the workings of the parliamentary arena diverges markedly from any previously advanced conception. If policy horizons exist and are reasonably constraining, coalition behaviour becomes much more focussed on maintaining external support and less concerned with seizing immediate opportunities; party leaders become much less like calculating machines, much more like the limited human beings we all know they are. The policy horizon hypothesis points to an understanding of the working of parliamentary government that is thus novel as well as plausible, and it deserves further investigation on both counts.

Appendix 1: The *Horizons 3D*© Program

This appendix contains instructions for installing and operating *Horizons 3D*©, the computer program that was used to perform all of the calculations involving policy horizons and their intersections for this study. *Horizons 3D*© can operate under Windows 98, 2000, or XP, or MacIntosh OS 10 operating systems. It is a stand-alone Java program that runs on the desktop, rather than in a browser window, and it utilizes the standard toolbar format with a choice of drop-down menus or buttons for inputting data and executing calculations and simulations.

1. Installing *Horizons 3D*©

Horizon 3D© requires the prior installation of the Java 2 Platform. The relevant version is Java Standard Edition, version 1.4.1_05. (More recent versions will almost certainly work, but this cannot be guaranteed.) This version is available for download at no charge from the following website: http://java.sun.com/products/archive/j2se/1.4.1_05/index. html. The Java site also provides instructions for installing it.

The *Horizons 3D*© program is contained in a compressed file, *Horizons.xxxx.zip* ('*xxxx*' gives the date the version was uploaded), which is available free of charge at the following website: http://www.sfu.ca/~warwick/. Its installation consists simply of placing it in a folder of the user's choice and uncompressing it (by double-clicking on the file name and following the instructions).

Uncompressing the file yields several files, including *Horizons.jar*, the main application file, and three versions of the graphical component of the programme, *ViewHorizons.exe*, *ViewHorizons.ogl.exe*, and *ViewHorizons.app*. The first is based on the DirectX application programming interface (API), which is the default version for Windows systems. An alternative is OpenGL, which Linux systems (and others) use. If no image appears after the data for at least one party has been entered, the OpenGL version may be required. To implement this version, delete the default version and change the file name of the 'ogl' version to *viewHorizons.exe*. Two other files that appear are *Msvcp70.dll* and *Msvcr70.dll*, which are libraries required for operating V*iewHorizons.exe* in a Windows environment. They may be left where they are or placed in the Windows/System folder.

For MacIntosh users, the appropriate graphics file is V*iewHorizons.app*. No other files are required for its operation.

2.   Launching *Horizons 3D*©

For Windows users, *Horizons 3D*© is launched by double-clicking on the *Horizons.jar* file in the Windows Explorer or by creating a desktop short-cut to this file and double-clicking on it. An alternative is to execute the following steps:

1. Select Run from the Windows Start menu.
2. Type cmd and click OK.
3. Navigate to the folder that contains *Horizons.jar*.
4. Type java –jar –Xmx96m Horizons.jar and hit Enter.

This second method is recommended when the objective is to perform simulations on legislatures with large numbers of parties, since it provides a means of expanding the amount of memory the programme uses. The available memory can be increased by replacing the '96' in the last command line with some larger specification, such as 256, 512, or 1024.

When *Horizons* is launched, three additional files are created in the folder where *Horizons.jar* and *ViewHorizons.exe* reside: *windowConfig.txt*, *config.txt*, and *log.txt*. The first two store information on the position and sizing of the various windows displayed by the programme. Any *Horizons* window can be moved by dragging and dropping its top panel and reshaped by pulling on its borders; the configuration created in this fashion is saved in these files so that it will appear the next time *Horizons 3D*© is launched. The third file, *logfile.txt*, contains the error message when *ViewHorizons* is unable to interpret and display the horizon data. This type of problem is also indicated by a failure of the *ViewHorizons* window to open. This typically occurs because some user-supplied parameters are internally inconsistent, for example a party's position does not fall within its horizon bounds on at least one dimension, or a horizon with a negative or zero radius has been specified. Correcting the erroneous parameter(s) will solve the problem.

3.   Inputting data

When *Horizons 3D*© is launched, the Horizons task-bar will appear. Two functions on the taskbar control the entry of data: 'Legislature' and 'Party'. These functions may be invoked by clicking on the word in the taskbar or by clicking the appropriate taskbar button (passing the cursor over the buttons will reveal their functions).

3.1.   Legislature properties

Data entry begins with the 'Legislature Properties' dialogue box, which appears when 'New' is selected from the legislature menu or the 'New Legislature' button is clicked. *Horizons 3D*© deals with legislatures one at a time and the identity of the particular legislature that is to be analysed is indicated here. The number of seats in the legislature and the number of ideological or policy dimensions for which data are available are also specified in this dialogue box. The dimensions are labelled x, y, and z, and the user can specify either two or three of them by clicking on the appropriate boxes. When displayed in *ViewHorizons*, the first dimension identified (which will normally be the *x* dimension) will be located horizontally, the second dimension will be located vertically, and the third dimension, if there is one, will appear as the 'forward–backward' direction.

The legislature data can be changed at any time by selecting 'Edit' from the Legislature menu. Normally, this will be a rare occurrence, but a useful exception occurs when data for three dimensions have been entered but the user wishes to confine the analysis, at least for the time being, to just two dimensions – without losing the data for the dimension to be excluded. This can be achieved by unchecking one of the Dimensions in the dialogue box, which will cause the data for the excluded dimension to be set to default values and greyed out in the Party dialogue boxes. The original data can be restored at any time simply by re-checking the dimension in the Legislative Properties dialogue box.

This flexibility will be compromised, however, if any of the 'Party' dialogue boxes has been opened in the interim. In this circumstance, the data for the excluded dimension can still be recovered, but only by closing the file without saving it and then re-opening it. If the purpose of opening a dialogue box was to make changes to the data, closing the file without saving it will cause these changes to be lost. Thus, if any party data are to be changed in any way, the user should ensure that all dimensions for which data are available are checked in the Legislative Properties dialogue box first.

3.2. Party properties

The next step is to enter information for each party in the legislature, using the 'Add Party' item on the Party menu or by clicking the 'Add Party' button. The information for each party consists of a party description, a specification of its ideal point or position, and a specification of the nature and positioning of its policy horizon. *Horizons 3D*© can accept a maximum of twelve parties per legislature.

3.2.1. The party description

The first two pieces of party information are its name and a short version of the name (which could be a number) that will be used to identify the composition of the various possible coalitions or 'proto-coalitions' in the legislature. The additional descriptive information consists of the number of seats held by the party and, optionally, an indication of whether the party is the 'First Formateur', that is the first party chosen to form a government in the current formation situation. The rationale for this specification is that providing a party with the initial opportunity to form a government may confer on any proto-coalition in which it participates a greater likelihood of emerging as the government. A first formateur is indicated by clicking on the relevant box.

3.2.2. The ideal point specification

The next subsection of the 'Party' menu is the ideal point or policy position specification. This consists of up to three types of information. The first is simply the party's location on each of the policy dimensions (again labelled *x*, *y*, and *z*). This is the only required information.

A measure of the salience or importance the party attaches to each dimension may also be provided. The default is '1'. Values other than this indicate the proportional extent to which the party deviates from this value; thus, a salience of '2' would indicate that the party attaches twice the salience to the dimension in question; '0.5' would indicate that it attaches only half (50 per cent). These values are used to calculate salience-weighted policy distances for each proto-coalition.

The final type of position information concerns the error in locating the party's ideal point. The purpose of this error specification is to allow each party's position to be altered in simulations according to the specific level of uncertainty associated with it. The default error specification is 0, which is appropriate if no parameter-specific estimates of measurement uncertainty are available. (Uncertainty may still be captured in simulations by means of a 'global' error specification, as discussed below.)

Party-specific information on uncertainty will normally be available when the position estimate is the mean of several separate estimates, for example the mean of several survey responses. In this case, the uncertainty associated with these responses can be represented by the standard error of the mean, and this value can be entered as the parameter's error. Specifying the nature of the error distribution as 'normal' will cause an error term to be drawn from a normal distribution with a standard deviation equal to this value and added to the party's position parameter in each iteration. If the number of respondents is small, a t-distribution can be specified instead, in which case the degrees of freedom (one less than the number of respondents) would also be specified. It is also possible to specify a uniform distribution. In this case, the error to be entered consists of the range of the distribution. For instance, a range of 0.5 would indicate that error terms are to be drawn from a uniform distribution ranging from 0.5 units below the party position to 0.5 units above it.

3.2.3   The horizon specification

The right-hand side of the Party menu is devoted to the specification of the party's policy horizon. The horizon may be a sphere, an ellipsoid, or it may take on an irregular, user-defined shape. In addition, each of the parameters that define the horizon may have associated with it an error specification for use in simulations. As before, the error distribution may be normal, t (which requires the additional specification of the degrees of freedom), or uniform.

The first and simplest type of horizon is a sphere. If only two dimensions have been specified, this automatically reduces to a circle. The key defining information for a horizon of this type consists of a radius or distance from the party's ideal point to the horizon. This distance must be greater than zero.

A more complicated horizon specification is an ellipsoid (which becomes an ellipse in two dimensions). This format allows the breadth of the horizon to vary across dimensions and it requires a separate radius (greater than zero) to be specified for each dimension.

The final option is a 'user-defined' horizon, which allows for a wide variety of irregular shapes. Here, the user inputs the positions of the horizon bounds on each dimension in either absolute terms or relative to the position of the party's ideal point. For instance, if a party's compromise limits on a given dimension extend 1.5 units above its ideal point of '5' and 2 units below, this information can be entered in relative terms by giving its upper and lower limits as '1.5' and '2' or in absolute terms by giving them as '6.5' and '3'. The default is relative bounds; absolute bounds are specified by means of the 'Bounds' box. User-defined horizons are created by joining up the bounds specified by the user with a (nearly) smooth, concave surface, as discussed in Chapter 2.

Once the data for a party are entered, two more windows will appear. One is the 'Legend' that lists the parties, gives their colour codes, and provides instructions for manipulating the image; the second is the image itself. The default image is in solid colours with no shading; switching to the wire-frame view (by pressing 'w') allows the user to capture better the three-dimensional nature of the image (or simply to see the intersections more clearly). Visual inspection of the image and, in particular, the horizon intersections is also facilitated by rotating the image. Rotation in any of three directions is available (F1 to F6) and the speed of the rotation can be controlled (r/R toggle). It is also possible to move the image in any direction (page up, page down, left and right directional arrows) and to zoom in on or out from the image (up and down directional arrows). As noted earlier, the overall size of the display can be increased by pulling on the margins of the ViewHorizons window.

Party information can be changed, and parties can be added or removed, at any time. This is achieved by selecting the appropriate choice in the Party menu or by clicking on the appropriate toolbar buttons ('Add a Party', 'Edit a Party', or 'Remove a Party'). The only limitation is that a new party can be added, or an existing party increased in size, only if there are available seats in the legislature. In other words, a new party cannot be added to a 100-seat legislature that already has two 50-seat parties; either the size of the legislature would have to be increased or the size of one of the existing parties would have to be reduced first.

4. Performing calculations and simulations

4.1. Calculations

Once information on all parties in the legislature has been entered, calculations and simulations can be performed. Selecting 'Calculate' from the Calculations menu or simply clicking on the Calculations button launches the process. A progress indicator window appears and when the calculation is completed, the Results window is displayed automatically. If more than one procedure is run, the results of each will be displayed on a separate tab, numbered in the order they were produced. By default, the most recent calculation will appear on top.

During a calculation, the programme builds a list of all the possible coalitions that the parties in the current legislature can form. It then creates the following variables for all of these proto-coalitions. (Note that each dichotomous indicator variable is coded '1' if the proto-coalition has the trait and '0' otherwise.)

- *Coal.* – the current proto-coalition's name, composed of the short names of all the parties in the coalition separated by dashes (e.g. a-b-c-d or 3-4-5-6).
- *# P* – the total number of parties in the proto-coalition.
- *Size (%)* – the percentage of the total seats in the legislature held by the proto-coalition.
- *FF* – an indicator of whether the proto-coalition contains the first party chosen as formateur in the current formation situation.

- *Maj.* – an indicator of whether the proto-coalition contains a legislative majority.
- *MW* – an indicator of whether the proto-coalition is minimal winning.
- *Int.* – an indicator of whether the horizons of all parties in the proto-coalition intersect.
- *Int.Size* – the size (i.e. the area in two dimensions or the volume in three dimensions) of the proto-coalition's horizon intersection (it is coded '0' if all horizons do not intersect).
- *EWM* – an indicator of whether the intersection encompasses the proto-coalition's weighted mean (it is coded '0' if all horizons do not intersect).
- *SMI* – an indicator of whether the proto-coalition is a subset of a majority intersection (it is coded '0' if the proto-coalition is majoritarian).
- *CbD* – the maximum city-block distance between any two parties in the proto-coalition.
- *EuD* – the maximum Euclidean distance between any two parties in the proto-coalition.
- *AMCbD* – the assumed-majority city-block distance of the proto-coalition. This is the minimum city-block distance that would have to be spanned for the proto-coalition to command a legislative majority (it equals its actual city-block distance if the proto-coalition is majoritarian).
- *AMEuD* – the assumed-majority Euclidean distance of the proto-coalition. This is the minimum Euclidean distance that would have to be spanned for the proto-coalition to command a legislative majority (it equals its actual Euclidean distance if the proto-coalition is majoritarian).
- *SCbD* – the maximum salience-weighted city-block distance between any two parties in the proto-coalition.
- *SEuD* – the maximum salience-weighted Euclidean distance between any two parties in the proto-coalition.
- *SAMCbD* – the assumed-majority salience-weighted city-block distance of the proto-coalition. This is the minimum salience-weighted city-block distance that would have to be spanned for the proto-coalition to command a legislative majority (it equals its actual salience-weighted city-block distance if the proto-coalition is majoritarian).
- *SAMEuD* – the assumed-majority salience-weighted Euclidean distance of the proto-coalition. This is the minimum salience-weighted Euclidean distance that would have to be spanned for the proto-coalition to command a legislative majority (it equals its actual salience-weighted Euclidean distance if the proto-coalition is majoritarian).

4.2. Simulations

A simulation run differs from a calculation run in that the above calculations are performed more than once, with different values attributed to position and/or horizon parameters each time. A simulation run is specified by selecting 'Simulate' from the Calculations menu or by clicking on the simulations button in the taskbar. Three types of information must be provided to conduct a simulation run: the number of iterations or simulations to be performed, the type of error to be used in altering party ideal points, and the type of error to be used in altering party horizons.

The number of iterations refers to the number of times parameters are to be changed and calculations re-performed. For instance, specifying '500' would cause 500 calculation runs to be performed on the legislature. Before each of these calculations, the ideal points of the parties may be altered either according to the error specifications provided for them in the Party menu or according to some 'global' specification, or they may be left as they are. The same holds for the horizons. (Of course, if 'No error' is chosen for both the ideal point error specification and the horizon error specification, the simulation run will simply reproduce the results of a calculation run in each iteration).

If the 'predefined error' option is chosen, a random error term will be drawn from the error distribution specified for each parameter in the Party menu and will be added to that parameter to give it a new value; a calculation run will then be performed using this altered set of parameter values. This process will be repeated as many times as the number of iterations requested. The user has the option of changing the magnitude of these errors by specifying a 'multiplier' (the default is '1'). Thus, specifying a multiplier of '2' would cause all the error specifications to be doubled in the simulations.

The 'global error' specification allows the user to provide a single error specification for altering the values of all ideal point or horizon parameters. This is the only viable option if errors have not been specified for the individual parameters in the Party dialogue boxes; it may still be chosen, however, even if parameter-specific errors have been provided in the data entry process. The errors may be drawn from either a normal or a uniform distribution, and the size of the error specified follows the same principles as before: it represents the standard deviation if a normal distribution is chosen and the range if a uniform distribution is chosen. Thus, specifying a normal distribution and an error of '0.5' for ideal point parameters will cause each party position parameter to be altered in each iteration by adding to it a term drawn from a normal distribution with a mean of zero and a standard deviation of that value; the same error specification associated with a uniform distribution will cause the error terms to be drawn from a uniform distribution with the range of ±0.5.

Once these specifications have been made and the 'OK' button clicked, the simulation run is launched. A progress indicator window is displayed while a simulation is running and once the simulation is completed, the Results dialogue box will appear. As noted earlier, simulations on legislatures with large numbers of parties and/or horizon intersections may require additional memory; users are strongly advised to specify as much memory as possible when launching the *Horizons 3D©* program if a simulation run is contemplated (see Launching *Horizons 3D©*).

The output from a simulation run is the same as for a calculation run, with the following exceptions. First, all indicator variables now record the number of iterations in which the condition in question is met. For instance, *Int.* reports the number of iterations in which the horizons of all parties in the proto-coalition intersect. (Converting any of these variables to rates is simply a matter of dividing by the total number of iterations.) Second, all continuous variables give the mean value of the variable across the iterations. Thus, *EuD* reports the average Euclidean distance between the two parties in the proto-coalition that are the furthest apart. The one exception to these rules concerns the intersection size: it gives the average size across only those iterations in which a common horizon intersection exists (it is coded '0' if no iteration yields a common horizon intersection). Multiplying this value by the intersection rate will produce the mean intersection size across all iterations, if this is desired.

Very rarely, simulations can produce a highly deviant final value. It is not clear that this represents a defect in the algorithm; due to the memory-intensive nature of simulations, the random number generator used in obtaining a new parameter in each iteration may become 'stuck', that is it may generate numbers that are very similar from iteration to iteration. It is recommended that you compare simulation and calculation values for the proto-coalitions and re-do any simulation run that has yielded a highly deviant result for any proto-coalition.

5. Exporting results and saving horizon files

The Results dialogue box that appears whenever a calculation or simulation run is performed also contains an option allowing the user to export the results; that is, to save the results in a separate file for further analysis. The user may select any or all of the variables to be saved and must indicate how the variables are to be separated or delimited, that is by tabs, spaces, commas, or pipes. The selected variables will be saved as a raw data file and, by default, it will receive the file name extension of '.hop' (*Horizons* output). The user will be prompted to provide a name for the file to be saved (including a different extension name, if desired) and a location.

Any legislature created in *Horizons 3D©* may be saved for further use. This option can be invoked from the 'Legislature' menu or by clicking on the 'Save' button in the toolbar. When a file is saved, the user is prompted to provide a name and location for the file. The file will be saved with the extensions '.hdt' (*Horizons* data), which is the only data file extension that *Horizons 3D©* recognizes. Saved files may be opened simply by selecting 'Open' from the Legislature menu or clicking on the 'Open an Existing Legislature' button.

It is recommended that the save procedure be invoked immediately after the data for a legislature have been entered. The results of calculations or simulations performed on a legislature can also be saved, a particularly useful feature if the results in question are those emanating from a lengthy simulation run. If any results are present in the Results dialogue box when the save procedure is invoked, they will automatically be saved with the rest of the file. Results that are not to be saved must therefore be removed (by clicking the 'Remove this result' button on the Results tab) before the file is saved.

6. Further information

There are two documents that provide technical information related to the *Horizons 3D©* program. The first is Eberly (2002), *3D Geometric Support for Horizons*, which explains exactly how horizons are constructed and intersections identified and measured by the program. The second is Jercan (2003), *Horizons 3D© Results*, which describes the implementation of the various calculations that *Horizons 3D©* performs. Both are available for download from http://www.sfu.ca/~warwick/.

Appendix 2: Results from the Expert Survey

This appendix contains the information from the expert survey of party systems used to derive estimates of policy distance, horizon intersections, and related variables. For each country, three ideological or policy dimensions are identified; these are the ones most often given the three highest salience scores by the respondents to that country survey. For each party on each dimension, the survey elicited estimates of its position, the upper and lower limits of its range of acceptable compromise for the purpose of entering coalition governments, and the salience it attributed to the dimension (if different from the dimension's overall salience in that system, which was requested separately). The question format and guiding instructions were discussed in Chapter 4. The following tables list the mean estimate of each of these parameters, followed by the standard error of that mean, and finally the number of respondents providing estimates.

Austria

Party	Dimension 1: Left/right				Dimension 2: Libertarianism/authoritarianism				Dimension 3: Materialism/postmaterialism			
	Lower bound	Position	Upper bound	Salience	Lower bound	Position	Upper bound	Salience	Lower bound	Position	Upper bound	Salience
Kommunistische Partei Österreichs (KPÖ)	0.36	1.08	2.39	0.98	–	–	–	–	5.47	7.09	9.95	0.68
	.21	.17	.28	.02	–	–	–	–	1.74	.60	.05	.18
	7	12	7	12	–	–	–	–	3	8	3	6
Die Grünen/Die Grüne Alternative (GA)	1.28	2.68	4.96	0.97	0.55	2.84	4.23	1.00	0.25	1.76	5.13	1.06
	.33	.17	.45	.03	.26	.40	.47	.21	.19	.21	.51	.32
	8	14	8	14	4	7	4	4	5	14	5	4
Sozialdemokratische Partei Österreichs (SPÖ)	2.58	3.70	6.53	0.98	3.19	4.76	7.88	0.80	3.80	6.52	9.16	1.03
	.20	.19	.48	.02	1.34	.64	.31	.14	.97	.44	.57	.31
	8	14	8	14	4	7	4	4	5	14	5	8
Österreichische Volkspartei (ÖVP)	4.19	6.40	8.19	0.98	4.08	6.50	8.95	.80	4.03	6.63	9.36	1.03
	.50	.16	.31	.02	1.31	.29	.37	.14	1.09	.36	.39	.31
	8	14	8	14	4	7	4	4	5	14	5	8
Freiheitliche Partei Österreichs (FPÖ)	4.66	7.94	9.19	0.99	5.84	8.96	9.93	1.05	4.39	7.43	9.73	0.95
	.66	.35	.15	.01	1.14	.26	.05	.24	.76	.45	.21	.31
	8	14	8	14	4	7	4	4	4	14	4	8
Liberales Forum (LIF)	3.59	4.84	7.35	0.95	.53	1.92	4.25	1.08	2.43	2.83	7.38	1.06
	.69	.38	.51	.05	.28	.55	.75	.25	.59	.31	.38	.34
	8	14	8	14	4	7	4	4	4	13	4	7

Belgium

Party	Dimension 1: Left/right				Dimension 2: Clerical/secular				Dimension 3: Centralization/decentralization			
	Lower bound	Position	Upper bound	Salience	Lower bound	Position	Upper bound	Salience	Lower bound	Position	Upper bound	Salience
Ecologistes confédérés (ECOLO)	1.28 / .36 / 11	2.35 / .31 / 10	5.19 / .45 / 11	1.09 / .10 / 12	1.61 / .49 / 7	3.85 / .60 / 10	7.61 / .65 / 7	.83 / .14 / 10	2.09 / .97 / 4	3.17 / .74 / 6	6.80 / .42 / 4	.96 / .21 / 6
Anders gaan leven (AGALEV)	1.29 / .35 / 11	2.55 / .24 / 10	5.41 / .32 / 11	1.14 / .13 / 12	2.25 / .57 / 7	4.20 / .51 / 10	7.80 / .41 / 7	.82 / .14 / 10	2.10 / .97 / 4	3.92 / .76 / 6	6.53 / .47 / 4	1.13 / .20 / 6
Parti Socialiste (PS)	2.17 / .29 / 11	3.36 / .27 / 10	6.00 / .26 / 11	1.19 / .09 / 12	.56 / .38 / 7	2.16 / .27 / 10	5.29 / .90 / 7	1.16 / .22 / 11	3.33 / .55 / 4	6.00 / .50 / 6	7.50 / 1.02 / 4	1.19 / .15 / 6
Socialistische Partij (SP)	2.25 / .32 / 11	3.51 / .19 / 10	5.91 / .28 / 11	1.18 / .09 / 12	.69 / .50 / 7	2.34 / .25 / 10	5.80 / .78 / 7	1.12 / .19 / 11	2.79 / 1.17 / 4	5.57 / .85 / 6	6.31 / .83 / 4	1.18 / .13 / 6
Vlaamse Liberalen Demokraten (VLD)	4.32 / .36 / 11	7.01 / .21 / 10	8.28 / .27 / 11	1.10 / .05 / 12	1.29 / .50 / 7	3.64 / .43 / 10	6.94 / .76 / 7	.91 / .14 / 10	3.83 / 1.33 / 4	6.50 / .76 / 6	7.70 / .53 / 4	1.22 / .10 / 6
Parti réformateur libéral (PRL)	4.25 / .33 / 11	6.70 / .17 / 10	8.46 / .17 / 11	1.11 / .05 / 12	1.11 / .38 / 7	3.92 / .33 / 10	6.81 / .82 / 7	.89 / .13 / 10	3.28 / 1.53 / 4	4.58 / .88 / 6	6.49 / 1.23 / 4	1.13 / .16 / 6

(Continued)

Party	Dimension 1: Left/right				Dimension 2: Clerical/secular				Dimension 3: Centralization/ decentralization			
	Lower bound	Position	Upper bound	Salience	Lower bound	Position	Upper bound	Salience	Lower bound	Position	Upper bound	Salience
Christelijke Volkspartij (CVP)	3.58	5.70	7.60	.99	4.56	7.87	9.31	1.21	2.24	5.50	6.64	1.28
	.30	.29	.21	.03	.99	.25	.26	.22	1.16	1.15	.52	.08
	11	10	11	12	7	10	7	11	4	6	4	6
Parti social chrétien (PSC)	3.48	5.61	7.65	.99	4.04	7.66	9.19	1.21	1.78	2.33	5.04	1.14
	.32	.19	.20	.03	.84	.28	.36	.22	1.13	.42	.76	.16
	11	10	11	12	7	10	7	11	4	6	4	6
Front dém. francophone (FDF)	4.48	6.40	8.52	.99	1.31	4.61	7.15	.82	6.66	6.90	9.51	1.54
	.58	.31	.22	.08	.46	.39	.77	.14	1.24	1.14	.37	.34
	11	10	11	12	7	10	7	11	4	6	4	6
Volksunie (VU)	3.15	5.16	7.48	.95	2.11	4.60	7.64	.87	6.90	8.67	9.50	1.74
	.43	.41	.29	.04	.56	.50	.49	.14	.99	.42	.35	.28
	11	10	11	12	7	10	7	10	4	6	4	6
Vlaams Blok (VB)	3.15	5.16	7.48	.95	2.11	4.60	7.64	.87	6.90	8.67	9.50	1.74
	.43	.41	.29	.04	.56	.50	.49	.14	.99	.42	.35	.28
	11	10	11	12	7	10	7	10	4	6	4	6

Denmark

Party	Dimension 1: Left/right				Dimension 2: Libertarianism/authoritarianism				Dimension 3: Materialism/postmaterialism			
	Lower bound	Position	Upper bound	Salience	Lower bound	Position	Upper bound	Salience	Lower bound	Position	Upper bound	Salience
Unity List (EL)/Left Socialists (VS)	.28 .13 11	1.33 .12 13	3.71 .42 11	1.08 .08 13	.98 .77 3	2.30 .61 12	4.33 1.33 3	.80 .15 10	.91 .53 4	2.25 .33 11	3.85 .64 4	.89 .16 10
Socialist People's Party (SF)	.96 .21 11	2.56 .13 13	4.85 .43 11	1.02 .04 13	1.03 .80 3	2.85 .45 12	4.50 1.26 3	.77 .14 10	1.05 .63 4	2.85 .28 12	5.23 .95 4	.87 .15 10
Social Democratic Party (SD)	2.23 .23 11	4.04 .15 13	6.41 .36 11	1.00 .00 13	2.83 .33 3	5.34 .33 12	6.17 .44 3	.71 .13 10	2.63 .72 4	5.48 .35 12	7.76 .31 4	.72 .13 10
Radical Liberals (RV)	2.83 .26 11	4.90 .14 13	7.13 .32 11	.97 .02 13	1.82 .34 3	3.30 .29 12	5.17 .93 3	.77 .14 10	1.60 .70 4	3.51 .29 12	6.31 .70 4	.87 .15 10
Progress Party (FRP)	6.51 .35 11	8.61 .25 13	9.69 .12 11	1.03 .09 13	3.30 .70 2	5.41 1.01 11	8.50 1.50 2	.88 .14 10	6.63 .66 3	7.50 .55 11	9.50 .50 3	.78 .13 10

200

(Continued)

Party	Dimension 1: Left/right				Dimension 2: Libertarianism/authoritarianism				Dimension 3: Materialism/postmaterialism			
	Lower bound	Position	Upper bound	Salience	Lower bound	Position	Upper bound	Salience	Lower bound	Position	Upper bound	Salience
Centre Democrats (CD)	3.70	5.67	7.69	.95	3.33	5.05	7.18	.71	3.15	6.24	8.44	.73
	.12	.17	.30	.05	.83	.45	1.00	.13	1.27	.39	.46	.13
	11	13	11	13	3	12	3	10	4	12	4	10
Liberals (V)	4.85	4.65	9.05	1.04	3.67	5.31	7.20	.80	3.76	6.94	8.08	.74
	.28	.21	.21	.04	1.17	.71	1.56	.15	.95	.43	.83	.13
	11	13	11	13	3	11	3	10	4	11	4	10
Christian People's Party (KRF)	3.20	5.83	7.72	.86	3.68	6.35	7.97	.86	3.01	5.17	7.96	.77
	.32	.17	.24	.06	.89	.50	.78	.16	.73	.54	.62	.14
	11	12	11	12	3	12	3	10	4	12	4	10
Conservative People's Party (KF)	4.58	7.07	8.70	1.04	4.02	6.38	7.83	.71	4.50	6.95	8.66	.69
	.33	.19	.16	.04	1.03	.56	1.09	.13	1.14	.31	.48	.12
	11	13	11	13	3	12	3	10	4	12	4	10
Danish People's Party (DF)	5.78	8.75	9.88	.95	2.60	5.83	7.00	.77	6.45	8.25	9.25	.79
	.87	.48	.12	.05		.93		.37	1.10	.25	.75	.08
	4	4	4	4	1	3	1	3	2	4	2	4

Finland

Party	Dimension 1: Left/right				Dimension 2: Materialism/postmaterialism				Dimension 3: Urban–centre–EU/rural–periphery–anti-EU			
	Lower bound	Position	Upper bound	Salience	Lower bound	Position	Upper bound	Salience	Lower bound	Position	Upper bound	Salience
Left–Wing Alliance (VAS)	.73	2.08	6.76	1.25	2.60	5.56	7.47	.85	1.64	4.19	6.64	1.23
	.12	.16	.62	.10	.82	.51	.47	.08	.55	.54	.35	.22
	9	11	9	11	6	10	6	9	4	8	4	8
Green League (VIHR)	1.43	4.25	7.71	.88	.51	2.09	5.48	1.25	1.00	2.58	5.99	1.35
	.32	.31	.35	.09	.27	.27	.25	.13	1.00	.51	.78	.19
	9	11	9	11	6	10	6	9	4	8	4	8
Social Democratic Party (SDP)	1.50	3.68	7.64	1.06	3.27	6.14	7.97	.84	.78	2.41	6.03	1.25
	.28	.20	.44	.03	.68	.46	.33	.10	.26	.24	.02	.14
	9	11	9	11	6	10	6	9	4	8	4	8
Rural Party (SMP)	2.15	5.91	8.75	.89	4.43	6.77	8.94	.95	5.51	8.84	9.39	1.46
	.42	.41	.27	.06	.78	.58	.49	.10	.84	.31	.45	.10
	9	11	9	11	6	9	6	8	4	8	4	8
Centre (KESK)	2.12	5.76	8.31	1.01	4.44	7.03	8.78	.92	4.88	8.38	9.70	1.44
	.44	.25	.30	.01	.38	.38	.44	.08	.31	.16	.24	.10
	9	11	9	11	6	10	6	9	4	8	4	8
Liberal People's Party (LKP)	2.83	5.73	8.51	1.01	2.42	4.65	7.41	.86	.80	2.93	5.13	1.19
	.51	.32	.24	.01	.94	.51	.81	.10	.50	.30	.13	.24
	9	11	9	11	6	10	6	9	4	7	4	7

(Continued)

Party	Dimension 1: Left/right				Dimension 2: Materialism/postmaterialism				Dimension 3: Urban–centre–EU/rural–periphery–anti-EU			
	Lower bound	Position	Upper bound	Salience	Lower bound	Position	Upper bound	Salience	Lower bound	Position	Upper bound	Salience
Swedish People's Party (SFP)	2.66	6.94	9.26	.99	2.28	5.40	8.27	.71	1.50	4.62	8.03	1.15
	.79	.21	.18	.02	.49	.44	.40	.12	.66	.54	.82	.25
	9	11	9	11	6	10	6	9	4	8	4	8
Christian League (SKL)	3.38	7.45	9.00	1.01	2.25	5.08	6.86	.97	2.28	6.51	8.03	1.19
	.68	.31	.14	.04	.40	.58	.47	.10	.85	.52	.41	.23
	9	11	9	11	6	10	6	9	4	8	4	8
National Coalition (KOK)	2.88	7.55	9.13	1.05	3.61	5.95	8.30	.84	1.02	2.30	6.03	1.31
	.56	.15	.07	.02	.78	.56	.18	.10	.41	.24	.41	.19
	9	11	9	11	6	10	6	9	4	8	4	8
Progressive Finnish Party (NUORS)	4.23	8.05	9.32	1.08	2.83	4.60	7.43	1.07	.30	1.33	3.40	1.31
	.83	.19	.14	.08	1.24	.73	.87	.14	.24	.40	.53	.14
	9	11	9	11	6	10	6	9	4	8	4	8

France (V)

Party	Dimension 1: Left/right				Dimension 2: Libertarianism/ authoritarianism				Dimension 3: Materialism/ postmaterialism			
	Lower bound	Position	Upper bound	Salience	Lower bound	Position	Upper bound	Salience	Lower bound	Position	Upper bound	Salience
Parti communiste	1.05	2.10	4.24	1.36	3.15	4.34	6.81	.73	5.63	8.07	9.16	.84
	.46	.24	.37	.13	1.27	1.50	1.13	.15	.38	.25	.38	.18
	8	7	8	10	4	5	4	3	5	9	5	9
Les Verts	1.60	3.58	6.19	.75	1.25	1.62	3.70	.73	.29	1.67	3.37	.96
	.33	.42	.47	.09	.92	.29	.87	.15	.20	.30	.22	.23
	8	6	8	10	4	5	4	3	5	9	5	8
Parti socialiste	1.60	3.56	6.06	1.15	.93	3.55	4.37	.97	2.22	4.56	6.20	.68
	.31	.20	.41	.09	.46	1.14	.86	.03	.71	.69	.64	.12
	9	7	9	10	3	5	3	3	5	9	5	8
Progrès et Dém. moderne (PDM) (1967–68)	4.20	6.14	7.91	.89	4.34	5.47	7.24	.57	3.71	6.16	7.18	.59
	.45	.35	.27	.06	.71	.45	.51	.09	.55	.42	.90	.10
	9	7	9	10	4	5	4	3	4	8	4	6
Centre démocrate et progrès (1973)	4.18	6.09	7.79	.95	4.16	5.34	7.01	.57	4.15	6.55	7.43	.59
	.35	.32	.28	.03	.68	.37	.49	.09	.43	.22	.97	.10
	9	7	9	10	4	5	4	3	4	8	4	6

(Continued)

Party	Dimension 1: Left/right				Dimension 2: Libertarianism/authoritarianism				Dimension 3: Materialism/postmaterialism			
	Lower bound	Position	Upper bound	Salience	Lower bound	Position	Upper bound	Salience	Lower bound	Position	Upper bound	Salience
Radicaux de gauche	2.56	4.16	6.48	.94	1.56	3.35	4.11	.83	2.84	4.98	6.30	.68
	.31	.32	.52	.05	.38	.50	.50	.09	.78	.54	.74	.10
	8	7	8	10	4	5	4	3	4	8	4	6
Mouvement réformateur (1973)	3.63	5.30	6.93	.97	3.25	4.53	6.10	.53	3.80	5.63	6.88	.59
	.42	.44	.36	.03	.13	.28	.44	.09	.58	.63	.91	.10
	8	7	8	9	4	5	4	3	4	7	4	6
Union pour la Démocratie française	4.34	6.66	8.54	.99	4.45	5.61	7.44	.70	3.03	6.22	6.90	.64
	.39	.17	.24	.05	.62	.39	.56	.00	.42	.32	.99	.09
	9	7	9	10	4	5	4	3	4	7	4	6
Républicains indépendents (1962–73)	4.81	7.28	8.33	.98	4.34	5.87	6.98	.57	3.94	6.29	7.28	.63
	.38	.15	.22	.03	.71	.55	.59	.09	.65	.39	1.21	.10
	9	7	9	10	4	5	4	3	4	8	4	6
Rassemblement pour la République	4.85	6.86	8.42	1.04	5.33	7.01	7.96	.73	4.28	6.94	7.78	.72
	.38	.17	.20	.06	.24	.24	.41	.03	.76	.29	.61	.12
	9	7	9	10	4	5	4	3	4	8	4	6
Front national	7.32	9.01	9.93	1.03	7.76	9.29	9.74	1.17	5.73	8.63	8.36	.96
	.27	.29	.03	.12	.50	.34	.25	.28	1.41	.31	1.46	.17
	8	7	8	10	4	5	4	3	4	8	4	7

Germany

Party	Dimension 1: Left/right				Dimension 2: Clerical/secular				Dimension 3: Materialism/postmaterialism			
	Lower bound	Position	Upper bound	Salience	Lower bound	Position	Upper bound	Salience	Lower bound	Position	Upper bound	Salience
Alliance 90/Greens (G)	1.43	2.78	5.29	.99	.22	.82	3.11	.96	.60	1.92	5.24	.94
	.23	.15	.42	.07	.20	.27	.58	.19	.19	.28	1.02	.11
	12	12	12	12	5	7	5	7	7	12	7	12
Social Democrats (SPD)	2.24	3.94	6.45	1.04	1.24	2.38	4.79	.71	2.15	5.03	7.55	.64
	.23	.14	.30	.08	.40	.25	.58	.09	.34	.46	.65	.09
	12	12	12	12	5	7	5	7	7	11	7	11
Free Democrats (FDP)	3.68	5.44	7.33	.90	1.04	1.51	4.89	.77	3.24	4.77	7.96	.62
	.35	.27	.32	.07	.47	.42	1.02	.10	1.08	.55	.94	.07
	12	12	12	12	5	7	5	7	7	12	7	12
Christian Democratic Union (CDU)	3.94	5.82	7.68	.98	4.69	6.35	8.11	.89	4.17	6.13	8.20	.66
	.27	.30	.29	.07	.21	.52	.39	.16	.60	.38	.30	.09
	12	12	12	12	5	7	5	7	7	12	7	12
Christian Social Union (CSU)	4.72	6.92	8.25	1.00	5.86	7.48	8.73	.97	4.92	6.67	8.50	.67
	.30	.24	.26	.02	.29	.42	.44	.19	.86	.43	.39	.10
	12	12	12	12	5	7	5	7	7	12	7	12
Party of Democratic Socialism (PDS)	.40	1.20	3.80	1.32	.03	.41	2.85	.87	2.50	5.69	6.95	.59
	.17	.16	.34	.14	.03	.17	.65	.18	.72	.71	.79	.08
	12	12	12	12	5	7	5	7	7	11	7	11

Iceland

Party	Dimension 1: Left/right				Dimension 2: Materialism/postmaterialism				Dimension 3: Internationalist–Pro-West/isolationist–nationalist			
	Lower bound	Position	Upper bound	Salience	Lower bound	Position	Upper bound	Salience	Lower bound	Position	Upper bound	Salience
People's Alliance (PA)	.81	2.49	5.56	1.19	1.38	3.48	5.83	.53	.18	1.69	4.73	1.06
	.25	.14	.50	.12	.55	.30	.32	.15	.18	.44	.37	.20
	8	8	8	9	4	8	4	6	3	5	3	5
Women's Alliance (WA)	1.02	2.25	4.92	.97	.14	1.99	3.85	.92	.85	1.51	4.00	.80
	.28	.37	.64	.07	.14	.38	.68	.24	.15	.22	1.00	.12
	7	7	7	7	4	7	4	6	2	5	2	4
Union of Liberals and Leftists (ULL)	1.85	3.93	6.46	.90	3.38	5.92	8.63	.38	2.42	5.10	7.08	.87
	.21	.23	.43	.16	.69	.37	.24	.06	1.18	.17	.63	.13
	7	7	7	7	4	6	4	5	2	4	2	3

Social Democrats (SDP)	2.97	4.88	8.04	.98	2.88	5.63	8.15	.42	4.20	8.35	9.47	1.06
	.46	.30	.33	.02	.66	.32	.15	.06	.20	.32	.27	.20
	8	8	8	9	4	8	4	6	3	5	3	5
Progressive Party (PP)	2.89	5.52	7.89	.98	5.25	6.83	9.36	.48	2.20	4.89	6.95	.82
	.36	.33	.43	.02	1.38	.59	.38	.11	.42	.52	.53	.13
	9	9	9	10	4	9	4	6	3	5	3	5
Independence Party (IP)	4.62	7.37	8.89	1.07	5.38	7.39	9.38	.40	5.97	7.18	9.28	.90
	.47	.29	.22	.05	1.11	.47	.47	.05	.61	.63	.49	.16
	9	9	9	10	4	9	4	6	3	5	3	5
Citizens' Party (CP)	3.47	7.18	9.31	.86	5.66	7.95	9.95	.38	5.50	6.26	8.68	.87
	.66	.28	.28	.14	.94	.70	.05	.06	.05	.79	.77	.13
	7	7	7	7	4	6	4	5	2	4	2	3
People's Movement (PM)	2.57	4.15	6.38	.98	2.33	4.88	7.33	.45	.80	4.94	6.50	.95
	.36	.28	.30	.02	.33	.28	.67	.08	.20	.89	2.50	.13
	8	8	8	8	3	8	3	6	2	5	2	4

Ireland

Party	Dimension 1: Left/right				Dimension 2: Clerical/secular				Dimension 3: Materialism/postmaterialism			
	Lower bound	Position	Upper bound	Salience	Lower bound	Position	Upper bound	Salience	Lower bound	Position	Upper bound	Salience
Labour Party	2.24	3.60	6.41	1.26	1.91	3.52	6.38	.91	3.64	5.64	8.24	.65
	.28	.25	.23	.09	.38	.52	.46	.11	.96	.55	.85	.15
	14	14	14	15	6	9	6	10	4	9	4	8
Progressive Democrats (PD)	4.40	7.44	8.71	1.27	2.47	3.69	7.13	1.01	6.35	6.59	9.69	.65
	.29	.23	.21	.09	.76	.79	.31	.16	1.19	.70	.31	.16
	14	14	14	15	6	9	6	10	4	9	4	8
Fianna Fáil (FF)	3.12	5.32	7.24	.89	3.78	6.96	8.98	1.03	5.88	7.24	9.45	.60
	.32	.23	.28	.03	.40	.23	.47	.12	1.43	.48	.55	.13
	14	14	14	15	6	9	6	10	4	9	4	8
Fine Gael (FG)	3.44	5.89	7.76	.94	2.83	5.58	8.44	1.00	5.50	6.29	9.48	.54
	.28	.17	.16	.05	.58	.27	.28	.12	1.38	.58	.53	.10
	14	14	14	15	6	9	6	10	4	9	4	8
Greens	2.09	3.30	5.88	.81	1.53	2.86	5.18	.88	.01	2.32	4.67	1.25
	.37	.34	.39	.08	.55	.45	.81	.11	.01	.31	.38	.14
	14	14	14	15	6	9	6	10	5	12	5	11
Democratic Left (DL)	1.44	2.67	5.34	1.27	1.16	1.90	5.06	1.01	1.98	5.31	6.56	.63
	.26	.33	.41	.09	.55	.50	.66	.14	.71	.78	.97	.18
	11	13	11	13	5	7	5	8	4	8	4	7
Sinn Féin (SF)	1.53	3.06	6.02	.81	1.22	3.44	6.50	.88	4.93	5.37	8.33	.57
	.34	.30	.52	.10	.45	.52	.42	.12	2.58	.78	1.20	.17
	12	14	12	15	6	9	6	10	3	8	3	7

Italy before transition

Party	Dimension 1: Left/right				Dimension 2: Clerical/secular				Dimension 3: Materialism/postmaterialism			
	Lower bound	Position	Upper bound	Salience	Lower bound	Position	Upper bound	Salience	Lower bound	Position	Upper bound	Salience
Communists (PCI)	.20	1.95	4.83	1.04	1.00	2.69	5.55	.93	4.20	5.96	7.70	.52
	.13	.21	.32	.03	.63	.55	.97	.16	1.02	.70	.93	.08
	10	13	10	13	5	9	5	8	6	11	6	10
Socialists (PSI)	1.84	4.09	6.96	1.02	1.00	2.53	5.05	.98	3.54	5.30	7.82	.56
	.29	.27	.30	.02	.63	.49	.90	.16	.98	.65	.98	.07
	10	13	10	13	5	9	5	8	6	11	6	10
Radicals	1.29	3.84	7.06	.65	.00	.66	1.72	1.46	.00	1.98	2.32	.69
	.39	.35	.84	.10	.00	.20	.54	.26	.00	.78	.44	.10
	9	13	9	13	5	9	5	8	6	11	6	10
Social Democrats (PSDI)	2.83	4.93	7.65	1.02	1.18	3.80	7.24	.84	3.10	6.15	8.37	.52
	.27	.19	.18	.02	.72	.44	.87	.19	1.01	.57	.92	.08
	9	13	9	13	5	9	5	8	6	11	6	10

(Continued)

Party	Dimension 1: Left/right				Dimension 2: Clerical/secular				Dimension 3: Materialism/postmaterialism			
	Lower bound	Position	Upper bound	Salience	Lower bound	Position	Upper bound	Salience	Lower bound	Position	Upper bound	Salience
Republicans (PRI)	2.74	5.01	7.28	1.02	1.00	2.30	4.12	1.04	4.40	5.79	8.05	.52
	.26	.22	.31	.02	.63	.25	.27	.16	.75	.52	.87	.08
	10	13	10	13	5	9	5	8	6	11	6	10
Christian Democrats (DC)	2.59	5.64	8.28	1.02	6.29	8.84	9.60	1.35	4.21	6.34	8.87	.52
	.31	.26	.30	.02	.36	.32	.24	.20	.50	.43	.60	.08
	10	13	10	13	5	9	5	8	6	11	6	10
Liberals (PLI)	4.19	6.84	8.67	1.02	1.30	3.98	5.54	1.07	5.23	6.98	8.88	.52
	.37	.33	.20	.02	.89	.76	1.15	.17	.65	.44	.80	.08
	10	13	10	13	5	9	5	8	6	11	6	10
Italian Social Movement (MSI)	6.69	9.36	10.00	1.10	4.90	8.32	9.80	.87	6.37	7.35	9.50	.52
	.52	.15	.00	.07	1.38	.75	.20	.18	.73	.50	.50	.08
	10	13	10	13	5	9	5	8	6	11	6	10

Italy after transition

Party	Dimension 1: Left/right				Dimension 2: Clerical/secular				Dimension 3: Materialism/postmaterialism			
	Lower bound	Position	Upper bound	Salience	Lower bound	Position	Upper bound	Salience	Lower bound	Position	Upper bound	Salience
Comunisti Italiani	.17	2.05	4.53	1.13	1.25	2.01	3.06	.81	1.91	4.40	6.08	.52
	.17	.32	.38	.08	.75	.65	.82	.20	.42	1.21	1.46	.05
	6	8	6	8	4	5	4	5	4	6	4	6
Partito Democratico della Sinistra (PDS)	.29	2.71	5.39	1.07	.00	2.17	6.06	.85	.97	3.49	6.74	.54
	.18	.30	.29	.05	.00	.38	1.63	.17	.43	.70	.99	.09
	7	9	7	9	4	6	4	6	5	7	5	8
Verdi	.90	3.20	5.71	.75	.19	2.01	3.74	.84	.00	1.45	2.47	.85
	.35	.29	.31	.08	.19	.42	1.32	.11	.00	.37	.43	.15
	10	13	10	13	5	9	5	8	6	11	6	10
Lista Pannella	1.15	5.52	8.95	.66	.00	1.12	1.70	1.43	.33	1.88	2.94	.66
	.47	.47	.41	.10	.00	.62	.60	.24	.33	.51	.51	.10
	10	13	10	13	5	9	5	8	6	11	6	10
Partito Popolare (PPI)	1.69	4.55	6.39	1.00	5.56	7.57	9.00	1.34	3.70	5.39	7.56	.47
	.26	.26	.62	.00	1.21	.76	.71	.13	.50	.37	.97	.06
	7	9	7	9	4	6	4	6	4	7	4	7
Centro Dem. – Crist. Dem. Uniti (CCD–CDU)	4.15	6.41	8.56	1.00	6.23	8.49	9.28	1.11	4.18	6.40	8.19	.52
	.24	.37	.30	.00	.43	.57	.58	.19	.34	.54	.60	.08
	9	13	9	13	5	9	5	8	6	11	6	10

(Continued)

Party	Dimension 1: Left/right				Dimension 2: Clerical/secular				Dimension 3: Materialism/postmaterialism			
	Lower bound	Position	Upper bound	Salience	Lower bound	Position	Upper bound	Salience	Lower bound	Position	Upper bound	Salience
Forza Italia	4.63	7.07	9.14	1.00	3.54	7.17	9.40	.85	5.85	7.31	9.17	.52
	.30	.21	.23	.00	1.15	.31	.40	.18	.59	.55	.65	.08
	10	13	10	13	5	9	5	8	6	11	6	10
Alleanza Nazionale (AN)	5.15	8.56	9.84	1.07	4.89	7.96	9.80	.89	5.71	7.24	9.50	.52
	.26	.18	.11	.05	1.51	.44	.20	.18	.44	.48	.22	.08
	10	13	10	13	5	9	5	8	6	11	6	10
Prodi/I Democratici	1.08	4.05	5.71	1.00	1.80	3.38	7.28	.94	1.93	4.23	7.07	.52
	.27	.22	.48	.00	.83	.63	1.17	.21	.35	.28	1.08	.05
	6	8	6	8	3	4	3	4	4	6	4	6
Lega Nord	4.30	7.05	9.16	.83	1.25	5.06	8.00	.83	6.24	7.28	9.00	.56
	.13	.39	.23	.08	.75	.81	1.22	.13	.72	.60	.63	.07
	10	13	10	13	4	8	4	7	6	11	6	10
Rifondazione Comunista (RC)	.00	1.07	3.49	1.17	.40	1.57	3.89	.90	2.87	4.83	6.73	.53
	.00	.17	.41	.10	.40	.33	1.57	.17	.96	.88	1.13	.07
	10	13	10	13	5	9	5	8	6	11	6	10
Lista Dini–Rinnovamento Italiano	2.31	5.04	7.13	1.00	1.93	4.89	7.85	.96	4.55	6.04	8.33	.52
	.44	.19	.32	.00	.84	.68	.57	.17	.47	.42	.92	.08
	10	13	10	13	5	9	5	8	6	11	6	10

Netherlands

Party	Dimension 1: Left/right				Dimension 2: Clerical/secular				Dimension 3: Materialism/postmaterialism			
	Lower bound	Position	Upper bound	Salience	Lower bound	Position	Upper bound	Salience	Lower bound	Position	Upper bound	Salience
Pacifist Socialist Party (PSP)	.38	1.53	3.14	1.11	1.00	.95	3.49	.95	.75	2.13	3.75	.90
	.16	.26	.39	.08	1.00	.32	1.20	.17	.48	.52	1.11	.17
	10	10	10	11	4	8	4	8	4	10	4	10
Radical Reform Party (PPR)	1.42	2.77	5.15	1.02	1.75	4.00	6.25	.95	.50	1.68	3.75	1.00
	.27	.27	.32	.05	1.03	.79	1.11	.12	.29	.53	1.11	.19
	10	10	10	11	4	8	4	8	4	10	4	10
Labour Party (PvdA)	2.23	3.68	6.07	1.10	1.58	2.52	4.96	.71	2.20	4.82	8.20	.67
	.15	.10	.35	.05	.37	.41	.40	.09	.66	.47	.37	.11
	12	12	12	13	6	10	6	10	5	12	5	12
Democrats 66 (D66)	2.93	4.73	6.86	.95	.87	1.88	3.96	.68	1.00	2.64	6.18	.88
	.25	.17	.27	.04	.31	.38	.51	.09	.63	.29	.86	.15
	12	12	12	13	6	10	6	10	5	12	5	12
Christian Democratic Appeal (CDA)	3.97	5.91	7.69	.95	4.82	7.14	8.73	1.07	2.54	4.94	7.62	.65
	.26	.23	.25	.03	.65	.13	.32	.10	.23	.45	.77	.10
	12	12	12	13	6	10	6	10	5	12	5	12
People's Party for Freedom and Democracy (VVD)	4.52	6.90	8.07	1.06	1.02	2.48	5.27	.70	4.40	6.63	9.58	.68
	.27	.26	.20	.04	.39	.42	.74	.10	.68	.35	.24	.10
	12	12	12	13	6	10	6	10	5	12	5	12

(Continued)

Party	Dimension 1: Left/right				Dimension 2: Clerical/secular				Dimension 3: Materialism/postmaterialism			
	Lower bound	Position	Upper bound	Salience	Lower bound	Position	Upper bound	Salience	Lower bound	Position	Upper bound	Salience
Political Reformed Party (SGP)	6.73	8.25	9.02	.94	8.47	9.46	9.93	1.82	4.00	6.10	7.03	.62
	.41	.25	.19	.07	.18	.16	.07	.18	1.78	.74	1.56	.16
	11	12	11	13	6	10	6	10	4	11	4	11
Reformed Political Union (GPV)	6.34	7.40	8.71	.90	7.98	9.17	9.92	1.81	3.50	5.63	6.75	.62
	.41	.39	.19	.05	.20	.20	.08	.18	1.55	.70	1.49	.16
	11	12	11	13	6	10	6	10	4	11	4	11
Reformed Political Federation (RPF)	6.31	7.34	8.82	.90	7.80	9.20	9.96	1.81	3.35	5.68	6.76	.62
	.41	.43	.17	.05	.24	.19	.04	.18	1.41	.70	1.49	.16
	11	12	11	13	6	10	6	10	4	11	4	11
Centre Democrats (CD)	6.99	8.74	9.95	.96	2.82	3.86	7.21	.64	6.00	7.94	9.75	.55
	.75	.38	.03	.06	1.46	1.00	1.39	.08	.82	.60	.25	.11
	11	12	11	13	5	9	5	9	4	11	4	11
Green Left	1.28	2.45	4.77	1.10	.53	1.68	3.63	.64	.40	1.98	4.00	.88
	.21	.22	.42	.07	.24	.35	.35	.10	.24	.31	.95	.14
	12	12	12	13	6	10	6	10	5	12	5	12

Norway

Party	Dimension 1: Left/right				Dimension 2: Clerical/secular				Dimension 3: Materialism/postmaterialism			
	Lower bound	Position	Upper bound	Salience	Lower bound	Position	Upper bound	Salience	Lower bound	Position	Upper bound	Salience
Socialist Left (SV)	1.18	2.41	4.24	1.10	.29	1.68	4.67	.61	.60	2.38	4.41	.92
	.17	.11	.22	.07	.18	.19	.57	.06	.31	.32	.40	.09
	17	18	17	18	7	16	7	15	8	17	8	17
Labour (DNA)	2.66	4.32	6.17	1.22	1.22	3.69	6.57	.57	3.79	6.28	8.67	.48
	.18	.14	.17	.07	.34	.26	.72	.03	.62	.27	.37	.04
	17	18	17	18	6	15	6	14	8	17	8	17
Liberals (V)	3.91	5.91	7.76	.92	1.77	4.53	8.58	.60	.97	3.43	5.65	.74
	.23	.18	.24	.06	.61	.30	.45	.04	.31	.36	.38	.09
	16	18	16	18	6	15	6	14	8	17	8	17
Christian People's Party (KrF)	3.80	5.56	7.51	.84	5.64	8.45	9.57	1.31	1.73	4.11	6.35	.57
	.16	.16	.22	.05	.47	.22	.30	.14	.23	.16	.36	.08
	17	18	17	18	7	16	7	15	7	16	7	16

(Continued)

Party	Dimension 1: Left/right				Dimension 2: Clerical/secular				Dimension 3: Materialism/postmaterialism			
	Lower bound	Position	Upper bound	Salience	Lower bound	Position	Upper bound	Salience	Lower bound	Position	Upper bound	Salience
Centre (SP)	2.79	4.37	6.47	.82	2.42	6.13	8.59	.65	1.75	4.46	6.29	.60
	.15	.17	.19	.05	.71	.21	.46	.05	.68	.44	.42	.08
	17	18	17	18	6	15	6	14	7	16	7	16
Conservatives (H)	5.24	7.28	8.55	1.23	2.17	5.19	8.25	.59	4.42	7.01	9.14	.45
	.20	.18	.21	.07	.60	.32	.36	.03	.55	.24	.36	.05
	17	18	17	18	6	15	6	14	8	17	8	17
Progress (FrP)	5.63	8.03	9.40	1.07	1.41	4.42	7.68	.59	5.60	8.17	9.67	.47
	.21	.21	.21	.05	.37	.41	.58	.03	.46	.28	.22	.07
	17	18	17	18	6	15	6	14	8	17	8	17
Red Electoral Alliance (RV)	.04	.85	2.06	1.13	.12	.67	4.25	.66	1.00	3.88	5.90	.60
	.04	.13	.24	.09	.12	.17	.79	.08	1.00	.51	.60	.08
	16	18	16	18	6	15	6	14	5	16	5	15

Portugal

Party	Dimension 1: Left/right				Dimension 2: Clerical/secular				Dimension 3: Materialism/postmaterialism			
	Lower bound	Position	Upper bound	Salience	Lower bound	Position	Upper bound	Salience	Lower bound	Position	Upper bound	Salience
United Democratic Coalition (CDU)	1.10	2.06	3.72	1.27	.64	1.82	3.71	1.01	2.33	4.94	7.35	.69
	.26	.21	.33	.08	.32	.33	.43	.11	1.20	.55	1.33	.15
	10	14	10	15	7	13	7	12	3	14	3	13
Socialist Party (PSP)	3.29	4.45	6.44	.99	1.53	4.23	5.94	.87	1.87	4.19	7.65	.68
	.14	.11	.29	.05	.43	.24	.57	.11	1.04	.24	.88	.13
	9	14	9	15	7	13	7	12	3	14	3	13
Social and Democratic Left (UEDS)	1.89	2.78	4.32	1.06	1.14	2.67	4.61	1.03	2.00	4.24	7.37	.69
	.33	.45	.63	.04	.41	.38	.59	.09	1.15	.82	.88	.15
	5	7	5	8	6	7	6	7	3	7	3	7
Independent Social Democratic Ass'n (ASDI)	3.50	4.64	6.15	.96	3.10	5.18	6.66	.90	2.37	4.33	7.33	.70
	.50	.36	.54	.13	1.08	.59	.24	.10	1.17	.77	.88	.18
	4	4	4	5	4	6	4	6	3	6	3	6

(Continued)

Party	Dimension 1: Left/right				Dimension 2: Clerical/secular				Dimension 3: Materialism/postmaterialism			
	Lower bound	Position	Upper bound	Salience	Lower bound	Position	Upper bound	Salience	Lower bound	Position	Upper bound	Salience
Social Democratic Party (PSD)	4.69 / .13 / 10	6.08 / .15 / 14	7.86 / .23 / 10	1.00 / .00 / 15	4.40 / .37 / 7	6.55 / .44 / 13	8.71 / .34 / 7	.95 / .10 / 12	4.68 / .66 / 3	6.11 / .28 / 14	9.03 / .03 / 3	.72 / .15 / 13
Social Democratic Centre–People's Party (CDS–PP)	6.04 / .24 / 10	7.56 / .18 / 14	8.65 / .18 / 10	1.11 / .05 / 15	6.49 / .37 / 7	7.68 / .56 / 13	9.81 / .14 / 7	1.11 / .12 / 12	5.67 / .88 / 3	6.99 / .41 / 14	9.67 / .33 / 3	.68 / .15 / 13
Democratic Renewal (PRD)	3.36 / .33 / 7	4.18 / .34 / 10	6.49 / .42 / 7	.82 / .10 / 11	2.28 / .66 / 5	3.76 / .39 / 8	6.48 / 1.08 / 5	.83 / .09 / 8	2.87 / .94 / 3	4.84 / .31 / 7	7.33 / .88 / 3	.54 / .17 / 7
Popular Monarchist Party (PPM)	5.83 / .57 / 6	7.57 / .34 / 10	8.65 / .43 / 6	.90 / .06 / 11	6.07 / .67 / 6	7.53 / .59 / 9	9.53 / .33 / 6	1.03 / .13 / 9	2.35 / .33 / 3	4.40 / .76 / 10	8.33 / 1.20 / 3	1.07 / .18 / 10

Sweden

Party	Dimension 1: Left/right				Dimension 2: Libertarian/authoritarian				Dimension 3: Materialism/postmaterialism			
	Lower bound	Position	Upper bound	Salience	Lower bound	Position	Upper bound	Salience	Lower bound	Position	Upper bound	Salience
Communist Left (VPK)	1.23	2.75	4.64	1.10	2.78	4.48	6.00	.68	.69	3.95	6.13	.62
	.27	.26	.19	.05	.66	.76	1.66	.12	.34	.68	.85	.11
	10	11	10	12	3	6	3	6	5	11	5	11
Social Democrats (S)	2.68	4.26	6.22	1.00	3.07	5.48	7.92	.52	3.29	6.87	9.09	.43
	.25	.19	.15	.01	.84	.45	.73	.07	1.30	.47	.78	.05
	10	11	10	12	3	6	3	6	5	11	5	11
Centre Party (C)	3.75	5.40	7.83	.93	5.63	6.56	8.20	.72	2.99	5.89	8.41	.48
	.16	.14	.24	.04	1.00	.72	1.10	.11	1.12	.55	.68	.07
	10	11	10	12	3	6	3	6	5	11	5	11
Liberals/People's Party (FP)	4.51	6.28	8.25	.97	1.63	3.33	3.52	.68	2.52	5.45	7.69	.47
	.26	.22	.19	.03	.74	.70	1.28	.12	1.04	.53	1.21	.06
	10	11	10	12	3	6	3	6	5	11	5	11

(Continued)

Party	Dimension 1: Left/right				Dimension 2: Libertarian/authoritarian				Dimension 3: Materialism/postmaterialism			
	Lower bound	Position	Upper bound	Salience	Lower bound	Position	Upper bound	Salience	Lower bound	Position	Upper bound	Salience
Moderate Party (M)	5.60	7.75	8.99	1.03	1.83	4.21	5.77	.63	4.83	7.57	9.79	.42
	.21	.18	.22	.03	.55	.66	1.05	.12	1.27	.29	.20	.07
	10	11	10	12	3	6	3	6	5	11	5	11
Green Party (MP)	2.17	3.77	5.86	.86	4.58	5.96	8.43	.62	.09	1.63	4.74	.66
	.23	.20	.22	.07	.82	.68	.22	.07	.06	.24	.90	.12
	10	11	10	12	3	5	3	5	5	11	5	11
Christian Democrats (KDS)	4.68	7.05	8.50	.91	5.55	6.98	8.25	.82	2.46	4.49	8.20	.47
	.32	.22	.19	.06	.87	.54	1.13	.17	.84	.53	.87	.06
	10	11	10	12	3	6	3	6	5	11	5	11
New Democracy (NYD)	6.54	8.46	9.59	1.03	1.65	4.29	6.50	.74	4.15	7.27	9.83	.52
	.69	.26	.24	.07	–	1.48	–	.26	1.15	.61	.17	.10
	5	7	5	8	1	5	1	5	3	8	3	8

Notes

1 Introduction

1. The 'other things' that are considered to be equal include dimension saliences. As we shall see in Chapter 2, unequal saliences can produce cases where a closer policy is more costly to a party than one further away. In these situations, calculations of closeness must take differences in salience into account.
2. This is a little harsh, since common sense tells us that people do miscalculate at times, but most theorists, especially rational choice theorists, are unwilling to abandon the fundamental premise that people maximize utility in an efficient manner.
3. The Socialists and Communists were able to overcome their policy differences in the 1970s through a prolonged period of policy readjustment, with the Socialists moving significantly to the Left and the Communists moderating some of their more extreme positions. With the Socialist government now committed to more centrist policies, a gap had again opened up. By the way, the electoral system reform did not thwart the emergence of a coherent right-wing government; even with the National Front's sizeable parliamentary presence in 1986, the UDF and the Gaullists were able to govern on their own.
4. The Communist parties did eventually decline or disappear, but this probably had more to do with the collapse of the Soviet Union than with a failure to achieve cabinet representation.
5. Abstention from alienation suggests that voters are not content simply to vote for the closest party; if no party is close enough, they will opt out of the process entirely. This factor has figured in the US voting literature since Riker and Ordeshook (1968).
6. This space is commonly referred to as a 'policy space', but I shall use the term 'ideological space' which communicates the basic idea that each dimension represents a fundamental axis of political competition, not the range of possible positions on a particular policy.
7. *Horizons 3D*© is a Java 2 SDK, Standard Edition, Version 1.4.1 program for creating ideological spaces and calculating distances and horizon intersections among parties. It is available from my website (http://www.sfu.ca/~warwick).

2 The nature and testing of the policy horizon hypothesis

1. Points on as well as within a horizon could be considered acceptable for the purposes of joining governments, but it would mean that we would have to deal with the linguistic inelegance of talking about horizon intersections or tangencies in the remainder of this book. As a programming matter, it turned

out to be more straightforward to detect intersections than intersections plus tangencies. The upshot is that the *Horizons 3D©* program (see pp. 29–32) treats horizons that just touch as lacking an intersection and therefore having no single policy on which they can agree. Since even extremely small intersections are detectable by the program, however, this decision is inconsequential.

2. This distinguishes the policy horizon framework from the well-known 'veto players' framework advanced by Tsebelis (2002). Consider again the indifference contours for parties A and B in Figure 2.1(a). Since the contours intersect, some of these preferences are shared by the two parties. If A and B together commanded a parliamentary majority, they could upset the current government and form one of their own based on any of these policies. (Both parties would have to agree to take this action, however, which is what makes them veto players.) Doing so would cause the SQ to change and therefore all the indifference contours that pass through it; new configurations of policies and parties that could defeat the SQ would probably emerge. In contrast, the policy horizons and the configurations of parties that could form governments under the horizon hypothesis would stay the same. A change in government policy would have no effect on expectations concerning government formation under the horizon hypothesis, at least in the short term.

3. In Sened's (1995, p. 289) notation, party i's utility from membership in cabinet r is defined as: $U_{ir} = \alpha P_{ir} - \beta d(x_i, x_r)^2$, where P_{ir} is the portfolio payoff and $d(x_i, x_r)$ is the distance between party and government ideal points.

4. In previous research (Warwick 2001b), for example, I found that the strongest influence on government policy in coalition governments derives from the sizes of the various coalition parties.

5. Some supporters may stand to gain when party leaders assume cabinet positions because those positions may allow leaders to distribute patronage and other benefits to supporters. This is unlikely to compensate fully for the policy costs, however, since it represents only part of what has been gained in the exchange.

6. The expert survey that was administered to measure horizons (see Chapter 4) asked respondents to estimate the extent to which leaders can compromise on party policy for the sake of coalition membership without provoking serious intra-party dissension, but that does not prove that this concern is indeed their source.

7. In common with other logit methods, this method assumes independence from irrelevant alternatives (IIA). In simple terms, this means that the choice between any two alternatives does not depend on the other alternatives present in the choice set. The capacity of the models estimated in this study to meet this assumption will be evaluated. An alternative that does not require the IIA assumption is the conditional probit model. Probit models, however, can be very difficult to estimate and perhaps for this reason, the conditional probit model is not generally available in statistical packages.

8. One-dimensional spaces draw a lot less theoretical attention because they are not vulnerable to the instability of the chaos theorem (see Chapter 1); nevertheless, systems dominated by a single policy dimension can be handled by attributing very low salience values to the other dimension(s), as discussed in p. 34.

9. To capture shapes accurately, the number of facets increases with the degree of curvature of the horizon. Full details of the method *Horizons 3D*© uses to represent horizons and calculate their intersections are available from my website (http://www.sfu.ca/~warwick/).

10. All distances are calculated in *Horizons 3D*© using both a Euclidean and a city-block metric, although in this study only the former is used. This practice is in keeping with the vast majority of previous theoretical and empirical work and fits better the manner in which horizons are constructed here.

11. It could be argued that the minimum distance should be used since a lesser distance for one party implies that it is more willing to compromise to meet the expectations of the other party. In practice, the issue makes little difference. In the survey-based data, the correlation between the minimum weighted distance and the maximum weighted distance between pairs of parties is $r = .912$ ($N = 427$, $p < 001$). The rank-order (spearman rho) correlation, which is more relevant here since what matters is how parties order their options is .966.

12. Data analyses normally follow the different procedure of treating each variable score as a realization of some underlying distribution, sampling new scores from those distributions and re-estimating the relationships a large number of times to estimate a central tendency and a standard error for each effect parameter. In the present application, however, this procedure is not feasible. Since each legislature constitutes a separate *Horizons 3D*© file, implementing it would involve changing the positions and bounds for every party in all dimensions in a very large number of files, running each of these files individually and outputting the data from each run, and concatenating the sets of output data to produce a single data file – then repeating the entire process, say, 500 times. Months of (extremely tedious) work would be involved simply to gain a more reliable estimate of one parameter, the horizon effect, and experimentation with different model specifications would involve re-running the 500 data files numerous times and combining results each time. With the present procedure, just one final data set is produced and all statistical analyses can be run on it.

13. It is also possible to amplify or diminish the errors by specifying a multiple of the default value of '1'. For instance, specifying a multiple of '2' would cause the error terms to be drawn from distributions with standard errors (normal and student's t) or ranges (uniform) twice their specified values.

14. The number of proto-coalitions is given by 2^p-1, where p is the number of parties.

3 Behaviour-based horizons and government formation

1. If different parties apply different saliences to all dimensions, however, broader estimated horizons might simply indicate lower salience levels, rather than discrete limits on the willingness to compromise. Ideally, therefore, horizons should be tested against salience-weighted distances, which we do not have here. Fortunately, saliences as estimated by the expert survey respondents affect relative distance calculations only slightly. For instance, the average rank-order correlation within countries between the unweighted and weighted policy distances of proto-coalitions is .965.

2. The policy distance, D_h, at which the probability of joining the government is 50 per cent is given by:

$$\ln\left(\frac{0.5}{1-0.5}\right) = 0 = \alpha + \mathbf{X'B} + \gamma D_h \text{ or}$$

$$\frac{-\alpha - \mathbf{X'B}}{\gamma} = D_h$$

where $\mathbf{X}$ is the vector of party dummies and $\mathbf{B}$ is the vector of associated coefficients. To avoid having to enter the large $\mathbf{X'B}$ vector, D_h can be estimated from

$$\frac{-\left[\ln\left(\frac{\hat{p}}{1-\hat{p}}\right) - \gamma D\right]}{\gamma} = D_h$$

where $\hat{p}$ is the predicted probability of government membership and D is the distance between government and party ideal points.

3. The advantage of this strategy is that it makes it likely that several parties will have their horizons estimated on the basis of the same set of formation situations, thereby reducing the number of cases that are consumed by the measurement process.

4. To be specific, a re-estimation of Model 4 of Table 3.5 based on a split-sample approach to estimating logit horizons results in an effect coefficient for the horizon dichotomy of $\beta = 1.19$ $(SE = 0.25, p < .001)$.

5. The distinction is thus one between intermediate and prior causes. The hypothesis allows that there may be a variety of factors that influence the willingness of parties to join governing coalitions, but, with respect to policy, it asserts that they converge in the establishment of a distinct distance threshold for each party. The data at hand cannot tell us which factors are involved in producing these thresholds, only where they are likely to be located, if they exist. Much empirical research follows a similar format: it may reveal that two variables are related, but not which of several possible explanations for the relationship is the true one.

6. The initial coordinates for the parties are (3, 4), (4.5, 6.6), and (6, 4). These positions are altered by adding terms drawn from a normal distribution with mean of 0 and standard deviation of 1.

7. The decision to have six minority governments is arbitrary. It represents a smaller proportion than actually occur in West European systems but, since the policy distance spanned by these governments is 0 (again, unlike reality), their presence tends to favour the policy distance hypothesis.

8. This decision is usually justified by face validity alone but, as noted in Chapter 2, there is empirical evidence indicating that government positions in West European systems largely conform to it (Warwick 2001b).

9. Note that conditional logit models do not produce intercepts (constants).

10. The 'semi-presidential' French Fifth Republic is included because its parliamentary component functions very much as in pure parliamentary systems: parties must form coalition (or minority) governments that can command the support of the National Assembly.

11. These data are described and distributed in Ian Budge *et al.* (2001).

12. This results from the procedures for measuring horizons. The MJD method is unaffected and the logit method, because of the presence of party dummies, is only slightly affected by the use of a cross-national data set.

13. Whether this dimension has to do with postmaterialism *per se* or with libertarianism/authoritarianism (Flanagan 1987) is open to debate. With the survey data, we will be able to distinguish between these two conceptions, but it makes little sense to do so here. As for the importance of this dimension, which may surprise some readers, it is supported by the survey data, which reveal postmaterialism and/or libertarianism to be the second or third most important ideological dimension in all countries but one (Ireland). See Chapter 4 for details.

14. An alternative would be to use the left/right and 'new politics' additive scales proposed by Budge and Laver (1992, pp. 27–9). While the former scale seems to work quite well, the same cannot be said of the latter. As they note, 'References to it comprise much less of the total manifesto than references to the variables comprising the left–right scale, however, while its interpretation is potentially ambiguous in certain countries' (p. 29).

15. The general pattern is one in which the more often a party participates in government, the larger its horizon (ceteris paribus). The effect is moderate except when the party always participates in government; for these parties, the horizons 'explode'. The adjustment was performed by regressing the parties' estimated horizons on their participation rates and a dummy variable identifying parties with a 100 per cent participation rate. The coefficient estimated for the dummy variable was then subtracted from these parties' horizons to move the latter to the trend established for the other parties. Note that, even with this adjustment, these parties still have very large horizons.

16. The consequence is that 60.1 per cent of all governments in the data set are majoritarian, even though the policy distance spanned by majority proto-coalitions exceeds that spanned by minority ones by an average of about one-half (0.58) a standard deviation, a difference significant at $p < .0001$.

17. An alternative possibility is that it is not the amount of external support a proto-coalition would need in order to survive in office that matters, but rather the amount of additional policy distance that it would have to span. This can be measured with the aid of the *Assumed Majority Distance* variable produced by *Horizons 3D*[©]. This variable records the minimum amount of policy distance that would have to be taken on by a proto-coalition in order to achieve majority status (it is set to zero for majority coalitions). The difference between this distance and a proto-coalition's actual policy distance can be considered its 'policy gap'. Testing reveals, however, that the relevant consideration is the size gap, not the policy gap. This evidence is not reported here, but is available on request.

18. In *Stata: Release 8* (StataCorp 2003), the software used to produce these results, it is possible to cluster the observations by country, which would allow the standard errors to take account of any dependency that exists across the formations of each country. This option, however, is not implemented for imputed data sets, which we will be using quite frequently. To maintain consistency across results, clustering has not be specified here or for any of the other conditional logit analyses. We shall, however, examine country effects in Chapter 6.

19. The proto-coalition that formed the government must be included in the analysis, otherwise the entire formation situation would be lost.
20. The assumption that one of the estimators is efficient is violated if the model is mis-specified. There are also small-sample problems that could affect any sample that is finite.
21. Specifically, a party's anti-system score is its total score on CMP categories classified by Laver and Budge (1992, p. 24) as 'anti-establishment views' (Martin and Stevenson 2001, p. 40).
22. The task of replicating the Martin–Stevenson analysis was guided by a copy of the data set supplied by the authors, to whom I am grateful.
23. In addition to the various Communist parties, this list includes the Flemish Bloc in Belgium; the Danish Left Socialists; the Gaullists in the French Fourth Republic and the National Front in the Fifth; the Irish Workers' Party; Proletarian Unity, Proletarian Democracy, and the Neo-Fascists (MSI) in Italy; the Socialist People's Party and its successors in Norway; and the Portuguese Popular Monarchists.
24. Martin and Stevenson include Canada and Israel and exclude Finland, France and Portugal. In general, their data end in the 1980s, whereas the present data mostly terminate in the mid to late 1990s.
25. Given the multivariate normal distribution of the imputation model, King *et al.* (2001, p. 58) recommend applying an appropriate transformation to variables that violate this condition, such as a logistic transformation for proportions, to make them unbounded and symmetric. Since some variables are dichotomous and highly skewed, while others, such as the intersection rate, are proportions that have high concentrations of cases at the extremes (0 and 1), this tactic is not viable. Fortunately, the imputation model is often quite robust to violations of this sort and the results were examined carefully to determine whether they are reasonable. To ensure that dichotomous variables remain dichotomous, their imputed values were recoded so that values below 0.5 became zero and values of 0.5 and above became 1.0.
26. These results, moreover, are very similar to those produced when the analysis is based just on those cases for which complete information is available.
27. Intersections (as opposed to intersection rates) were not calculated for MJD horizons for reasons noted earlier. As for minority coalitions, the situation is more difficult to assess because being more compact may simply mean being smaller (i.e. further from majority status).
28. The correlation between MJD and logit-based intersection rates is $r=.758$.
29. An intersection is likely to exist in nearly twice as many proto-coalitions under the MJD method (31.2 per cent of all proto-coalitions) as under the logit method (17.9 per cent).

4 Expert estimates of ideological spaces and party bounds

1. The numbers of parties per country are too small to determine if the same patterning occurs in individual countries.
2. Although libertarianism and secularism tend to go together in general, the two characterizations of this dimension need not be in total agreement since it is possible to see extreme left parties as both secular and authoritarian.

3. Respondents were given two rationales for this injunction. The first is that basing estimates on parties' coalition behaviour would make it 'circular' to use the estimates to explain that behaviour. The second is to make it possible to define regions of acceptable compromise even for parties that have never entered coalition governments.

4. James N. Druckman provided valuable help in this search and both he and James Adams shared some of the burden of mailing and re-mailing the surveys.

5. Part of the problem is that the Huber–Inglehart survey did not include Luxembourg. Laver and Hunt (1992, pp. 35–6) also experienced this problem and resolved it by using political and media figures as respondents. That option is not pursued here.

6. The present survey averages 13 respondents per country. For countries covered in this survey, the corresponding averages are 6.8 for the Castles and Mair (1984) survey, 14.2 for the Laver and Hunt (1992) survey, and 8.8 for the Huber and Inglehart (1995) survey.

7. Correlations between the ratings of different respondents were examined in cases where there was reason to believe that different names may have been used for what in fact is the same basic dimension, for example centre/periphery and urban/rural. High correlations allowed these to be treated as the same dimension. This is indicated in Table 4.1 by listing all of the synonyms.

8. If some of the saliences for other dimensions seem too high, it is worth bearing in mind that the alternatives – using just the left/right dimension or ignoring dimension saliences entirely (which would cause all dimensions to be weighted equally) – are very likely to be much more unrealistic.

9. The dimensions selected in this manner are not necessarily those with the highest mean salience scores, as reported in Table 4.1 (relying on the latter would have made the influence of each respondent's choices on the final selection a function of the extremeness of his or her salience ratings).

10. From the responses of respondents who provided horizon estimates, the correlations between horizon width and dimension salience for the second and third dimensions are just $r = -.064$ and $r = -.094$, respectively.

11. Both Barnard and Gary King, one of the authors of *Amelia*, were contacted about this problem, but no suggestions were forthcoming.

12. The greater uncertainty over horizons is probably due to the unfamiliarity of respondents with the concept, but it may also be an artefact of the way in which they interpreted the concept of bounds. If respondents were thinking of bounds in terms of distances from ideal points, the uncertainty associated with any bound may combine their uncertainty over the location of the relevant ideal point plus their uncertainty over that distance, resulting in a greater total uncertainty for the bound. I am grateful to James Adams for bringing this possibility to my attention.

13. Strictly speaking, it ought to be called 'a coefficient of determination' or 'squared correlation', but by convention it is referred to simply as a correlation.

14. The reliability of salience levels cannot be assessed effectively by this method because differences in salience scores across parties tend to be small or non-existent.

15. Browne *et al.*'s (1984b) is in fact an updating of Dodd's (1976) first or economic conflict scale and, with a few further updates, is used in its place in the comparisons in Table 4.3.
16. Intraclass correlations are not used here because their purpose is to assess inter-rater reliability of ratings of the same objects. Here, raters are usually groups of experts and the objects may have changed over time. As it happens, the ICCs are all reasonably high and broadly similar to the correlations reported in the table.
17. Incidentally, positions on the left/right dimension also correlate reasonably well ($r=-.804$) with mean positions on the first principal component of the manifestos data, used in the analyses of Chapter 3.
18. Budge (2000, pp. 107–8) also argues that 'Closeness of location [policy distance] would not tell us anything about policy agreements if the positions concerned were based on different substantive criteria for different parties, countries, and time periods.' Actually, country and time period differences can be controlled; the use of these data would only be undermined if respondents were evaluating different parties in the same system on the same dimension according to different criteria, which seems improbable.

5 Survey-based horizons and government formation

1. Note, however, that since it is no longer necessary to calculate government positions in order to estimate horizons, cases need not be excluded because information is lacking on a party that falls below this threshold but happens to be a government member.
2. As noted in Chapter 4, the importance of a dimension was determined by counting the number of respondents placing it among their top three choices, rather than by averaging salience scores across respondents.
3. In this data set, 60 per cent of the governments are majoritarian, even though the policy distance spanned by the average majority proto-coalition exceeds that of the average minority proto-coalition by 28 per cent.
4. Of the remaining ten anomalies, five are Icelandic cases involving the Communists (PA) and the Progressive party, which occasionally share power despite their policy differences.
5. In contrast, the Christian Democrats never appeared in government with the MSI. Despite their common horizon intersection, the MSI was never regarded as an acceptable coalition partner.
6. This interpretation brings to mind Laver and Shepsle's (1996) well-known portfolio allocation model of government formation, which holds that ministers have the power to impose their parties' own policies in the ministerial portfolios they control. This would not explain why the anomalies are concentrated in these particular cases, however. An alternative possibility is that the other parties may have been willing to defer because the issues in question mattered so much less to them than they did to the six Christian Democratic/ Centre parties. Since the six parties are central players in their party systems – Laver and Schofield (1990, p. 136) list most of them as occupying the core in their systems – it is also plausible that they may have been able to exploit that position to oblige other parties to accept compromises outside their horizons.

7. The width of their horizons on the corresponding dimensions (clerical/ secular or rural/urban) average 3.88 units; the Christian Democratic and Centre parties, despite attributing much higher salience levels to these dimensions, have an average width of 4.06. This comparison does not include Sweden because a rural/urban dimension is not one of its three dimensions.

8. Further evidence indicates that this was not part of a more general failure to produce horizons that conform to salience levels. A rough indicator of the overall tightness of a party's horizon is its average width across the three dimensions. For these parties, the correlation of this indicator with Laver and Hunt's (1992) 20-point scale measuring the importance parties place on policy-seeking versus office-seeking is an insignificant $r = .205$ ($p = .463$, $n = 15$). For the other parties rated in both surveys, in contrast, the correlation is a much stronger and highly significant $r = .526$ ($p < .001$, $n = 68$).

9. The test consists of estimating the standard model without the intersection rate on both the full and reduced data sets. The most relevant effect is the policy distance effect, since it correlates well with horizon intersections. It changes from $\beta = -0.50$ ($SE = 0.03$) in the full sample to $\beta = -0.68$ ($SE = 0.07$) when all anomalous non-intersections, including the Icelandic ones, are excluded, indicating that the distance effect changes only modestly as the sample becomes smaller.

10. Note that not all anomalous non-intersections have been recoded; only those that fit a repeated pattern. The rest are assumed to be the result of random measurement error and are left as they are. Since the horizons of any party involved in an anomalous non-intersection might be inaccurate, another strategy would be to recode the intersection rates of all proto-coalitions that include a party involved in an anomalous non-intersection to missing data. The problem here is that 59.1 per cent of all intersection rates would become missing data.

11. As noted in Chapter 3, the imputation model assumes a multivariate normal distribution and King *et al.* (2001, p. 58) recommend transforming variables, where necessary, to make them unbounded and symmetric. For the intersection rate, the intersection size, and the probability of an encompassed weighted mean, the high concentrations of cases at one or both extremes (0 and 1) render such a transformation pointless. The imputation model can often handle such violations well, however, and in any case the likely effect of nonsensical imputed values would be to weaken, not strengthen, the horizon effect. Because these variables were not transformed, imputed values sometimes fell outside their logical limits; in these cases, the imputed values were recoded to equal those limits. As before, the imputed values of dichotomous variables were re-dichotomized at the cutting-point of 0.5.

12. The value of 0.5 was chosen to introduce approximately the same error as in Chapter 3. In that analysis, positions were measured in *z*-scores, which gave them an effective range of about six units; since the surveys use a scale that is approximately twice as large (ten units), the size of the global error specification was also doubled.

13. If the standard model (Model 3 of Table 5.2) is re-estimated without these cases, the distance effect changes from −0.34 to −0.33 and the intersection rate effect remains the same at 1.35.

14. This analysis is based on five data sets containing imputed values for missing data in the Martin–Stevenson variables. These values were generated in the same imputation procedure that produced imputed horizon intersection rates for the anomalous non-intersections.

15. As before, majority status and the size gap have also been added to prevent under-estimation of the distance effect. The horizon intersection effect becomes slightly stronger ($\beta = 0.69$, $SE = 0.38$, $p = .035$ in a one-tailed test) if these variables are excluded.

16. The same conclusion holds if horizons are estimated by means of the logit method. The intersection rate effect declines only modestly from $\beta = 5.63$ (Model 4 of Table 5.3) to $\beta = 4.92$ ($SE = 0.45$).

17. Of the respondents 88.0 per cent provided horizon estimates for at least one dimension. The degree of constraint is illustrated by the fact that 69.6 per cent of the horizons estimated on the left/right dimension spanned less than five units on the 10-point scale and 95.8 per cent of respondents provided at least one horizon of that width or less.

6   Elaborating the horizon framework

1. Approximately 70% of single-party proto-coalitions meet the SMI condition versus about 20% (logit horizons) or 30% (MJD horizons) of other minority proto-coalitions.

2. The interaction of this variable with the SMI rate is excluded because both versions correlate so highly (approximately $r = .90$) with the indicator variable. If included, the SMI rate remains highly insignificant in both cases. Another way to show that the SMI effect is spurious is to confine the analysis to proto-coalitions with more than one party. The SMI rate shows no significant net effect in these analyses.

3. Note that the interaction between the EWM rate and the 'single-party' indicator cannot be included because it is coterminous with the latter variable (single-party proto-coalitions always include their weighted mean). If the analysis is to be confined to multiparty proto-coalitions, the EWM rate continues to play a significant net role in both data sets.

4. For multiparty proto-coalitions, the skewness of the intersection size variable is 6.15 (logit horizons) and 5.03 (MJD horizons).

5. Taking the ninth root is simply one of an infinite number of possible transformations and, in an approach reminiscent of Box-Cox transformations, one might search for the transformation that produces the strongest relationship to the dependent variable. A little experimentation revealed that the ninth root appears to work reasonably well not just for logit horizons, but for MJD and survey horizons as well. Although it is not optimal in any of these applications, the improvements to be gained through further fine-tuning appear to be relatively minor.

6. The EWM rate in Model 4 is insignificant because it is incorrectly signed. This is the result of excessive collinearity with the single-party variables (all single-party proto-coalitions have a perfect EWM rate, by definition), rather than an indication that encompassing the weighted mean position actually harms a proto-coalition's formation prospects. Further testing also shows

that the marginally significant distance effect in Model 4 is entirely due to the presence of this perversely signed EWM variable.

7. For the survey-based data, the means are based on four trials in each of five partially imputed data sets.

8. For the survey-based data, the mean coefficient across the five partially imputed data sets is shown, followed by the mean difference between it and the corresponding full-sample coefficient and the standard error of those differences.

9. The analyses for these countries show symptoms of severe over-determination, such as two or more effects that are significant at $p > .99$ and non-concave likelihood functions.

10. Majority status is included because the covariate that eliminated it, the interaction of majority status and the intersection expected value, is being left out.

11. Specifically, the minority proto-coalition that formed the government has a predicted probability that equals or exceeds that of the most probable majority proto-coalition in 44.4 per cent of the formations based on logit horizons and in 45.3 per cent of the formations based on MJD horizons.

12. This is based on predicted probabilities averaged across the five partially imputed data sets. Thus, it takes some account of the anomalous non-intersections.

13. This is the mean predictive success rate across the five partially imputed data sets.

14. This does not mean that support could not be elicited from parties whose horizons do not intersect those of the coalition, just that it need not look that far afield for that support. The issue of whether external support can be provided by parties for policies outside their horizons, and the implications of this issue for coalition formation theory, will be taken up in the concluding chapter.

15. The distance effect is $\beta = 0.04$ ($SE = 0.22$, $p = .42$ in a one-tailed test) in the six-variable model based on logit horizons and $\beta = 0.31$ ($SE = 0.11$), which is wrongly-signed, with survey horizons. Using MJD horizons, the effect is $\beta = -0.42$ ($SE = 0.17$, $p < .01$), but with the addition of the Martin–Stevenson variables, it becomes $\beta = -0.05$ ($SE = 0.24$, $p = .41$).

7 Policy horizons and government survival

1. In principle, a model of government formation could be devised that includes the possibility that post-election formation situations may result in different outcomes, but I am not aware of any rationale that would sustain such an expectation. Post-election governments, however, clearly do survive longer.

2. The government might also be a minority government based on one of these intersections, as we saw in Chapter 6, but this possibility is excluded here to avoid unnecessary complexity.

3. They might have relatively high scores on both, but not low scores on both; the exclusion of these cases is what biases the sample of governments.

4. This is done by assessing the contribution of these cases to the likelihood function by means of the survivor function, which gives the probability of surviving to time *t* or beyond, rather than with the density function.

5. Whether the second government should be treated as having different survival prospects because it is a repeat of the first government will be discussed below.

6. Governments that are repeated two or more times are placed in a single category because there are too few cases (a total of just 14) for finer distinctions.

7. The 1994 study tested various ways of measuring ideological diversity and found that the ideological distance spanned by the two parties in the coalition that are the farthest apart produced the most successful predictors of government survival. This is, of course, the conceptualization used to measure policy distance throughout the present study.

8. A government's returnability score is calculated as the total number of government parties that returned immediately following a government termination (excluding those occasioned by regular elections) in the present government plus the preceding four governments, divided by the total number parties included in these governments. The first four governments in each system receive missing values (values were not imputed in these cases because of the likelihood that the actors simply do not know the prospects of returning to power at this early stage of the system's post-War history). Another version that based the variable on a moving average rate of return across the five governments was also calculated, but was found not to perform as well and will not be used for that reason.

9. Non-invested governments are indeed short-lived, but there are too few of them (seven) to make the effect significant at the .05 level. Without the non-invested governments, the significance level for investiture remains essentially the same ($p = .087$).

10. Part of this result is undoubtedly due to the fact that policy distance is measured on the basis of government parties only; I showed that including support parties in the calculation of the policy distance spanned by minority governments increases the strength of the policy distance effects (Warwick 1994, p. 121).

11. Two features of the construction of this variable should be noted. First, formateur parties could not be identified in several French cases where a non-partisan individual formed the government and for Ireland, where there is no formateur (Mitchell 2000, p. 131). In these instances, the largest government party took its place. Second, the exclusion of the formateur party occasionally left no alternative majority coalition. This should be mathematically impossible since there are no majority parties in the governments under consideration here, but it occurred in practice because of the existence of missing data for the occasional small party. In these cases, imputed values were calculated using the *Amelia* program (Honaker *et al.* 2003). Since the multiple imputation procedure implemented in *Stata* is not available for duration models, the imputed values used in the analysis are the average values across the five imputed data sets.

12. Nyblade's version of the variable, which excludes alternative majority proto-coalitions that contain the largest party, was also tested. It yields results that

are virtually indistinguishable from Model 4, but proved to be slightly less effective in the data sets that utilize MJD and survey horizons.

13. Further testing shows that this assumption is correct: relative predicted values do perform better than predicted values in accounting for government survival.

14. Again, two other variants of this variable were tried, one of which considers all majority alternatives and the other of which excludes majority alternatives that contain the government's largest party, but neither proved to be noticeably superior to this version.

15. The effect of this version of the relative predicted value and its intersection are much less significant when MJD horizons are used, but this turns out to be due to just one deviant case (the 1970–1971 Kreisky government in Austria). Without this one case, the effects are as pronounced with MJD as with logit horizons.

16. Three of the Martin–Stevenson variables have missing data, for which imputed values have been calculated using the *Amelia* program. Because the multiple imputation routine is not implemented for survival models in *Stata*, the new value for each missing datum is the average imputed value across the five imputed data sets. This procedure is discussed more fully below. Another point to note is that the 'repeat government' variable differs slightly from Martin and Stevenson's definition. The difference is that it does not count as a repeat government whose mandate was renewed in an election, which is a more appropriate interpretation for the purpose of modeling survival.

17. These results are not shown here, but are available on request.

18. A case's Schoenfeld residual is the difference between its covariate value at its time of termination and a weighted average of the covariate values of all cases still at risk of termination. If the proportional hazards assumption is met, the regression of these residuals against time should not produce a slope that is significantly different from zero (Cleves *et al.* 2004, pp. 178–9).

19. Cox-Snell residuals provide an estimate of the cumulate hazard and can therefore be thought of as the expected number of terminations in a given time interval (Box-Steffensmeier and Jones 2002, p. 122), rather than a residual as the term is normally used.

20. This censoring regime distinguishes between early elections that were occasioned by political difficulties and early elections that were held despite the absence of any indication (primarily from *Keesing's*) of political problems or pressures. Only the latter were censored.

21. A Weibull model with a duration dependency parameter of 1 reduces to an exponential model. In the Weibull models estimated here, this parameter is never significantly different from that value. Thus, for terminations that end in replacements, the event theorists' suggestion that the hazard be modelled by an exponential distribution is affirmed (although not their belief that systematic factors have no role to play in government survival).

22. This was done as follows. The predicted values from both the full formation model and the reduced model that consists of just the three intersection expected value variables were calculated for each of the imputed data sets. Since the conditional logit analyses that generated these predicted values showed similar, highly significant effects on government formation in all

five data sets, corresponding predicted values tend to resemble one another very closely. These values were averaged across the data sets to yield a final predicted value and a final intersection predicted value for each proto-coalition. These values were then made relative in the same manner as before, that is by scanning the corresponding predicted values for all other proto-coalitions in each formation situation to identify the highest score among majority proto-coalitions that exclude the formateur, and subtracting this value from the government's predicted value. Similarly, any data gaps in the Martin–Stevenson variables were replaced by their mean imputed values across the data sets (as was the case in the analysis of the manifesto-based data).

23. As noted earlier (note 8), missing data for the first four governments in each system were not imputed because it is not clear that actors could form an impression of the chances of returning in the next government.

24. There are two exceptions to the overall similarity of the diagnostic test results. The first is that the proportionality tests reveal significant non-proportionality with respect to the returnability variable. Further investigation shows that the effect of this variable declines with duration time; in other words, high prospects of returning to power in the next government are less likely to induce the collapse of the present one the longer it stays in power. (There was, in fact, some indication of this tendency in the analysis of the manifesto-based data, but it failed to achieve statistical significance.) The introduction of an interaction between returnability and the square root of duration time eliminates the non-proportionality in both models. The second exception is that testing the Martin–Stevenson variables reveals a significant effect for the variable indicating the presence of a VSP in the government, as defined and measured by Laver and Shepsle (1996). This effect is puzzling not just because it is at odds with the corresponding finding from the manifesto-based data set, but also because of its direction: it indicates that having a VSP in the government increases the risk of collapse. In any case, the important point for present purposes is that its presence in the models, like that of the returnability/duration time interaction, does not weaken the roles played by the variables conveying the influence of relative predicted values.

25. In Chapter 6, I noted that most governments do not have the highest predicted values in their choice sets, but those comparisons involve all other proto-coalitions. Incidentally, the percentages are even higher when the predicted values are generated solely from the intersection expected value variables.

8   Conclusion

1. Aldrich (1995) and Miller and Schofield (2003) extend this to all parties by emphasizing their need not just for voluntary labour but also for financial support from activists.

2. It does form part of the relative predicted value but since the predicted values in question are calculated from the formation models, its role is minor or non-existent.

3. Comparing between manifesto-based and survey-based data sets produces results that are nearly as strong. The task of matching proto-coalitions in the manifesto-based data set with those in the survey-based data set is greatly facilitated if we confine the matching to formation situations that have precisely the same choice sets (differences in parties included in the two data sets often means that this condition is not met). Excluding the formations involving anomalous non-intersections, the two behaviour-based methods agree with each other 89.3 per cent of the time and have agreement rates with the survey method of 86.8 per cent (logit) and 84.9 per cent (MJD).

4. If the original intersection dichotomies are used, the rates are approximately the same, although slightly lower in the survey data.

References

Adams, James, Jay Dow, and Samuel Merrill. 2001. 'The Political Consequences of Alienation-Based and Indifference-Based Voter Abstention: Applications to Presidential Elections'. Presented at the Annual Meeting of the *American Political Science Association*, San Francisco, CA.

Aldrich, John. 1995. *Why Parties?*, Chicago: The University of Chicago Press.

Boehmke, Frederick J., Daniel S. Morey and Megan Shannon. N.d. 'Selection Bias and Continuous-Time Duration Models: Consequences and a Proposed Solution'. *American Journal of Political Science* (forthcoming).

Box-Steffensmeier, Janet and Bradford Jones. 2002. *Timing and Political Change: Event History Modeling in Political Science*. Ann Arbor, MI: University of Michigan Press.

Browne, Eric and Mark Franklin. 1973. 'Aspects of Coalition Payoffs in European Parliamentary Democracies'. *American Political Science Review*, 67: 453–69.

Browne, Eric, John Frendreis, and Dennis Gleiber. 1984a. 'An 'Events' Approach to the Problem of Cabinet Stability'. *Comparative Political Studies*, 17: 167–97.

Browne, Eric, Dennis Gleiber, and Carolyn Mashoba. 1984b. 'Evaluating Conflict of Interest Theory: Western European Cabinet Coalitions 1945–80'. *British Journal of Political Science*, 14: 1–32.

Browne, Eric, John Frendreis, and Dennis Gleiber. 1986. 'The Process of Cabinet Dissolution: An Exponential Model of Duration and Stability in Western Democracies'. *American Journal of Political Science*, 30: 628–50.

Budge, Ian, David Robertson, and Derek Hearl, eds. 1987. *Ideology, Strategy, and Party Change: Spatial Analyses of Post-War Election Programmes in 19 Democracies.* Cambridge: Cambridge University Press.

Budge, Ian and Hans Keman. 1990. *Parties and Democracy: Coalition Formation and Government Functioning in Twenty States.* Oxford: Oxford University Press.

Budge, Ian and Michael Laver. 1992. 'Coalition Theory, Government Policy and Party Policy'. In Michael Laver and Ian Budge, eds., *Party Policy and Government Coalitions*, pp. 1–40. New York: St. Martin's Press.

Budge, Ian. 2000. 'Expert Judgements of Party Policy Positions: Uses and Limitations in Political Research'. *European Journal of Political Research*, 37: 103–13.

Budge, Ian, Hans-Dieter Klingemann, Andrea Volkens, Judith Bara, and Eric Tanenbaum, eds. 2001. *Mapping Policy Preferences: Estimates for Parties, Electors, and Governments 1945–1998.* Oxford: Oxford University Press.

Castles, Francis, and Peter Mair. 1984. 'Left-Right Political Scales: Some 'Expert' Judgments'. *European Journal of Political Research*, 12: 73–88.

Cleves, Mario, Wiliam Gould, and Roberto Gutierrez. 2004. *An Introduction to Survival Analysis Using Stata®.* College Station, TX: Stata Press.

Cox, David. 1972. 'Regression Models and Life Tables (with Discussion)'. *Journal of the Royal Statistical Society*, B, 34: 187–220.

Cox, David. 1975. 'Partial Likelihood'. *Biometrika*, 62: 269–76.

Crombez, C. 1996. 'Minority Governments, Minimal Winning Coalitions and Surplus Majorities in Parliamentary Systems'. *European Journal of Political Research*, 29: 1–29.

Diermeier, Daniel, and Randolph Stevenson. 1999. 'Cabinet Survival and Competing Risks'. *American Journal of Political Science*, 43: 1051–68.

Dodd, Lawrence. 1976. *Coalitions in Parliamentary Government*. Princeton, NJ: Princeton University Press.

Downs, Anthony. 1957. *An Economic Theory of Democracy*. New York: Harper and Row.

Eberly, David. 2002. *3D Geometric Support for Horizons*. Published at website: http://www.sfu.ca/~warwick.

Flanagan, Scott. 1987. 'Changing Values in Industrial Societies Revisited: Towards a Resolution of the Values Debate'. *American Political Science Review*, 81: 1303–19.

Friedman, Milton. 1953. 'The Methodology of Positive Economics'. In M. Friedman, ed., *Essays in Positive Economics*. Chicago: University of Chicago Press.

Gabel, Matthew and John Huber. 2000. 'Putting Parties in their Place: Inferring Party Left-Right Ideological Positions from Party Manifestos Data'. *American Journal of Political Science*, 44: 94–103.

Gordon, Sanford. 2002. 'Stochastic Dependence in Competing Risks.' *American Journal of Political Science*, 46: 200–17.

Honaker, James, Anne Joseph, Gary King, Kenneth Scheve, and Naunihal Singh. 2003. *Amelia: A Program for Missing Data, Version 2.1*. Cambridge, MA: Harvard University.

Huber, John and Ronald Inglehart. 1995. 'Expert Interpretations of Party Space and Party Locations in 42 Societies'. *Party Politics*, 1: 73–111.

Jercan, Monica. 2003. *Horizons 3D Results*. Published at website: http://www.sfu.ca/~warwick.

Keesing's Contemporary Archives. 1945–2000. London: Keesing's Publications.

King, Gary, James Alt, Nancy Burns, and Michael Laver. 1990. 'A Unified Model of Cabinet Dissolutions in Parliamentary Democracies'. *American Journal of Political Science*, 34: 846–71.

King, Gary, James Honaker, Anne Joseph, and Kenneth Scheve. 2001. 'Analyzing Incomplete Political Science Data: An Alternative Algorithm for Multiple Imputation'. *American Political Science Review*, 95: 49–69.

Klein, John and Melvin Moeschberger. 1997. *Survival Analysis: Techniques for Censored and Truncated Data*. New York: Springer-Verlag.

Laver, Michael and Norman Schofield. 1990. *Multiparty Government: The Politics of Coalition in Europe*. Oxford and New York: Oxford University Press.

Laver, Michael and W. Ben Hunt. 1992. *Policy and Party Competition*. New York: Routledge.

Laver, Michael and Ian Budge, eds. 1992. *Party Policy and Government Coalitions*. New York: St. Martin's Press.

Laver, Michael and Kenneth Shepsle, eds. 1994. *Cabinet Ministers and Parliamentary Government*. Cambridge and New York: Cambridge University Press.

Laver, Michael and Kenneth Shepsle. 1996. *Making and Breaking Governments*. Cambridge and New York: Cambridge University Press.

Laver, Michael and Kenneth Shepsle. 1999. 'Understanding Government Survival: Empirical Exploration or Analytical Models?'. *British Journal of Political Science*, 29: 395–401.

Laver, Michael and John Garry. 2000. 'Estimating Policy Positions from Political Texts'. *American Journal of Political Science*, 44: 619–34.

Laver, Michael, Kenneth Benoit, and John Garry. 2003. 'Extracting Policy Positions from Political Texts Using Words as Data'. *American Political Science Review*, 97: 311–31.

Luebbert, Geoffrey. 1986. *Comparative Democracy: Policy Making and Government Coalitions in Europe and Israel*. New York: Columbia University Press.

Lupia, Arthur and Kaare Strøm. 1995. 'Coalition Termination and the Strategic Timing of Parliamentary Elections'. *American Political Science Review*, 89: 648–65.

Martin, Lanny and Randolph Stevenson. 2001. 'Government Formation in Parliamentary Democracies'. *American Journal of Political Science*, 45: 33–50.

McFadden, Daniel. 1973. 'Conditional Logit Analysis of Qualitative Choice Behavior.' In P. Zarembka, ed., *Frontiers of Econometrics*. New York: Academic Press, pp. 105–42.

McFadden, D. 1974. 'The Measurement of Urban Travel Demand'. *Journal of Public Economic*, 3: 303–28.

McKelvey, Richard. 1976. 'Intransitivities in Multidimensional Voting Models and Some Implications for Agenda Control'. *Journal of Economic Theory*, 16: 472–82.

McKelvey, Richard. 1979. 'General Conditions for Global Intransitivities in Formal Voting Models'. *Econometrica*, 47: 1085–111.

Miller, Gary and Norman Schofield. 2003. 'Activists and Partisan Realignment in the United States'. *American Political Science Review*, 97: 245–60.

Mitchell, Paul. 2000. 'Ireland'. In W. Müller and K. Strøm, eds., *Coalition Governments in Western Europe*. Oxford: Oxford University Press, pp. 126–57.

Müller, Wolfgang, and Kaare Strøm, eds. 2000. *Coalition Governments in Western Europe*. Oxford: Oxford University Press.

Nyblade, Benjamin. 2004. 'Reconsidering Ideological Diversity and Government Survival'. Unpublished manuscript.

Powell, Bingham. 1982. *Contemporary Democracies: Participation, Stability, and Violence*. Cambridge, MA: Harvard University Press.

Rabinowitz, George and Stuart Elaine Macdonald. 1989. 'A Directional Theory of Issue Voting'. *American Political Science Review*, 83: 93–121.

Ragin, Charles C. 2000. *Fuzzy-Set Social Science*. Chicago: University of Chicago Press.

Riker, William, and Peter Ordeshook. 1968. 'A Theory of the Calculus of Voting'. *American Political Science Review*, 62: 25–42.

Saalfeld, Thomas. 2001. 'Cabinet Survival in Parliamentary Democracies'. Paper presented at Annual Meeting of the *American Political Science Association*, at San Francisco, CA.

SAS Institute. 2001. *SAS: Version 8*. Cary, NC: The SAS Institute.

Sened, Itai. 1995. 'Equilibria in Weighted Voting Games with Sidepayments'. *Journal of Theoretical Politics*, 7: 283–300.

Sened, Itai. 1996. 'A Model of Coalition Formation: Theory and Evidence'. *The Journal of Politics*, 58: 350–72.

StataCorp. 2003. *Stata Statistical Software: Release 8.0*. College Staton, TX: Stata Corporation.

Strøm, Kaare. 1990a. 'A Behavioral Theory of Competitive Political Parties'. *American Journal of Political Science*, 34: 565–98.

Strøm, Kaare. 1990b. *Minority Government and Majority Rule*. Cambridge and New York: Cambridge University Press.

The Guardian Weekly. 28 February 2002 and 12 February 2004.

Tsebelis, George. 1990. *Nested Games: Rational Choice in Comparative Politics*. Berkeley and Los Angeles: University of California Press.

Warwick, Paul V. 1994. *Government Survival in Parliamentary Democracies*. Cambridge and New York: Cambridge University Press.

Warwick, Paul V. 1996. 'Coalition Government Membership in West European Parliamentary Democracies'. *British Journal of Political Science*, 26: 471–99.

Warwick, Paul V. 1998. 'Policy Distance and Parliamentary Government'. *Legislative Studies Quarterly*, 23: 319–45.

Warwick, Paul V. 1999. 'Ministerial Autonomy or Ministerial Accommodation? Contested Bases of Government Survival in Parliamentary Democracies'. *British Journal of Political Science*, 29: 369–94.

Warwick, Paul V. 2000. 'Policy Horizons in West European Parliamentary Systems'. *European Journal of Political Research*, 38: 37–61.

Warwick, Paul V. 2001a. 'Towards a Common Dimensionality in West European Policy Spaces'. *Party Politics*, 8: 101–22.

Warwick, Paul V. 2001b. 'Coalition Policy in Parliamentary Democracies: Who Gets How Much and Why'. *Comparative Political Studies*, 34: 1212–36.

Warwick, Paul V. and James N. Druckman. 2001. 'Portfolio Salience and the Proportionality of Payoffs in Coalition Governments'. *British Journal of Political Science*, 38: 627–49.

Warwick, Paul V. 2005a. 'Do Policy Horizons Structure the Formation of Parliamentary Governments? The Evidence from an Expert Survey'. *American Journal of Political Science*, 49: 373–87.

Warwick, Paul V. 2005b. 'When Far Apart Becomes Too Far Apart: Evidence for a Threshold Effect in Coalition Formation'. *British Journal of Political Science*, 25: 383–402.

Warwick, Paul V. and James N. Druckman. 2005. 'The Portfolio Allocation Paradox: An Investigation into the Nature of a Very Strong but Puzzling Relationship'. *European Journal of Political Research* (forthcoming).

Index